D0900216

TIME'S REASONS

TIME'S REASONS

PHILOSOPHIES OF HISTORY
OLD AND NEW

LEONARD KRIEGER

THE UNIVERSITY OF CHICAGO PRESS
CHICAGO AND LONDON

LEONARD KRIEGER, University Professor Emeritus in the
Department of History at the University of Chicago, is the
author of seven books, including *The Politics of
Discretion, An Essay on the Theory of Enlightened
Despotism,* and *Ranke: The Meaning of History,* all of
which are published by the University of Chicago Press.

The University of Chicago Press, Chicago 60637
The University of Chicago Press, Ltd., London
© 1989 by The University of Chicago
All rights reserved. Published 1989
Printed in the United States of America

98 97 96 95 94 93 92 91 90 89   5 4 3 2 1

Library of Congress Cataloging-in-Publication Data

Krieger, Leonard.
    Time's reasons : philosophies of history old and new /
Leonard Krieger
        p.   cm.
    Bibliography: p.
    Includes index.
    ISBN 0-226-45300-6
    1. Historiography   2. History—Philosophy.   I. Title.
D13.K7   1989
907'.2—dc 19   88-29407
                                                  CIP
⊚ The paper used in this publication meets the minimum
requirements of the American National Standard for
Information Sciences—Permanence of Paper for Printed
Library Material, ANSI Z39.48-1984.

To Esther

CONTENTS

PREFACE

The related occasions to which this book should be considered a response are the radical doubt which has arisen of late in our Western culture about history as a mode of knowledge and the special form which this doubt has taken in sponsoring new and presumably more valid approaches to history within the discipline itself. The uncertainties which this doubt and these current alternatives foster cast suspicion on not only the value but also the very credibility of history as it has been practiced traditionally. They indict the genre not only for producing truths that are neither applicable to present life nor relevant to past life, and that are therefore not worthwhile. This is old stuff. Charges like these have been raised against the practice of history from both outside and inside the discipline from time immemorial. Now they indict history for propounding the truths of a past which cannot be breached by traditional methods and whose pretended truths are no truths at all —this is new.

The implications of the charges and of the response to these charges are of interest here. What have been the reasons that historians, both old and new, have given to back their claim that they should be believed? Why do these reasons no longer hold? What reasons can be given that remedy former weaknesses and that may therefore carry some conviction about belief in history? It is toward the elucidation of these reasons in their historical form that the following essay is addressed. As the questions indicate, the focus of this book will be on developments within the discipline of history rather than on the external cultural attack upon the historical dimension of things as such. The one external factor to be included in this study will be the philosophy of history; for while philosophers of history tend to be philosophers rather than historians and while the philosophy of history, vis-à-vis historiography, does view historical reality from the outside as against the inside view of a historical method or theory, philosophy of history is connected with history proper usually through the pattern of a universal history as well as through the specific application of a general view of reality to the past and to the work of the historian on it. The goal of the book can be viewed as a vehicle whereby the individual becomes a part of the subject matter of the book. My conclusions are put forth in the spirit of teaching and with a mind toward rejuvenating the traditional discipline of history.

The crisis we experience usually seems more profound and more convulsive than the crisis we read about, and this truism certainly seems to hold for the latest installment of the "new history" that we have witnessed in the past generation. Traumatic as past bouts of historical innovation may have seemed in their time, we are wont to absorb them into the continuing story of a single developing discipline. This effort contrasts with the serious doubts about the integrity of the discipline which have been recently engendered by the crucial divergence between traditional and novel practitioners in their notions of what history is and how historians should approach it. This divergence can be discussed now—and frequently enough has been discussed—as an issue of contemporary experience, both by partisans and nonpartisans. From it we have come to understand the variant attitudes toward the concepts and techniques of the humanities and the social sciences, the classes and the masses of past societies, narrative and structural patterns, representative individuals and statistical samples, even the cognate disjunctions in the commitments of today's historians. But it does seem fair to say that even when the argument provides more light than heat the contemporary perspective is still more apt to illuminate differences than connections. Aside from a joint concern with the past—a formal concern that provides only the most tenuous community and is, besides, hardly exclusive to historians—the two historical sects would seem to have little in common. Clearly, a complementary perspective is needed for a full answer to the question of what constitutes the integrity of the discipline, if there is any integrity left to it at all, and this perspective can itself only come from the past—that is, from a historization of the current conflict that assesses its place in the long history of the discipline. Just such a history is attempted here.

To judge the relationship of the new to the old history from the standpoint of their mutual antecedents requires a common measure. Perhaps the most indicative such measure, because it has had such a continuous career, is the set of time's reasons which, mutatus mutandis, has ever served as the distinctive answer to the historian's quest for communicable guarantees of his truth. In any period, then, what constitutes the grounds of credibility for the community of historians? Certainly the grounds have changed from community to community and especially from period to period, but two stipulations from time's reasons have remained constant: the credibility of historians has always entailed what was noteworthy of belief as well as what was entitled to belief. Thus time's reasons apply as much to history as to the historian: they answer the question of why events deserve to be reported, just as they answer the question of why reports should be deemed faithful to their events.

Characteristically, the reasons which justify history, as distinct from the historian, have required the evaluation of events in proportion to their compatibility with other events—in proportion, that is, to their propensity for coordination into larger patterns of events. Thus the full range of time's reasons which make up the common measure for assessing the relationship between different communities of historians calls for the comparative confrontation both of the reasons for believing historians—that is, confrontation of their respective paradigmatic methods for getting at the facts—and of the forms of reason in history itself—that is, confrontation of the over-arching coherences that constitute the variant versions of rationality in the historical process. This historical perspective on contemporary historiography requires, too, that the discipline rather than the profession be the focus of inquiry. To be sure, it is within the historical guild—locally (that is, departmentally), nationally, and internationally—that the factional struggle is more palpable; but to be led by this location of the overt conflict to identify the practitioners of history wholly with the people who call themselves historians is to invite serious distortion.

Since the specialized profession of history is less than two hundred years old it is evident a priori that a historical perspective on the practice of contemporary history must cover more of the current scene than is occupied by the scholar-teachers who inhabit history departments, and this formal presumption acquires substance through the important persistence of extraprofessional history in today's cultural world. The point is not the familiar—and trivial—one of finding a place for the continuing production of amateur historians, since they either have been or can be easily accommodated within the profession. The point is rather the commitment to the historical approach on the part of those who are professionally natural or social scientists, philosophers, theologians, scholars of literature and the arts, or the like. The implication of this broadened horizon is more qualitative than the mere inclusion of nominal nonhistorians within the scope of contemporary historiography. It means that the current rift in the practice of history is more than an intraorganizational feud and that its provenance is more than an intrahistorical split.

The fact is that what has happened within the discipline has been conditioned by what has happened to history as a generic dimension of life in the world at large. In order to judge the relationship of both directions of current history to the long tradition of historiography and thereby to each other, we must ascertain what, under the unprecedented cultural conditions of our time, the respective orientations which are to be related have become. My narrative is meant to be objective, based upon what I have found interesting in this history. I ask of my fellow historian only that he make continued reference to nature, and that he continue to celebrate the variety in history, the view toward unity, the particular and the individual, as the stuff of history proper.

No one, in these days which see the interrelation of all things, can escape both institutional and personal obligations when writing, and this is all the more the case when the book is as general as the one proposed here. What follows is a partial list of these obligations. Institutionally, I am beholden to the University of Chicago for providing the time and inspiration for publication, as well as for funding my student/graduate assistant, editor, and friend, Myron L. Brick. This manuscript could not have been completed without his patient and able assistance. He skillfully contributed to the manuscript's final form, amplifying my emphasis where needed for the sake of clarity and comprehension. Mr. Brick is the kind of reader for whom I have always written as well as the kind of student for whom I have always taught.

I am also personally grateful to my old friends, the Professors Edward Shils, Felix Gilbert, and Carl E. Schorske, of the University of Chicago, the Institute for Advanced Study, and the Princeton University history department, respectively, for their contributions to this project both in terms of the general example which they have offered of the historian who is open to tradition and to novelty alike and in terms of their specific assistance. I am also appreciative of the special services of Mrs. Elizabeth Bitoy and Mrs. Augustine Lehman, who typed a manuscript that was not of the neatest. And I should, of course, acknowledge the help given by my wife, Esther, who, as was usual with her, lent her unflagging support to this project and the indomitable spirit that assured its successful completion. The bulk of the research and writing for *Time's Reasons* was done between 1978 and 1982. Naturally, the content of this work belongs to me alone, and all of the usual caveats apply.

INTRODUCTION

The most potent cotemporary influence on the discipline of history, bearing on its new and critical practitioners alike, is the challenge to the very substance of the historical approach to life that has been mounted by antithetical agents of the general culture. What is new and especially lethal in the current rejection of history as such is that it is mounted not in the name of science—the older kind of rejection which historians have become quite adept at countering or evading—but in the name of the very life and vitality which historians have prided themselves on recreating. The emphasis in contemporary culture is on spontaneity, on discontinuity, on simultaneity, on plasticity, and on the interpenetration of the traditional three dimensions of time. These emphases clearly imply the inherent independence of every impression, sensation, and experience. They imply the sovereignty of the living human individual who puts these aspects of everyday life together for himself, since it is only through and by individuals that experience can be put together and made meaningful at all. They imply the essential irrelevance of past moments to the actual life that is being lived and the equally essential irrelevance of the future to the better life that should and can be created—now.

This antihistorical tendency in contemporary culture is related, to be sure, to the vitalist tradition, which goes back at least to Nietzsche, and indicates history as the means of assuring the dominion of dead things over living people and of spawning, in effect, generation upon generation of historically minded zombies. But the challenge to history today is much more serious and much more radical than this. Nietzsche himself, after all, admitted that even if historians were beyond repair history itself could be used validly in the service of life by those men who were truly interested in living; and in any case, after Nietzsche's strictures, there have been philosophers of history and even historians in abundance who have vitalized the past by admitting its unbroken continuity with the life of the present.

The external challenge to history today is more lethal than even its most critical predecessors' challenge because it is a challenge of a different and more fundamental kind: where previous attacks have been directed in the first instance against history as a dimension of human life and then against historians derivatively, because they abet the evil by publicizing it. I use the term "evil" advisedly, because the moral judgment is a corollary of the new rejection of the human past as it has been lived. Certainly moral judgments have been levied upon the past before. St. Augustine took grim satisfaction in demonstrating that the Romans deserved the miseries they were getting. For men of the eighteenth-century Enlightenment, the Middle Ages were replete not only with tyranny and superstition but with knavery as well. And, in turn, for many nineteenth-century observers, the eighteenth century had been dominated by men who were malicious, cynical, and destructive. But always their judgments were selective: for most, it was some men in some ages past who were condemned; and even for those few, like Immanuel Kant, who looked with a jaundiced eye upon the whole lot, it was on the permanent traits of human nature and not upon the past or history in general, that the unfavorable judgment was cast.

What is so fundamental about the current crisis of history, then, is that it has been triggered by a profound revulsion, not merely against what some men have done in the past, not merely against what men as such do all the time with reference to the past, and not merely against what historians do with the past: it has been triggered by a profound revulsion against the simple and unselective fact of a past—any past. This categorical judgment has been produced by the merger of two kinds of historical criticism which between them have swept the board clean: the first is the cultural presentism which views any tie to the past as a kind of bondage; the second is the political radicalism which views any tie to the past as a guarantee of injustice. The first of these critiques removes history from spirit; the second removes history from power. What has changed fundamentally in these critiques, then, is not history as knowledge of the past, since the reliability and value of such knowledge has been deprecated, off and on, at least since Aristotle. Nor is it even the criticism of history as the actual process of the human past as such—a criticism which carries to their extreme conclusion the doubts about the continuity of history and the deprecations of its morality that have been raised, off and on, at least since Augustine. What has changed is that, whereas these two kinds of deprecations used to alternate, they have now combined with explosive effect. Men who used to concede the frailty of historical knowledge compensated by seeing in the actual past a meaningful and edifying pattern, revealed by God or nature, which imposed clear models even on the weak sensors of the historian. But then men lost their attachment to the actual past as the acceleration rate of change made the past seem both dispensable and regressive; yet since the same change also undermined the stability of divine and natural patterns in life as a whole, these same men could compensate for the devaluation of the lived past by exalting the historical knowledge of it as the only way of directing the process of change away from debilitating repetition. What we have now, however, is not simply the addition of the two kinds of doubt into a general suspicion of history but a multiplier effect of the merger which has escalated partial doubts into a general rejection. Not very long ago most of us endorsed Santayana's lukewarm defence that those who did not know history were condemned to repeat it. Many young men now believe flatly that those who do know history condemn themselves to persist in it.

But serious as it is (from our point of view here), this challenge from the outside is important primarily for its resonance within the historical discipline itself. Certainly there remain genuine antiquarians and exoticists who could have been born at any time and place apart from the object of their interest and still do what they now do; but it has become a truism that, detached as they try, and claim, to be, historians in general also are conditioned by the culture of their own age and that they reflect it in their own distorted way. The contemporary withdrawal from history outside the profession is reflected in profound cleavages between historians within the profession, although there are, to be sure, autonomous historiographical reasons for the current rifts in a discipline in which abortive claims to "new" approaches have been raised off and on for the greater part of the century. With the internal divisions as with the external challenge the gravity of the problem stems not from a single issue but from the convergence of two kinds of opposition to history as it has been hitherto approached—or, more precisely, to history as it is thought by its enemies and reformers to have been hitherto approached. Whereas in other disciplines academic radicalism and political radicalism have struck in separate, successive stages, in history the two oppositions are telescoped into one massive crisis. The behavioral—that is, mathematical and statistical—movement in the social sciences, like the New Criticism in literature and positivism in philosophy, had already carried the day against the institutional, historical, and theoretical schools of the academic establishment in this country and themselves become establishmentarian when the political radicals rose against them with the rallying cry of "social relevance." The current reverberations of this political cry within the historical profession are therefore not distinctive in kind—although the demand for relevance to social action in the present for the future must inevitably be more radical in degree when applied to a study of the past than to the social study of contemporary life, however scientific. What is distinctive in kind about the crisis of history is the overlap between the disciplinary effects of this political radicalism and the disciplinary effects of the academic radicalism being simultaneously propounded by the devotees of the new social history.

In many ways, then, the academic movement in history is the belated counterpart of the behavioral movement in the social sciences generally; it stresses the necessity of a scientific method, especially for the generalizations; it insists on an adequate range of facts for any inductive inference and deplores the traditional shortcuts to so-called "representative facts," whether these be the official acts of organizations, the policies of governments, or the publications of formal theories and programs; it penetrates instead to the "grass-roots" level of life, to the situations and relationships of the bulk of the ordinary individuals composing mankind; it stresses analytical and structural rather than narrative connections; and it uses quantification and correlation to get valid conclusions from the mass of social material.

This model of innovative historiography is obviously subject to qualification. For one thing, the techniques of quantitative history—computational and statistical—are not as essential to the new social emphases as the other conceptual and methodical attributes are. If the ancillary adduction of economics and sociology favors the conversion of historical data into numerical series, the absorption of categories and procedures from psychology, anthropology, geography, meteorology, and other purveyors of qualitative dimensions from ancillary sciences indicates certainly that quantitative methods are not necessary components of the new social history.[1] Moreover, beyond social history—both quantitative and qualitative—there are other kinds of new history which show an unprecedented appreciation for the autonomous and irreducible inner meanings and distinctive languages of past philosophies and arts and which thus challenge the conceptual laxity of traditional history on its individual side as seriously as the social historians do on its collective side.[2] But neither of these reservations essentially disturbs the partisan model. However spotty the actual use of quantitative methods may be among the new brand of social historians, not only are the attributes which we have seen associated with such methods prevalent among the practitioners of the whole social genre, thereby making the quantitative historians the most prominent and defiant advocates of social history in general, but it seems to be generally agreed among the protagonists of social history that quantitative methods represent what is most characteristic of the genre.[3] And although there are undeniable tensions between the traditional historians and the maverick cultural tendencies of the new intellectual history, the advocates of this genre are too few and their suspicion of the antithetical new social history too strong for them to establish a second front within the historical discipline. For all practical purposes, then, it is quantitative social history that organizes the new history into the program of an intradisciplinary party.

Like the behavioral movement in the social sciences generally, academic radicalism in history is essentially independent of political radicalism; it is, indeed, in scientific principle even more detached and value-free—that is, free from values—than the rival traditional documentary history with its casual methods and porous disciplinary standards. Among historians, consequently, academically conservative social radicals and socially conservative academic radicals are not mere eccentrics: they represent the mutually independent origins of their respective movements. Despite the loose usage of terms which tends to confuse them with each other, the scientific empiricism of behavioral history is categorically different from the social pragmatism of revolutionary history. Indeed, some politically radical historians are essentially traditional in their methods, raising the critical component of traditional historiography exponentially and applying wonted techniques to popular documents. This species of radical history is often recognized by the euphemism attached to it of "revisionist" history. As the generic label indicates, the conflict between this kind of radicalism and traditional history is reminiscent of analogous consanguine conflicts of political principle throughout the history of history.

Thus political-like academic innovators include subsections whose members seem more akin to traditional historians than to each other. But whether because of the simultaneity of their rise in the historical profession or because of the same distinctive trait in history as a discipline, the fact is that, however independent in their origins, the two kinds of radicalism do overlap and reinforce each other in their effects. The main area of their intersection is in the subject matter which they agree is the proper concern of history. For both kinds of radicalism, traditional history is elitist history, dealing with the activities and ideas of a small minority of humankind, for reasons that vary, depending on the academic or the political nature of the radicalism, from the convenience of seeing history through the eyes of the small group that has left formal documents in survivable form to the sympathy of the present class of exploiters and their epigones with their counterparts in the past. For both kinds of radicalism, then, the proper history of man is the history of all men alike, with due emphasis placed upon the way of life, painfully slow structural change, and the unstructured attitudes of whole anonymous populations whom the traditional historian has tended to neglect because they were inarticulate or because they were the silent witnesses of the continuing oppression of most men by a few. And so we have a makeshift alliance between the historical technologists and the abominators of all technologies.

In the face of this massive challenge to history, from both outside and within the ranks of its devotees, the old history which is the common target of the challengers may seem actually to be as unified and solidaristic as it appears to them. And yet there are not only many kinds but many vintages of histories which can be lumped together as "old" only by the special criteria of contemporary radicalism, academic and political, but which actually include species of history recent both from the point of view of their resemblance to contemporary radicalism in historical purpose, albeit not in method, and therefore of their comparative invulnerability to radical attack. This more recent kind of "old" history comes out of a generation of historians who learned from a contemporary society paralyzed by economic depression, mesmerized by totalitarianism, and convulsed by total war to be both politically and academically critical in its approach to history. These historians oppose the pretenses to political objectivity in the history *they* call old, equating nonpolitics with acceptance of an untenable status quo and therefore with conservative politics. For their own part, they define their distinctive function as politically committed intellectuals to be criticism of their contemporary society and their distinctive function as politically committed historian-intellectuals to be the knowledge and explanation of where this society has gone wrong. But they, too, oppose the academic blinders worn by the historians whom they call old: they proclaim the preoccupation with governmental politics in history to be trivial, the worship of facts in history to be idolatrous, and the alignment of facts for explanation in history to be superficial. This generation extends the academic scope of history to all the fields of human activity: intellectual, cultural, social, and economic, as well as political. It insists that historians must get inside their facts through analysis and must equip themselves with whatever special knowledge is required for such internal understanding. And because it frankly seeks explanations not only for history but also from history for life, it finds its historical explanations not in the mere chronological pattern of events but in the contribution of a past process to the understanding of a general, overarching issue common to both past and present. Finally, it insists upon the same critical determination of the coherence which assembles historical facts into a history that applies to the determination of historical facts as such.

Thus the distance between the radical and the critical historian is not as great as the rhetoric from either side might indicate. But the point is not to *deny* that there is a real difference between them; the point is to *define* this difference accurately, to the end that the relationship between the new and the old historical reasoning may find its proper contemporary form. Three distinguishing marks of critical history are especially pertinent here.

First, the critical historians believe that to whomever the future may belong, changes in the past were initiated and recorded by minorities and that the stabilized or inertial effects of these changes continue to dominate our present. They study elites, then—if that abused term be understood to mean the identifiable individuals and groups in all classes who have left durable traces of the changes in which they were involved—and they study the kinds of documents in which these changes were impressed. And the critical historians do it not on the assumption that such study covers all of history or exhausts the background of action in the present, but on the assumption that such study is the most appropriate approach to the process of change in history for those interested in the process of change in history; that the masters of change in the past anticipated the masters of power in the present; and that the study of these historical elites is a key to the understanding of the conditions of present action.

The second distinguishing mark of the critical, in comparison with the radical, historian—a mark perhaps impressed upon it in its tender years by a wartime culture which was always admonishing: Know Your Enemy—is the belief that abhorrent people and situations not only can be known in their own terms without corruption but must be known in their own terms for effective action upon them to be possible. It is *not* a belief, as the caricature would have it, in the objectivity and independence of knowledge from action—a belief which has certainly been used, as Marx said, to interpret the world rather than to change it. It *is* a belief in knowledge and practice as two kinds of action, dovetailing toward the same actionable end but each kind with its own rules, conditions, and contributions to make toward it.

The critical generation believes, finally, that every historian should be aware of his own assumptions and should confess them openly to his audience, just because it does believe in the unity of thought and action and therefore in the use and morality of avowing the actionable position from which it takes its historical sightings. Such a procedure implies its acceptance of the idea that there are several valid perspectives on truth, but again this idea which critical historians do in fact accept must not be confused with the caricature of it called "pluralism." For the pluralism in the caricature entails a belief in the equality of the several points of view, while the perspectival nature of the critical historian entails a hierarchy of points of view which posits the superiority of his own while maintaining the usability of the others.

Let us make plain, then, the reference to all kinds of historians who deliberately set themselves apart from the historical tradition as "new historians" with the understanding that the distinctions within the ranks of innovators is decisive for the understanding of the alleged crisis in history. We shall call the "new history" therefore whatever smacks of radicalism, academic or political. Moreover, as a necessary corollary, let us lump together as well the extant representatives of the historical tradition as "critical historians," thereby recognizing that both the latest emphasis in the development of traditional historiography and the attenuation of the interval differences among these historians is in the service of a common defense against the radicality of the innovators and the blindspots of the traditionalists. Where the radicals deny the necessity of the fact and the coherence of the assembled facts as the proper basis for any possible historical science they go too far; where the traditionalists fail to pay sufficient heed to, take for granted, or perhaps even ignore the importance of the critical determination of the coherence of the assembled facts they leave the door open to the charges of the radicals. If we allow the congruence of academic and political radicalism to stand for one party in the current historiographical struggle and if we allow the latest installment of critical history to stand for the other, then the question is: how do their apparently divergent attitudes toward the same historical reasoning of their common historical tradition help to explain the relationship of their attitudes to each other?

By way of suggesting an answer to this question a history of the various vintages of history qua history is proposed as the reconciling agent between these divergent ends. In advance of this history of history as a gradual dimension of knowledge, then, some conventional terminology must be decided upon; the critical and historical assumptions upon which such a reconciliation would depend must be made plain. There are four historical phases of critical history that are put forth here as a definition of critical history and three kinds of critically based coherence upon which traditional history's authority is seen to have depended.

The first phase of critical history is the critical approach toward fact and historical coherence the principles of which are still to be found in the works of ancient and medieval authors, principles which are spelled out in Chapter 1. The second phase of critical history pertains to the so-called historical revolution of the sixteenth and seventeenth centuries,

8

which, from the perspective of this history, is more rightly put forth as the historical definition of the term "historism." Historism signaled a change in our working relationship with the past and has everything to do with the study of history. In this sense it defined the early science of documents, of negotiation between the realities of the past and the understanding and interpretation of the present. New standards of authenticity were invoked, newly defined heuristic principles were relied upon, and these efforts, together with their common stress upon the legal, the political, and the religious aspects of history combine to define historism as an amalgam of ideas and events. This material comprises the whole of Chapter 2.

Chapter 3 introduces the third phase of critical history as well as the fourth. Together they account for the nineteenth century in history. The third phase of critical history pertains to the notion of the re-creation of the past, to the idea that the actuality of the past can be reconstructed from surviving documents. New hybrid-historians are generated here which derive from newly consolidated definitions of coherence, definitions which belong to traditional history. The fourth and final phase of critical history—historicity—emphasizes the historical coherence of the present. It strives to fix both the presence and the absence of the historical past within the historical present. Historicity represents that rare mixture of the definitive categories of historical science, the application of critical history to the sources of historical coherence themselves.

The three variants of coherent history which derive from the historism of the nineteenth century are rationalism and, again, historism and historicity. These last two terms act as conceptions of historical reasons and also serve to label the penultimate and ultimate phases of critical history. Rationalism in history stands for the *overt* importation of organizing concepts and methods from outside of history. Rationalism, or pan-rationalism as it might be called, has as its fundamental tenet the assumption that history evinces the same kind of coherent and intelligible patterns as do the more stable and determined phenomena of scientific inquiry. It signifies a rationality that both *is* and *is not* peculiar to history itself. In this context the term historism represents pan-rationalism's opposite while remaining its complement. Historism as a mode of historical coherence stands for the *covert* importation of organizing concepts and methods from outside of history. It, too, signifies a rationality that both *is* and *is not* peculiar to history; but in the case of historism, or auto-rationalism as it might be called, history is seen as particularly recalcitrant toward the kinds of rational and orderly patterns more commonly associated with the results of natural science. To the contrary, historism calls for a historical reason specific to history, a reason and as such a basis for historical coherence that is manifest in the continuity behind or between past events, a reason which abstracts extra-historical reality not from but rather into the distinctive historical reality it seeks to recreate. In this sense historicity, the deliberate search for the *overt* organizing methods and concepts from within history itself for the sake of a thoroughly historical science of history, is to be seen as the self-conscious corollary to the above-outlined historism. But as is the case with historicity, neither has succeeded totally in grounding the overt historicality of its principles.

The fourth chapter provides a historical definition of a term more frequently abused in critical discussions of history than any other term whatsoever: historicism. Here historicism is defined narrowly as the response of a seminal group of thinkers at the turn of the twentieth century to what was perceived as the universal dissolution of the absolute, any absolute, as an external source for intellectual and scientific definitions of coherence. This definition has the twin strengths, I believe, of maintaining the distinctness of historical epochs while leaving open the possibility of a true historicism, a historical reason in the guise of immanent critique.

Chapter 5 continues the discussion of these historical variants of critical history well into the twentieth century. It offers a tentative genealogy of twentieth-century historians who have confronted history's problems in the wake of historicism, as I have defined it, problems which remain to be confronted again if critical history is to retain its status as a mode of general knowledge. A tentative positing of what links together the efforts of our century's historians on the basis of their problematical relations to the element of coherence in their work is to be found there as well. As for my own prescriptions for the discipline, my recommendations for carrying on, they are to be found in the epilogue to this history.

I

THE HISTORY OF CRITICAL HISTORY
EARLY TESTIMONY

Prominent in the characterization of history as a Western discipline has been the requirement that there be some kind of coherence, whether explanatory or generalizing, among the facts. Without this quality, history by definition is no longer history; it becomes chronicle. The solution of the apparent paradox between the equivalent importance of coherence and facts and the subordination of coherence to criticism in the historical tradition lies in the distinction between the historical nature of its requirement and the unhistorical nature of its substance. Although the presence of a patterned truth beyond multifarious truths of verified discrete facts has always been deemed essential to both the actuality and the discipline of history in the Western sense, the patterns themselves have generally had to be imported from some sphere of general reality—whether religious, philosophical, or scientific—and from the field of knowledge appropriate to that reality—whether theology, metaphysics, ethics, aesthetics, biology, physics, or mathematics—transcending or suspending the flow of historical time and the particular methods devised to deal with events. The one kind of coherence that has ever been congruous with the manifold facts of history is narrative, since its structure consists in the temporal alignment of such facts, and this congruity helps to explain the longevity of narration as the typical historical mode of linkage. But even if we elide the thorny question of possible literary or philosophical models for the logic of historical narration and grant an irreducible historiographical character to it, we must still note that the coherence that has been seen in actual history and required by the historical discipline has been more general than narrative threads and has been constituted differently from them. Far from being resolved by narration, the relationship of coherence in history to narration has been as problematical as its relationship to the separate facts of which the narration was composed.

Thus just as characteristic of the historian as the question What truly happened? has been the question of why it happened. Indeed, the what has come to include the why, and the historian's answer to the problem of explanation has typically been to insert the event to be explained in a larger series of events, so that explanation becomes equivalent to coherence. The narrative series, or narrative coherence, constitutes a traditional type of such explanation, as does the presentation of motives for an action, for motivation has not only been adduced as the human version of causation but has also satisfied the need for explanation as the initial pole in a connected series of events where the act to be explained represents the terminus. The reason in history which betokens an intelligible pattern of coherence underlying or woven through the separate events is thus tantamount to the reason why historians should be believed.

Throughout the course of Western historiography there have been two equally distinguished and mutually opposed attitudes toward what I am specifying here as rationality-in-history. According to one view, human history shares the logical structure of all reality; hence it evinces the same kind of coherent and intelligible pattern as the more stable and determined phenomena do. Henceforward we shall refer to this as the rationalist or pan-rationalist view of history. According to the alternate view, human history is peculiarly recalcitrant to the kind of rational and orderly pattern which is appropriate to other fields of reality. Although protagonists of this approach could conceivably stand for the simple negation of rationality and could consequently insist merely on incoherent heterogeneity as the distinctive feature of human history, they have not actually done so. The drive for discovering unity, whether of principle or of relationship, is so strong in Western culture that even these devotees of historical skepticism who find the human past too eccentric to comport with more organizable forms of wordly appearance, far from denying the inherent patternability of history, wind up by asserting a special rationality for history, or at least for the capricious kind of reality most prominently represented by history. Henceforward we shall refer to this as the historistic, or auto-rationalist, view of history. Unquestionably the rationalist view is the older of the two, for before the modern era human history was conceived to be an extension in social time and space of stable orders that were essentially located outside of such time and space.

Moreover, from the very beginning of recognizably Western history, resort has been had to patterns of reality outside of history for application to the general meaningfulness of history. Traditional history refers to the continuous line of Western historians which goes back to Herodotus and develops, with several pronounced modulations but no essential breaks, into the familiar historical literature of the present. It is a line that defines history by two criteria: the truth of the facts and the coherence of the relationship among the facts. Without the first criterion, history is reduced to fiction; without the second, history is reduced to chronicle. But despite the equal necessity of both requirements for the definition of history in the Western sense, both the proportionate emphasis upon the two qualities and the respective status of them have been far from equal in the tradition of the discipline. Not only historical method but the very distinctiveness of historicity itself has been identified much more with the ascertainment of the truth of past facts than with the validation of the truth of their connections. Whereas the assertion of factual truth has been persistently explicit for the whole tradition from its very beginnings, the insertion of the links between the facts, joining them in some kind of process, has been just as persistently assumptive. Where the standards of factual truth have been openly discussed as the very foundation of what is historical, the principles of the conjunction process have usually been imported from outside the realm of history and have depended upon arguments outside the realm of history for the discussion of their validity. Where the criteria of factual truth have been developed primarily in the name of historical science, the construction of coherences has tended to attract justification in terms of the substantive arts or humanities outside of history. Finally, if both the warrant of factual truth and the identification of coherent principle have undergone significant changes throughout the history of Western historiography, the varieties of the first have been advanced under the common title of critical method while the sequence of the second has followed the mutations of the culture as a whole.

In a view of the repeated births of critical history in the modern period—its origins have been traced to "historical revolutions" of the sixteenth and seventeenth centuries, to the skepticism of the eighteenth, and to the scientific empiricism of the nineteenth—the explicit reverence paid to its principles even in the supposedly credulous ancient and medieval periods must come as something of a suspicious surprise. But even if this historical piety was mere lip service during most of the Western centuries, it remains a testimonial to the prominent role played by the critical approach to the sources of fact during the whole of the Western tradition.

There are two kinds of background to the modern critical as well as to the more prominent coherent qualities of Western history. First, there is the ancient Greek background, and indeed it is from the Greek that our very word for "history" comes. Second, our notion of history, like our notions of many other things, comes from the Old Testament and the Judaic part of the Judeo-Christian tradition.

The ancient Greeks began the notion that history deals with the truth of facts. The prevalence among the ancients of Herodotus' unfortunate reputation as a liar apparently stemmed from Thucydides, and it furnishes a negative proof of the indispensable role played by veracity and the methodical ascertainment of factual truth in the original justification of history. Herodotus himself laid himself open to such charges through his repeated claims to "base my account on those . . . authorities who seem to tell the simple truth" or even, in the case of conflicting testimony, to suspend "the truth or falsity" of the traditions he encountered and to "prefer to rely on my own knowledge."[1] Nor was the application of such rigorous standards by Thucydides merely polemical. Modern generations may retrospectively see in Thucydides a master of the integrated narrative and a genius at elucidating the patterns of human nature and the political power in concrete events, but his own methodic introduction and sporadic asides to the reader reveal what was patently at the forefront of his mind: an overwhelming concern with the factual accuracy of what he was writing. His complaint that men receive traditions "all alike as they are delivered, without applying any critical test whatsoever"; his preference for contemporary history because here he could cross-check his own observations with the testimony of others, "the accuracy of the report being always tried by the most severe and detailed tests possible," so as to yield "an exact knowledge of the past as an aid to the interpretation of the future"; his periodic self-restraint, as in his discussion of the great plague, when he abjured "all speculation as to its origin and its causes" and promised that "for myself, I shall simply set down its nature, and explain its symptoms"; as well as his scattered claims to factual impartiality, as in his preface to his description of the Athenian-Spartan truce, when he appealed to his firsthand experience of life on both sides during the years in question for the grounding of his claim "to know the exact truth about them":[2] all these indications articulated his commitment to specific truth as the distinction and provable hallmark of history. The general predilection of ancient historians for contemporary history and their suspicion of Herodotus for his reliance on more remote oral traditions confirm the prevalence of this commitment among the ancient Greeks.

The stature of Herodotus may have depended largely upon the veracity of the facts in "the story" he modestly claimed to tell—although his continual search for reasons pointed even in his case to connections beyond the facts[3]—but certainly the exemplary role which Thucydides has played for so many Western historians has to do as much with the integration of his account and with his propensity for general interpretation as with the critical caution which dominated his approach to his sources. There is, indeed, general consensus on one authoritative historian's "final judgment of him" to the effect that "he, more than any of his contemporaries, succeeded in allying standards of detailed accuracy with a deep and compelling sense of the generic"—that is, he effected "a union . . . between detailed fact and broad deduction."[4] But what must be emphasized in this centrality of what Thucydides "thought would be a recurrent pattern beneath the events of his time" is that the pattern was external to the events—that history was for him "a field of experiment to which the general laws of human response could be applied and by which the presumption of their truth could be established," and that these laws came from Sophistic philosophy, medical science, and other extrahistorical articulations of the Greek spirit in the fifth century, B.C.[5] Thucydides' famous statement of purpose—"I shall be content if it [my history] is judged useful by those inquirers who desire an exact knowledge of the past as an aid to the interpretation of the future, which in the course of human things it must resemble if it does not reflect it"—is obviously predicated in general on the presumption of a constant human nature which was a truism of Greek philosophy and science and in particular on the cyclical view of wordly destiny that would receive its epochal formulation in the natural philosophy of Plato's *Timaeus* and in the social philosophy of his *Republic*.[6]

Other categorical propositions which are scattered through *The History of The Peloponnesian War* are similarly apodictic principles imposed on the history rather than general inferences from the history. For instance: "Revolution brought on the cities of Greece many calamities, such as exist and always will exist until human nature changes. . . . In peace and prosperity states and individuals are governed by higher ideals because they are not involved in necessities beyond their control, but war deprives them of their easy existence and is a rough teacher that brings most men's dispositions down to the level of their circumstances."[7] And again: "But in their revenges men are reckless of the future and do not hesitate to annul those common laws of humanity on which everyone relies in the hour of misfortune for his own hope of deliverance; they forget that in their own need they will look for them in vain." Such dicta, declared by the historian in his own name, betrayed more persistent preconceptions but were themselves sporadic. With his addiction to the reconstructed speeches of his historical agents, however—especially at the climactic points of Pericles' funeral oration, the Melian Dialogue, and the debate between Nicias and Alcibiades on the Sicilian invasion—Thucydides had a persuasive device for applying general principles to historical circumstances. The second root of modern critical conceptions of history lay in the Old Testament, i.e., in the story of the ancient Israelite tribes.[8] Although none of the sources of the Old Testament are contemporary with the actions that are described therein, and although there is little distinction between fact and legend within Hebraic history, the circumstance that the Hebraic religion was based on history and that the Old Testament was a component of Western sacred literature made the perception of Hebraic traditions, whether actual or mythic, a part of the historical reality of the West and thereby enthroned the facts as well as the legends and interpretations of Hebraic history as basic to Western reality.

The enthronement of this second root of modern critical history's conception was made permanent by the establishment of Christianity as a universal religion. The most significant work in this respect from the standpoint of the history of historiography is the work of St. Augustine, and, specifically, of his *The City of God*. If Augustine initiated the medieval conception of historical theology in the sense that he joined the Judeo-Christian attitude toward the human past with the Greek theology of history, it is clear that the original Judeo-Christian attitude was an autonomous strand of the Western historical tradition originating in the history intellectually, but not terminologically embodied in the Old and the New Testaments. In these sacred books was thought to be embodied not only God's overall plan for the salvation of man but also the less grand connection of motive and discrete deed in the human past. By and large the less inclusive coherence, which includes the plurality of the traditions embodied in both the Old and the New Testaments, stems from the anthropology of the Jewish tribes, while the overall pattern of events comes from Hebraic monotheism and its successor, the Pauline God of the world.[9] Indeed, the early Christian dispensation, embodied in the New Testament, already prefigures the independence of the divine pattern in the world by enthroning its eschatological separation from the past with which it is otherwise entangled, but in any case it lies behind the conflict between the historical and the antihistorical interpretations of Augustine, who in this as in general theological respects lies on the borderline between the ancient and the medieval world (he wrote *The City of God* from 413 to 426 A.D.).

In fact, transcendent provenance of the coherence in history has nowhere been more obvious and more explicit than in the Christian classics of medieval historiography. It is well known that Christian history during the Middle Ages followed two paths. One path was exemplified first by Eusebius in his *History of the Church* and then reformulated in the "Eternal Gospel" of Joachim of Floris. The other was exemplified first jointly in Augustine's *City of God* and his disciple Orosius's *Seven Books of History Against the Pagans* and then reformulated by Otto of Freising in *The Two Cities*. But both paths referred equally to God's suprahistorical plan of human salvation for the coherence that medieval man found in the chaos and misery of man's earthly history.

For the line initiated by Eusebius, God's plan for man was in the world literally, for it was manifest in the Church and could be followed continuously through ecclesiastical history. Eusebius not only made the true faith, as revealed in the theology of Christ and as manifested in "the lines of succession from the holy apostles," the theme of his Church history; but the "men of each generation," "challenged by successive heresies," were by preaching or writing "ambassadors of the divine word." And he joined to this thematic ecclesiastical history a universal history which organized secular events around the same theme in terms of "the widespread, bitter, and recurrent campaigns launched by unbelievers both Jewish and gentile [i.e., Roman], against the divine message, [including] the martyrdoms of later days down to my own time." Not surprisingly, then, Eusebius's typical explanations of historical events had reference to God's timeless plan for human salvation—that is, to "heavenly providence . . . in order that the gospel message should . . . speed to every part of the world" and to "God's vengeance" for the causation of "the miseries" of men.[10]

In Joachim's version almost nine centuries later, the Christian role in history was still literal, but it was embodied in the succession of historical epochs determined by the Christian Scripture—specifically by the Revelation of St. John—rather than in the career of the visible Church. In Joachim's version, which has been called "theological historism," the truth of the Christian God conferred a general definition upon the succession of the historical epochs of man—the Age of the Father, the Age of the Son, and the Age of the Holy Spirit; and the character of these epochs—their embodiment in a process of integrated change and their cumulative progression upward toward a perfect salvation—was correspondingly providential in its figurative references of temporal events to the literal truth of an eternal gospel.[11]

The other line of medieval Christian history, the line associated with the historical pattern of the two cities in the versions of Augustine and Otto of Freising, dispensed with both the literal manifestation of eternal religious truth in historical form and the continuous career of that truth in its temporal incorporation; but their account of human history nonetheless continued to be held together by its imputed force. Not only did the pattern of the two cities—the City of God and the City of Man—provide Augustine with the scheme for the organization of world history, but he went to great lengths to show that God "is the source of every nature, of whatever sort or condition"; that the destiny of man's city as well as God's was therefore accountable to "neither fortune nor fate" but to "Divine Providence alone," because "the things of this earth are not merely good; they are undoubtedly gifts from God." For Augustine, human history is really one history, with the City of God "living like an alien within" the City of Man and providing it with its ostensive unity because "the two currents of development flowed in a single stream." The City of God and the City of Man should not be confused with the spirit and the flesh as two separate realms; they distinguish rather those who serve God from those who serve man within the same earthly realm, and the primary visible criterion of the two types is the unity which characterizes the one as against the diversity which characterizes the other. "There is, accordingly, a good which alone is simple and, therefore, which alone is unchangeable—and this is God. . . . The City of Man . . . is a single community. . . . Nevertheless, each individual in this community is driven by his passions to pursue his private purposes. . . . . The reason for this is that nothing but Absolute Being can satisfy human nature. The result is that the City of Man remains in a chronic condition of civil war. . . . God, in whose mighty providence lie both defeat and victory, has seen to it that wars brought supremacy to some people and subjection to others." Hence the City of Man has been split into many earthly empires "for the sake of earthly advantage or greed," as opposed to the linear and harmonious development of "that other City," with its "support of divine authority in the history of our religion." And to give express confirmation to this crucial role of religious faith in historical interpretation, Augustine exclaims: "Who can be a more trustworthy chronicler of things past than one who was also a prophet of things future which our eyes behold realized in things present?"[12]

So spiritual and invisible was Augustine's City of God, so attuned to the atemporal, otherworldly salvation of the individual soul, and so historically centered on the single event of the Incarnation, that the meaning of his scheme for history had to be transmitted by others. It was especially through Paulus Orosius, his younger contemporary and student, that the meaning of the Augustinian providence for the history of the human city initiated a definitive tradition of medieval historiography. Orosius was infinitely more attentive to man's earthly tribulations and he was infinitely more appreciative of man's worldly empires than was his mentor. He dwelt upon the follies, crimes, and miseries in the human record to demonstrate what Augustine had adumbrated, that the evils and misfortunes in the history of man were not the results of fortuitous events, as with the pagan view of the Christian establishment, but were rather the homogeneous expressions of God's designs for this world. And he developed the scheme of the

Four Monarchies, which Augustine had subordinated to the six epochs of the divine city, to make the last of the monarchies—the Roman Empire—the juncture of the Two Cities whose history evinced the divinely ordained protection of man against his own divinely fore-known depredations.

If Augustine demonstrated the extrahistorical source of historical coherence by placing a one-sided emphasis on the City of God and Orosius demonstrated it by placing an equally one-sided emphasis on the City of Man, some seven centuries later Otto of Freising established the high-medieval model of this provenance for later generations of historians by making the relationship between the two cities the organizing theme of universal history. Otto deliberately strove to combine Augustine and Orosius, and in so doing he not only added the absolute truth which defined the City of God to the providential misery which defined the City of Man, but he intensified the religious nature of this dual history by bringing it up to the time of the Holy Roman Empire and showing that in their protracted application the two cities exhibited a developing pattern which explained the whole historical process. Thus he identified Augustine's invisible City of God with the visible Catholic Church, in which both cities were represented, after the birth of Christ, in order to indicate that with the subsequent union of church and state, "since not only all the people but also the emperors (except a few) were orthodox Catholics, I seem to myself to have composed a history not of two cities but virtually one only, which I call the Church. . . . I must call them properly but one—composite however, as the grain is mixed with the chaff."[13] If, then, he emphasized the miseries of his age—as he did ("I wrote this history in bitterness of spirit, . . . and therefore I did not merely give events in their chronological order, but rather wove together, in the manner of a tragedy, their sadder aspects, and so ended with a picture of unhappiness each and every division of the books") it was not only to show, in the wonted way, the hold of God on earthly affairs "by what is surely a wise and proper dispensation of the Creator, . . . so as [for men] to be directed by the wretchedness of this fleeting life from the creature to the knowledge of the Creator." But even more so he wrote to show that the contemporary age of the one hybrid city, incorporated in the Holy Roman Empire, must be preliminary to a coming "third state"—the end of the world—which will be generally characterized by the renewed division of the two cities. Unlike the early division of the cities when the City of God was "abject," the division now will be ultimate and the City of God "perfect." "The one City is to attain to the highest blessedness, the other to fail and to descend to the utmost misery."[14]

The theological doctrine of the two cities, together with its affiliated scriptural teaching of the four monarchies, thus furnished the explicit theme which integrated Otto's history. But it did more: it supplied the main strand for both of the two concepts that Otto employed to insure the continuity of his history. The general notion that "all human power or wisdom" started in the East and then moved to the West, where it "began to reach its limits" and the particular notion of the translation of empire from the Romans to the Franks obviously linked the histories of the successive empires into a coherent account and extended the scheme to cover the Germanic Middle Ages. But it is clear that over and above the categories of politics and philosophy that characterize the notions themselves and Otto's elaboration of them, the supratemporal concern of Divine Providence for the triumph of the Christian truth was the determining factor in the historical pattern of humanity. Thus it was, when "the Lord wished His city to spread abroad and to be extended . . . to all nations," that "He established the sovereignty of the Romans over the rest"; and it was when "the sound of the word of God went out into all the earth and unto the ends of the world" that the empire of the Romans was translated to the Franks.[15] But even more telling than the simple force for political and intellectual diffusion was the crucial role of the religious model in the cohesion of otherwise divergent facts. It has been noted that Otto appears inconsistent in his assertions of both the destruction and the persistence of the Roman Empire and in his declarations of both the affiliation and the independence of the Romans and the Franks, and in his characterizations of the post-Frankish period as both relevant to and separate from the empire of the Franks.[16]

What should be noted is that these apparent vacillations get resolved and become coherent in the light of the transcendent theme of the two cities. Otto recognized the Catholic empire of the Middle Ages to the degree that he was concerned with presenting both the progress of the divine component and the decay of the earthly component within the single city and insofar as he was concerned with presenting this pattern of rising Christianity and declining secularity as the necessary prelude to the end of the world and of its history. This end would be signaled by the final division into a triumphant City of God and a moribund City of Man. His contemporary age was clearly continuous with the past in its divine dimension and discontinuous with it in its earthly dimension. For Otto's scheme called for the godly and the carnal to be both combined for the present and distinguished for the future, and he articulated his history to fulfill both requirements. "Since all the kingdoms of the earth have suffered overthrow, let us who are writing a history to display the changes of this world be absolved by this shift in earthly authority as by a sufficient argument for the immutability of the heavenly kingdom. . . . The Church, which is destined to obtain the glory of the eternal country and after the toil of this present life to attain rest, and at this very time is, besides, growing to mountainous proportions and has begun to reach great authority as the state declines. . . . But let no one because of these words suppose that we separate the Christian sovereignty from the Church. . . . For the good and the bad cannot be separated at present, inasmuch as the Church judges only the things which are on the surface and God alone . . . weighs the merits of individuals."[17] Thus Otto's heterogeneous historical reality was rendered coherent by its conformity to a suprahistorical process of eternal salvation.

Christian history was not, of course, the only kind of history that was written (or spoken) in the Middle Ages. Other historical genres, more secular and more limited, were in vogue as well: local and national history, political biography, and recreational history carried on traditions of lay scholarship and literature that went back to ancient Rome and would persist into modern times. But not only was Christian history the most distinctive product of medieval historiography, through its domination of universal history it was also the most influential, often enough supplying overt or tacit assumptions for local history. But in any case, all these kinds of history, religious, ecclesiastical and lay alike, shared one feature which confirmed the extrahistorical source of whatever general continuity they had: they were all essentially propagandistic in the sense that they were composed to defend and publicize a cause, and this cause provided the rationale for the connections of their edificatory events.[18]

Thus the special contribution of medieval historians to the historiography of the West seems to fall on the coherent rather than on the veridical side of historiography's dual composition. But even here the medieval adherence to the classical genres of history bore along with it the persistent acknowledgment of factual truthfulness as the practicable criterion of historicity. No less than "the Venerable Bede" felt the necessity to make fidelity to the facts the necessary condition of his edifying purpose "in order to avoid any doubts as to the accuracy of what I have written in the minds of. . . any who may listen to or read this history," and he was careful to specify "the authorities upon whom I chiefly depend" for the purpose of instilling confidence in his truthfulness and of exculpating himself from any violations of it. "Should the reader discover any inaccuracies in what I have written, I humbly beg that he will not impute them to me, because as the laws of history require, I have labored honestly to transmit whatever I could ascertain from common report for the instruction of posterity."[19] It is true enough that, as Bede implied, medieval historians make conformity to authorities rather than the individual inquiry into veracity the touchstone of truthfulness and that only the biblical writers, the Church fathers, and the great literary names from classical antiquity ranked as "authors" in this respect.[20] But as Eusebius was careful to show, despite his preponderant role in making the development of the Christian church the sacred thread through history, "the practice of religion as communicated to us by Christ's teaching" was not only true in the sense of its ultimate meaning for man, but "primitive, unique, and true" in the sense that it had long existed as "the first, most ancient, and most primitive of all religions."[21] Hence Otto of Freising may have adapted the Augustinian theology of history to the later Middle Ages, literally in the providential pattern of his *Two Cities* and figuratively in the supreme edificatory purpose of his more purely practical *The Deeds of Frederick Barbarossa*, where he justified "digression . . . from the simple diction of history to loftier—that is, to philosophic—heights" on the dubious ground that the ancients communicated the secrets of philosophy "in recording not only the distinction between history which was dedicated to factual truth and digressive philosophy which was dedicated to something else," but also his own commitment to objective truth as the historian's characteristic attitude. He interpreted the historian's license to select and compose his material not, as might be expected from Otto, to support the historian's synchronization of events but rather to buttress his veracious function. "It avoids lies and selects the truth," he wrote of the discretionary capacity, and he used the principle to justify his impartiality, refusing in the light of it "to abandon the function of an historian by covering up a loathsome sight by colors that conceal the truth."[22]

But my point here is not to discuss pro and con the criteria whereby certain ancient and medieval authors determined their issue of fact and historical coherence; nor is it to deal with these authors comprehensively or to cover exhaustively the contribution of this early testimony to a definition of scientific history,[23] although it is being put to this end. My point is simply to suggest that these concerns have always been and must necessarily remain central to the conception and practice of history. The quotations assembled here form an elementary genealogy of the principles which underwrite this study. They are as well the signs of commitment to what this author considers the basis of historical praxis, theoretical building blocks themselves the product of historical labors and hence an a priori example of historical method which, mutatis mutandi, remains of service today. The point is not to put forth any facile notion of continuity in history but rather to assert those elements of continuity thought necessary for its practice.

Obviously, "fact" and "coherence" are concepts of a historically relative nature, whose definitions have changed with the course of scientific culture at large. But surely the historian who follows Thucydides and Bede is on solid ground when insisting upon the factual basis of the historical enterprise. Surely the historian can and must continue to search out and record a coherent history, giving disjunction its due where the facts warrant it while assembling those facts in accordance with the critical standards of the day. As the formal subject of a history, fact and historical coherence offer their historian the opportunity to assess the long history of his discipline according to the light of his own critical acumen. They represent a set of conditions from which I deem it impossible for the historian to escape. Hereafter this study concerns itself with its proper subject, with the sources of fact and historical coherence deriving from the so-called "historical revolution" of the sixteenth and seventeenth centuries. The concept of historical coherence comes constantly into question. Its measure evolves with the subject itself.

2

HISTORISM: THE EARLY HISTORY OF
COHERENT HISTORY

The "historical revolution" of the early modern centuries or, as it is called here, historism, has been seen as a fundamental part of the cultural change which spawned the modern mentality. It was essentially a development of the critical approach to the sources.[1] Variously attributed to the sixteenth and the seventeenth centuries, this so-called revolution consisted primarily in the unprecedented methods which were worked out gradually and successively under legal and confessional auspices for the authentication of documents and the disengagement of the undiluted factual truth from them. "Historism," in fact, specifies an amalgam of applications of critical standards to a freshly proclaimed "historical" past during a period of history writing best thought of as "philosophical" in the classical sense. Thus it is important that this term be given a historical definition in the terms of its early modern proponents, for historism amounts to an important formal change in the status of historical thinking itself and the formulation of new schemas of coherence. Some, like the auto-rationalists, absorbed extrahistorical reality into the pattern of history they put forth; pragmatists explicitly stressed causal relations to elicit instructive rules for politics; still others maintained a plurality of principles for a plurality of realities; and still others must yet be discussed in terms of the particular case. Obviously, these developments were of great consequence for critical thinkers of every stripe and amount to a historical revolution of the first magnitude.

Now, it should be clear from what we have already seen of ancient and medieval historiography that the novelty in early modern historical methods was not the appearance of a critical attitude toward the sources where there had been an uncritical attitude before (the stated attitude, at least, had not been uncritical); rather, the extension of the sources to which the critical attitude applied and the elaboration of standard procedures that were tailored to the newly criticizable sources constitute our definition of historism. This development, in turn, bore with it consequences for the positing of relations of coherence between the new facts that derived from these newly criticizable sources. The most important of the new sources were the documents that were the depositories of historical events themselves. The most important new aspect of the methods that were now elaborated to standardize the procedures for getting at valid historical truth was the concern with the question of how the documents had come into existence where there had been previously no necessity felt for looking into this question. The novelties were connected, of course, because it was precisely documentary history that required explicit and formal methods for validating original documents.

The new concern for the authenticity of documents had two connected bases. In the first place, it stemmed from movements which, from the fifteenth century on, were vitally interested in origins and looked to authenticate documents to certify them. Humanism, now exemplified in Lorenzo Valla, exercised its passion for the precise recovery of classical models in its juncture of philology and history and in its consequent "justification for historical scholarship" in the joint "fidelity to the letter and to fact"—in the conviction that knowledge could be attained only "through the examination of particular things."[2] In the second place, the efflorescence of legal studies, abetted in its historical orientation by the influence of humanism and contemporaneously motivated by the service to princely masters through the researching of original lawful titles, was another of the prominent early modern movements that contributed to the documentary gloss of critical historical method. The impact of humanism was registered especially in Guillaume Budé, Jacques Cujas, and other devotees of "the French mode" of Roman law; the political incentive was registered especially in Bodin, Grotius, Pufendorf, and other jurists who doubled as historical scholars and/or official historiographers. Budé and Cujas approached the texts of the Roman law as historical documents, interpreting them in the light of the age contemporary with their composition and weeding out later interpolations. Bodin devised tests for establishing the reliability of historical sources—that is, in his terms, of the "facts" or "the true narration of things" in which "the best part of universal law lies hidden," and which confer knowledge "about the governmental form of states"—while Grotius and Pufendorf wrote, for the sovereign who employed them, archival histories which buttressed patriotism with claims for the critical impartiality of their methods.[3]

A final early modern current that produced paradoxical advances in the critical approach to a true history from partisan motives was the long ecclesiastical polemic arising from the confessional rivalries of the Reformation and Counter-Reformation. The obviously prejudicial church history in the *Magdeburg Centuries* on the Protestant side and the Catholic response of Cesare Baronio on the other sponsored rather than precluded the discovery and collection of archival sources for this history. Later practitioners of the genre, like Paolo Sarpi and Gottfried Arnold, could extend this interest in the documentary support of a partisan position to Sarpi's disingenuous insistence that "I shall follow the truth closely," even to the point of writing with "suspended judgment," and to Arnold's entitling his work *The Nonpartisan* [Unparteiische] *History of Churches and Heretics,*[4] although it was partisan in favor of the heretics.

But undoubtedly it was Jean Mabillon's establishment of the science of diplomatics—i.e., the scientific method of ascertaining the authenticity of documents—that clearly turned ecclesiastical history from adaptation to the construction of new critical standards for factual scholarship. Mabillon developed his methodological apparatus in the service of his primary intention to write ecclesiastical history—especially that of his own Benedictine congregation of St. Maur and of the early church fathers—and this determination was itself a function of his profound belief that sound knowledge of Christian doctrine depended preeminently upon correct knowledge of church history and that correct knowledge of church history rested, in turn, upon accurate knowledge of the sources. In the series of prescriptions which he gave for the study of Scripture, the church fathers, councils, canon law, and theology he repeated time and again the necessity for the methodical ascertainment of authentic sources and the critical judgment of claimant authorities as well as of primary documents. Mabillon thus set forth rules for a critical documentary history that would ground religious faith and not undermine it. "A wise and respectful critic," he wrote, "who seeks only to instruct himself, who is as careful to control his heart as to enlighten his mind . . . — this modest critic will profit from everything, will be improved by everything; and God will be pleased to transmit knowledge to him."[5]

Over and above this encouragement given to historical criticism by substantive intellectual movements of the sixteenth and seventeenth centuries, an important formal change in the status of historical study provided a second support to the developing tradition of documentary methodology in historical study. Classical humanism and religious reform not only sponsored the return to historical sources directly but also stimulated the teaching of history in the schools—especially in the universities—with the result that the literary standards of a history that was either communicated orally or taught derivatively as a subdivision of the medieval arts were increasingly replaced by the scientific procedures of a history that was based on written documents and taught as an autonomous profane or ecclesiastical history in preparation for the professional study of law or theology. Hence the start of the "revolution" in historical methodology was connected with the composition of instructions for students' reading of history, and at least in the Protestant universities of Germany the juxtaposed development of secular and church history was accompanied by the increasing prominence of manuals of method devoted to the elucidation of historical truth.[6] But it is not the institutionalization of the critical attitude toward the sources which now demands our attention, for it is obvious that the critical attitude became the norm. Rather, what must now be considered are the forms of coherence that derived from and attended this development.

The Early History of Coherent History: Two Variants

The historiographical revolution of the early modern centuries is notable, as we have seen, primarily for its sophistication in critical method. But what must not be overlooked is that, despite the intellectual inertia that would produce the astrological incongruities of a Bodin or the reversionary scheme of a Bossuet, these centuries of methodical revolution also produced a transformation of the scheme giving coherent point to the critically ascertained facts of history. The radical shift of perspective which underlay this transformation rendered the Christian dispensation in the form of "divine history" or "sacred history" irrelevant to the course of "human history" and undermined the terrestrial scheme of the four monarchies which had been associated, through the scriptural Book of Daniel, with that dispensation.[7] Yet there persisted a commitment to large patterns in human events which stemmed from sources under God but above history which must be acknowledged by historians. Hence the coherence of history continued to be universal but was not derived from secular or sectarian universals; in this way it yielded the traditional satisfaction of connecting individual events and created a novel relationship to them.

But the secularization of the coherence in human history that accompanied the birth of the modern era in the sixteenth century resulted not only in the exposition of patterns within as well as without history, through the pan- or auto-rationalist forms of a revived classical humanism and a novel logic of nature, but also in the origination of new internal historistic patterns exclusively within history itself. The pan-rationalist forms of early modern historiography are obvious enough. It might have been expected that a Machiavelli would revive the ancient notion of a natural cycle and apply it once more to human history; that a Hobbes would apply his political insights into natural and social man to his historical study of Thucydides and his contemporary history of

Cromwellian England (which he called *Behemoth*); and that the philosophical historians in the eighteenth century—Voltaire, Robertson, Gibbon, albeit not Hume—would assert a secular rational structure with the consistent organization of nature, man, and society manifest in history but not in history alone. But what might not have been expected was that a whole sequence of writers in the same period, ranging from Bodin to Hume and Herder, would find historical patterns of either a distinctive or paradigmatic kind of reality. These thinkers would be the founders of historism in both of the variants which have been its staples ever since.

What these historical thinkers asserted, in effect, was a peculiarly historical reason that was manifested in the continuity behind or between the events of the past. So distinctive were the patterns in this tradition maintained to be that they were seen as construing the patterns of human destiny. Often with point, history and human nature were seen as homologous. Where the thinker's focus was human nature historical pattern was thought to make the case. Where historical pattern was the thinker's focus human nature rendered coherent the disparate facts of a multivalent past. But to put historical pattern on equal epistemological footing with the figures of rationality, therein hangs the tale of the historical definition of auto-rationalism.

Indeed, the terminology of reason was generally denied to those thinkers who thought the truths of historical pattern the equal of truths of rationality precisely because rationality was the outstanding feature of all the patterns history was not. The alternate tradition which descried in history an exemplary form of providence or reason valid in all kinds of human endeavor was strong enough for the early advocates of a distinctive reason in history to be denied any historicity at all and to be labelled "unhistorical" by readers until very recently. But such a label is founded on a principle whose application to the putatively unhistorical character of such thinkers as Francis Bacon and Thomas Hobbes has become dubious to say the least. This appellation of "unhistorical" is usually traced to the familiar seventeenth-century distinction between truths of science, based on reasoning and equivalent to philosophy, and truths of fact, which as "a thing past, and irrevocable," is registered as history, as well as to the equally familiar and obvious seventeenth-century preference for the truths of rational science.[8]

Indeed, the well-known inhospitality of the seventeenth century to the pragmatic or general kind of history that doted on coherences may be attributed to the antihistorical—actually antirationalist in respect to history—tendency of the philosophy that was supposed to supply history with its principles of coherence. The distaste of Descartes and the Cartesians for history is a notorious aversion; but the grounds for this distaste are more obscure, since Descartes' celebrated statement of explicit dissatisfaction with history by reason of its factual unreliability, in the *Discourse on Method*, overshadows the mistrust of historical reasoning which was the more essential basis of his rejection.[9] The second of Descartes' *Rules for the Direction of the Mind* argues for the superiority of deduction over inferences from immediate experience—such as historical reasons must be—as the way to knowledge because "inferences from experience are frequently fallacious" whereas the sciences founded on deduction deliver "certitude," since "they need make no assumptions at all which experience renders uncertain, but wholly consist in the rational deduction of consequences."[10] Although Descartes' idea of literal "experience" was more ambiguous than his language here suggested, he accepted it only in the form of "clear and distinct ideas" which were intuited by the operation of the mind upon commonsensible experience and which were irrelevant to the presumed facts of history.[11] In any case it was the resistance of history to logical coherence rather than the dubiety of its facts as such that grounded the antihistorical bias of the Cartesians.

It is hardly remarkable, then, that even Hobbes, a rare Cartesian who appreciated history, identified history with mere "knowledge of fact," classifying every "chain" of such facts merely as "opinion" and contrasting it to "the knowledge of the consequence of one affirmation to another," which he called alternatively science or philosophy.[12] Hence the state of nature on which Hobbes based his morality and his politics was essentially "ahistorical and logically timeless"; it was only through the regressive invocation of God that he could find a pattern within which to set history.[13]

A fortiori, John Locke may not have been a Cartesian, but he too subscribed to the idea of a state of nature which he did not apply to historical coherence, and since he excluded God's providence as well he exercised an even more inhibitory effect on history than did Hobbes.[14] Even in his formal philosophy, where he conceded a value to the history he never practiced, Locke repeated the prevalent seventeenth-century distinction between the knowledge of existences and the knowledge of logical relations, aligning history with the first as a "knowledge . . . only of particulars" and delivering a merely probable truth in implicitly pejorative contrast to the "general and certain truths" which "are only founded in the habitudes and relations of abstract ideas."[15]

But this depreciation, associated undoubtedly as it is with Bacon's preference for the induction of rational axioms in "the course of nature," as well as with Descartes' preference for "self-evident intuition and necessary deduction" as demonstrated in the mathematical sciences over the uncertain facts of human or civil history, is doubly irrelevant:[16] the distinction was epistemological, focusing on the knowledgeability of history at a time when men's real attitude toward history was substantive—that is, their attitude was founded on possible patterns of what was done in the past rather than on the process by which historians knew it—and it was particularistic, focusing on the reliability of specific historical reports rather than on the coherence of what they reported. Hence the recent reinterpretations of such typical seventeenth-century figures as Bacon, Hobbes, and Pufendorf stipulating their historicity do not so much create a conflict of authorities as dwell on the actual stuff of their histories, rather than on their formal methodology, however unbeknownst to the revisers this shift of attention may be. If we regard the revision in terms of a relocation of attention from the epistemology to the substance of history, then we can perceive the beginnings of the two standard variants of the historistic tradition whose completion and perfection would come only with the nineteenth century.

In one of the two variants, represented most transparently in its preliminary stage by Francis Bacon for the seventeenth century, and perpetuated especially by historistic philosophers of history, the intelligible process of history is homologous with and furnishes the basis or model for the process of reality in general. Thus Bacon's thought has now been analyzed to indicate the intimacy of character and function linking his notion of civil or human history and the natural history which has always been recognized to lie at the base of his structure of knowledge. This analysis shifts Bacon's focus from the methodology of knowledge to the moral and social purpose of knowledge, pointing out that his thematic, causal, and interpretive emphasis in his *History of Henry VII* belies his problematical epistemological principle which restricted history to "individuals" and assigned philosophy to "general notions" and actually gave to his substantive history the determining role about which he was so vague in his pragmatic theories of learning, ethics, and politics.[17]

In the other of the two variants of the historistic tradition, incipiently represented by Hobbes and Pufendorf during the seventeenth century and taken up primarily by historians in all the eras that followed, the pattern that history reveals or can be made to reveal is peculiar to it; it is different from and unrelated to other patterns or processes which inform other kinds of reality. The vindication of Hobbes's historical-mindedness goes beyond the affirmation of the historical dimension in his anthropological history of man from the state of nature to membership in the body politic, since this kind of historical-mindedness is just an extension of his analytical philosophy and may well mean authentic temporality without history. Rather, the vindication of his historical-mindedness goes to his positive treatment of sacred history (in Parts III and IV of *Leviathan*), for in these contexts his history was thematic yet discontinuous with his political philosophy. In the testimony of a recent reviser, Hobbes's God was "a God of history," and if his warrant for belief was a faith in historical authorities far different from his usual philosophical sensationalism it also was integrated by a commitment to an eschatological future that worked as an independent structure for his history.[18] As for Pufendorf, he obviously turned to history as an alternative to his prior political theory of an ahistorical, natural law, in the attempt to understand the principles of human experience which had slipped through the grid of that theory.[19]

It should be noted that historism in both these variants stands for the general tendency to affirm an extrahistorical basis for historical connectedness and is to be distinguished both from historicism, which is the label given to the special doctrinal subset of historism that rose to predominance in the period from the aftermath of one world war to that of the second during our own century, and from historicity, a current movement of historical thought which seeks authentically for a ground of historical connectedness within the historical process itself. But this is to jump ahead of the development of the case.

As the examples of Bacon, Hobbes, and Pufendorf indicate, the historistic views of historical coherence pose very different problems for analysis than do the views of rationalists. Whereas the rationalists frankly set their organizing principles outside of history and openly apply these extrahistorical principles to history, both variants of historists insist that historical coherence is sui generis, whether coherence is to be found only in human history or serves as a model for human reality outside of history; and the task of tracing the actual extrahistorical roots of coherence is one of discovering a process that was unbeknownst to, or at least unadmitted by, the historists themselves. Hence the analysis of historism must inevitably be Janus-faced: it must treat of both the overt resistance of historists to the historical applications of the rationalists and its own covert absorption of congenial extrahistorical principles. Hence the ambiguity of attributing both historical and unhistorical qualities to such problematical early historists as Guicciardini, Bodin, the seventeenth-century historical critics of both Catholic (Mabillon) and non-Catholic (Spinoza and Bayle) persuasions, Vico, Herder, and Hume, as well as to the standard nineteenth-century historism associated with such great historians as Ranke, Michelet, Burckhardt, and Fustel de Coulanges. In each instance the structure of physical or human nature is conceived to be homologous with the pattern of humanity revealed in its history. The actual movement from the extrahistorical structure to the historical pattern is masked by the apparent consistency of the explicit movement in the other direction.

The rationalist alternative to the historist view of historical coherence, an alternative that expressly asserted the applicability of extrahistorical principles to history, had an equally notable and even more prominent representation in the early modern centuries. Rationalist writers and theorists of history can be recognized in this period by their adjectival qualification as "pragmatic" or "philosophical" historians. The pragmatic strain in history became literal during the sixteenth century, the first of the indisputably modern centuries. It stressed general connections explicitly. But despite its definition of history precisely in terms of such connections it still had to import them into history quite as much as the scholarly strain did covertly. The term "pragmatic history" was a German invention of the sixteenth century and, although it has remained restricted to German historiographical usage, the kind of history to which it refers—a large-scale political history approached primarily through the causal relationships behind its actions and analyzed primarily for the purpose of eliciting instructive rules of politics—was a prevalent genre throughout Europe in the early modern centuries.

The noteworthy feature of this pragmatic history, for our purposes, was the political or moral origin of the general connections it perceived in history. The general historical truth of the pragmatic school was, indeed, a kind of natural law,[20] and like the natural law it was a universal that held through the changes of time and the variations of space. Machiavelli's *History of Florence and of the Affairs of Italy* is a particularly prominent example supporting the general judgment about pragmatic history during the Italian Renaissance that in time "history became subordinated to politics." For Machiavelli prefaced his main historical sections with abstract disquisitions on the nature of politics— e.g., on the benefits of colonies, on the calamaties of civil strife, on the consequences of political cycles—and if from the perspective of his politics the history that followed served as mere examples of the principles, from the perspective of the history that he wrote the political principles served as the categories of selection and organization.[21] Since even a Machiavelli found the ultimate warrant for his principles of historical coherence in realms of thought and faith outside history, such reference was all the more transparent in those cases where the structure of the principle was homologous with the event recorded.

Needless to say, the historians of this period must more often than not be dealt with as individuals rather than under the rubric of any particular interpretive category, and the ambiguities of early historism revealingly attend the positions of its two leading sixteenth-century exemplars, Guicciardini and Bodin. In some ways Francesco Guicciardini, Machiavelli's younger contemporary and fellow Florentine historian, seems to represent a significant departure from the model of extrahistorical coherent historiography. Since both in his earlier *History of Florence* and in his later *History of Italy* he abjured theoretical discussions, rejected the relevance of general rules of human behavior to history, and appreciated the vital individuality of historical action, he severely limited the generalizing penchant of the rationalist historian. In the words of one authoritative commentator: "Guicciardini's fascination with history was too strong to permit him to obliterate the variety and richness of the past by the imposition of a theoretical structure."[22] Since, moreover, Guicciardini habitually posited the ubiquity of change in human affairs and tended consequently to seek causation in the individualized motivation and character of his historical actors, what there was of overt general coherence in his histories seemed to take the form of intrahistorical connections.[23] And yet, upon closer examination, it is clear that Guicciardini's apparent commitment to historical individuality and to the historization of connections was itself a congenial expression of the general moral and political principles he was trying to articulate. The key to this underlying structure can be found in Guicciardini's own nonhistorical works, the *Memoirs* (*Ricordi*) and the *Dialogue on the Government of Florence* (*Dialogo del Reggimento di Firenze*), for the first of these is replete with the general principles that take historical shape in the *History of Florence* and the *History of Italy* and the second offers a precedent wherein Guicciardini does integrate history into his political propositions. But the decisive evidence lies in Guicciardini's histories themselves, for aside from the scattered dicta that linked historical data by introducing or concluding them in thematic terms, the characteristic historical connections featured by these works turn out to be faithful applications of his two overriding general principles—the disastrous effects of irrationality in politics and the misery of man under the blind sway of incessant change.[24] The *History of Florence* had as its theme the series of ill effects caused by the changes perpetrated by irrational political leaders. The *History of Italy* also exhibited both principles but stressed rather the second—the drift of Italy into calamity and bondage under the buffeting of an inconstant fate. He himself projected the point of the work in his introduction: "It will appear from countless examples how unstable are human affairs—like a sea driven by the winds; how pernicious . . . are the ill-judged actions of rulers when they pursue only vain actions and present greed."[25]

Guicciardini, who was called both the author of "the last great work of theory in the classical pattern" and the modern "historian's historian," gave specific form to his ambiguities in his commitment to both the ancient humanist ideal of history and the empirical standards of modern history, and these ambiguities take the general form of his commitment to both the rational interpretation of human conduct, which presumed an extrahistorical analysis of human nature, and the random, "uncontrollable forces of Fortuna," which could be studied only by history and which comported only with a historical "inner logic."[26] Hence on the one hand he castigated Machiavelli for putting things, such as his *Discourses,* "too absolutely"—that is, too schematically—and in his *History of Italy* he underlined the particular characters of his historical agents. On the other hand, however, Guicciardini also did not hesitate to apply rational criteria in his historical judgments, and beneath the overt factuality of his account lay the pessimistic view of human nature that was rooted in the philosophical view of the miserable and irrational human conditions set forth in the prior reflections of his *Memoirs,* much of which was inserted literally in the *History of Italy.* Hence Ranke's criticism of Guicciardini for being "more concerned with ground and conclusion than with fact" echoed Guicciardini's own censure of Machiavelli and for an analogous reason, because Guicciardini's historical logic did subtly what Machiavelli's did openly—take its linkages from beliefs contracted outside of history.[27]

The young Bodin—that is, the Bodin of the *Method for the Easy Comprehension of History* (1566)—similarly imbedded, without acknowledgment, extrahistorical regularities in his history as the basis of its coherence. He addressed his whole critical method of reading history to articulating universal law, "so that from the very sources we may trace the main types and divisions of types down to the lowest, yet in such a way that all members fit together," since "the arts and disciplines . . . are not concerned with particulars, but universals" and "in history the best part of universal law lies hidden." It followed that fully one-third of his book on the *Method for the Easy Comprehension of History* was devoted to seeking—and finding—"more definite principles" of government "than those which have been suggested hitherto" by philosophers such as Aristotle, and he proceeded to define such political concepts as citizenship, sovereignty, the typology of states, and the patterns of change in empires by analytical arguments with historical examples.[28] It is equally well-known, moreover, that Bodin explicitly rejected the biblical and medieval schema of the four monarchies but replaced it with an equally thematic "system of universal time" to serve as the numerical basis of historical chronology.[29] Insofar as Bodin raised general questions of distinctively historical import—such as the factors making for the flowering or decay of cultures—he could characteristically come to no definite formulation.[30]

What makes the example of Bodin so striking as evidence of the extrahistorical source of historical coherence is his representation of the more scholarly, the more factual, the more critical wing of early modern historiography. It has become a truism in the history of history that two separate lines—scholarly (érudit) and what has been variously called pragmatic, universal, or literary history—traversed the sixteenth and seventeenth centuries, to converge only in the eighteenth. It is well known, too, that the great advances in critical historical method were produced by the first of these lines. Yet it must be remarked that despite their undoubted emphasis on the ascertainment and verification of historical facts the scholarly historians propounded a "new history" that would not only present true facts but would also explain them completely—it would, that is, uncover "the eternal connection which sustains the causes of human events."[31] And when these scholars progressed from the composition of programs to the writing of actual history, the same legal and sectarian interests which sponsored their concern for sources and their consequent innovations in critical method within history provided them with integrative concepts for application to history. In histories inspired by legal interest, for example, traditional constitutions and Roman or medieval laws supplied newfangled historians not only with their motivation and subject matter but, especially under the impress of royalist or corporate political interpretations of the constitutions and the laws, with their continuity as well.[32]

In ecclesiastical histories, similarly, even when religious divisions undermined the providential schemes of medieval vintage, partisan religious considerations could define a level of historical "reality" which embodied the rational explanation of a superficial and incomprehensible historical "appearance."[33] Thus the scholarly line of history in the sixteenth and seventeenth centuries, whether of the legal or the ecclesiastical type (the antiquarian type of scholarly history was short on coherence and is not relevant to the schema being developed here), was clearly representative of the historist view in its second, or exclusively historical variant. Its authors conceived of both a distinctive historical reality and of an extrahistorical reality that was different in kind from history, but through an osmotic process absorbed the structure of the extrahistorical reality into the pattern of historical reality to serve as its tacit foundation.

The historistic tradition was continued in the eighteenth century by Vico and Herder along the lines of the first variant—that is, the conception of all reality in historical terms—and by Hume along the lines of the second—that is, a rational history approached as an alternative to the principles governing the rest of reality. No revision has been required to mark these historicities.

These eighteenth-century historists, like the rationalists whom they overtly opposed, derived their principles of historical coherence from extrahistorical sources. But their role was distinctive in two ways; and if neither distinction violated the essential extrahistoricity of their historical connections, it did contribute importantly to the obscuration of this derivation. The application of philosophical and scientific concepts that were themselves dynamic, temporally conditioned, and therefore smoothly historizable; and the insistence on a genetic mode of understanding that converted human things into a coherent process comprehensible primarily through its beginnings; these contributions of Vico and Herder during the eighteenth century anticipated the triumphant independence of historical science, with its seemingly characteristic coherence as well as factuality, during the nineteenth century. But they also betray, more obviously than their successors, the scaffolding behind the apparently historical constructs.

Especially is Vico now credited with the first "vision of man as historical," a vision including both the faith that "minute attention to historical facts . . . alone revealed the pattern which determined what men were, had been and might have been, could and would be" and that the pattern itself is "immanent" in the historical facts, leading to the "absolute coordination of . . . the *'ragioni'* and the facts of events."[34] Vico accomplished this historization not only through a new "critical" approach to historical facts in the contemporary terms of the language and attitudes of the men who made them but also through three historistic changes in his approach to the connections among the facts. First, he qualified his well-known identification of *verum* and *factum*—i.e., his assertion of the proposition that men know to be true only what they have made themselves—with the provision that such knowledge must be "through causes" (*per causas*)—i.e., his assertion of the proposition that we know something to be true only when we know why or how it came to be what it is—and thereby he defined the historical facts which he rehabilitated from their Cartesian depreciation in terms of their coherence.[35] Second, he set the historistic prescription that all human activities must be understood by the changeable meanings of their particular times and places in a general context of an integrative pattern linking the varied expressions of particular time and place in a characteristic cultural style. Third, the preference for origins which was at the root of his genetic approach to history was part of a larger notion of successive, related stages in the life of each people in which the original qualities gave direction to the whole. As Vico wrote bluntly: "The inseparable properties of institutions must be due to the modification or guise with which they were born," and he proceeded to extend the connection even beyond the triadic succession in the life of each people by insisting on the doctrine of "recourse"—i.e., recurrence—to associate the courses of different peoples with one another.[36]

But despite this apparent historization of coherence through Vico's articulation of principles in terms of process, it is clear that his "new science" was not a historical replacement of philosophy but a historical modulation of philosophy. For one thing, as his *Autobiography*, which was written around the same time as the first edition of *The New Science*, shows unmistakably, Vico always prided himself on his possession of "the metaphysical mind whose whole labor is to know the truth throughout by genus and differentia." He characterized this mind as exercising itself, in his case, "in observing between the remotest matters ties that bound them together in some common relation, . . . to the end that all divine and human wisdom should everywhere reign with one spirit and cohere in all its parts"; and he consequently always emphasized the continuity leading from his metaphysical through his juristic to his historical studies. Thus he not only considered his prior work on *Universal Law* to be a sketch of *The New Science* but he explicitly gave to *The New Science* itself a hybrid definition which specified its philosophical as well as its historical component. In it he aimed, he wrote, at "a system so devised as to bring the best philosophy, that of Plato made subordinate to the Christian faith, into harmony with a philology exhibiting scientific necessity in both its branches, that of languages and that of things." He described *The New Science*, with corresponding duality, as "an ideal eternal history . . . traversed in time by all the particular histories of the nations, each with its rise, development, acme, decline, and fall."[37]

This duality could, and did, cut both ways: if it meant that such ingredients of the "ideal eternal history" as "the natural law of the gentes" had "separate origins among the several peoples" and that in general the "historical principles of philosophy" as well as of philology were knowable from their original forms in "sacred history" from the particular nations, it also meant that the "axioms" and "principles" which approach the "world of nations in its eternal idea"—i.e., through "the universal and eternal principles. . . on which all nations were founded and still preserve themselves"—"give form" to the specific materials of history and thus in their connective nature are distinct from the events and linguistic expressions that they order.[38] In Vico's formulation of their reciprocity, "the philosophers failed by half by not giving certainty to their reasonings by not appealing to the authority of the philologians, and likewise . . . the latter failed by half in not taking care to give their authority the sanction of truth by appeal to the reasoning of the philosophers."[39]

To underline the separate transcendence of coherence in history Vico assigned precisely this function to "divine providence," which was both knowable through history—"our new Science must be a demonstration, so to speak, of what providence has wrought in history"—and a force apart from the historical acts of men that did precisely those works of connection which the variegation of human choice cannot do. Corresponding in history to what in philosophy are "eternal truths that we cannot mistake or deny, and which therefore are not of our making," two of these coherent functions of providence were especially crucial for Vico's history. First, he made "divine providence" the author of that which was common among the inherently independent natural laws of the several *gentes;* and second, he made "divine providence" responsible for the difference between the variable things that men intend and the unintended linkages that result. On the first count, he attributed to providence sponsorship of "the common sense of the human race," by which the discrete nations recognized what was uniform among their respective natural laws, a recognition itself grounded in the harmony that providence gave them, as the author of the laws as well as of the commonsensical consciousness of them:

Uniform ideas originating among entire peoples unknown to each other must have a common ground of truth. This axiom is a great principle which establishes the common sense of the human race as the criterion taught to the nations by divine providence to define what is certain in the natural law of the gentes. And the nations reach this certainty by recognizing the underlying agreements, which, despite variations of detail, obtain among them all in respect of this law.

This criterion—"namely the common sense of the human race"—is "determined by the necessary harmony of human institutions," institutions which themselves "have been established by divine providence."[40]

On the second count, Vico assigned to the obviously suprahistorical function of providential coherence the function that would later be assigned to the more or less visible hand of nature (by Kant and Adam Smith) and to the cunning of reason (by Hegel)—the dual connection between the individual things that men purport and the very different social events that result and the irreducible linkage among the events themselves. In Vico's words:

> Our new Science must therefore be a demonstration, so to speak, of what providence has wrought in history, for it must be a history of the institutions by which, without human discernment or counsel, and often against the designs of men, providence has ordered this great city of the human race. For though this world has been created in time and particularity, the institutions established therein by providence are universal and eternal. . . . It is true that men have themselves made this world of nations, . . . but this world without doubt has issued from a mind often diverse, at times quite contrary, and always superior to the particular ends that men had proposed to themselves; which narrow ends, made means to serve wider ends, it has always employed to preserve the human race upon this earth.[41]

It is, then, "through the *order* of civil institutions" that "providence . . . makes itself palpable to us," and Vico did not shrink from showing that this organization was not only spatial but temporal— i.e., that providence was responsible not only for "the natural order" of families and for "the civil order" of monarchical states but also for the chronological passage from one general condition to the other and for the equally general development of the civil order through time.[42] Hence Vico's final call for "the study of piety" as an inseparable adjunct of the "new Science" was as indispensable to his history as it was satisfying to his religious faith.

The similarity of Herder's philosophy of history to Vico's was a matter of parallel creation rather than derivation, and it bespoke an alternative to the philosophical history of the Enlightenment that was more common than its presentation by a few apparently unaffiliated eccentrics might lead one to believe. Like Vico, Herder rejected the rational universalism of the philosophers' approach to natural structure and human history in favor of a pluralistic, individuated, genetic view of the historical process. But unlike Vico he attributed a creative rather than a formative role to transcendent divinity—and, revealingly enough, his history was all the more incoherent for it. Herder, indeed, propounded a more decisive and a more developed doctrine of individuality than did Vico. He emphasized far more the incommensurable distinctiveness of each people, popularizing the term *Volksgeist* to seal

39

it and importing the Leibnizian concept of the monad to finalize it; and he even tended to define totality, when he thought in holistic terms, as the progressive emanations of inimitable and incomparable forms which manifested the rich fecundity of the unifying ground of all things.

In the happy formulation which a recent commentator has given to Herder's attitude toward the components of history:

There was an infinite number of variations on the theme of man; each one had a finite existence; but as each came into being and was fulfilled in time, total humanity grew richer. In the course of history all possible combinations of human sensibility . . . would make their appearance. . . . Their filiations are tenuous. The possible cultural manifestations of the human are infinite, unpredictable, disorderly. . . . In bestowing significance upon the history of all peoples, Herder rather consistently refused to engage in comparisons among them. Each *Volk* contained the principle of its individuality within itself; it was a self-respecting monad. . . . All peoples partake of humanity in different forms. . .; they are variant renderings of the common Humanity. . . . Progress is the gradual expression of all possible *Volk* configurations. These forms are not created simultaneously, for it is the divine purpose that they be revealed through the passage of time.[43]

This Herderian individuation extends through time as well as space—it distinguishes moments as well as individuals from one another. "The whole course of a man's life is change," wrote Herder: "the different periods of his life are tales of transformation, and the whole species is one continued metamorphosis. . . . Thus the history of man is ultimately a theater of transformations, which He alone can review, who animates all these figures, and feeds and enjoys them all. The wanderer upon Earth, the transient emphemeron, can only admire the wonders of this great spirit in a narrow circle, enjoy the form that belongs to him in the general choir. . . ."[44]

Not that Herder was entirely indifferent to the problem of general coherence in history, or that, as an earthly wanderer, he refrained from considering human history as a whole. His preoccupation with the perennial tension between the One and the Many has been duly noted, and there has been no dearth of analyses showing his obligations to the universality of the Christian tradition and of the Enlightenment, however inconsistent these may have been to each other and to his pluralistic emphasis, to account for his preferential inclination toward Western culture and for the integrated presentation of it that emerged from his *Ideas Toward a Philosophy of History*. What is important about these specific judgments is their reference, in Herder, to a general and essential teleological orientation whose end was nonhistorical because it was as yet unrealized and hence outside of history but which yet provided a point of view for regarding what lay within history. Herder himself announced this orientation in the very midst of his assertion of the transient particularity in human affairs, thereby indicating his own conviction of their compatibility and, incidentally, accounting for his own performance more satisfactorily than with his verdict of *non possumus* on the very range of history that he travelled. "As the human intellect . . . seeks unity in every kind of variety, and the divine mind, its prototype, has stamped the most innumerable multiplicity upon the Earth with unity, we may venture from the vast realm of change to revert to the simplest position: *all mankind are only one and the same species.*"[45]

Indeed, "humanity"—in the joint anthropological and moral sense of the enlightened virtues which define the human species—is, for Herder, "the end of human nature," so established by "the beautiful and sublime laws of nature, by which [the tumultuous scenes through which we have been wandering] have been governed," and this end is what ties together man's history. "In all his earthly institutions man can conceive no other end, than what lies in himself, that is, in the weak or strong, base or noble nature, that God gave him. Now if throughout the whole creation we know nothing, except by what it is, and what it effects, man's end upon Earth is shown us by his nature and his history, as by the clearest demonstration." Despite the principle of spontaneous self-activity which nature implanted in man and despite nature's organization of man "as variously as the human species could be organized on this Earth"—provisions which make for the heterogeneity in human history—Jesus' Christianity and the "gift of reason" in man are two unifying forces which "have promoted the progress of humanity in our species, and . . . will continue to promote it," for "there is no doubt, generally speaking, that what has not yet appeared upon Earth will at some future period appear."[46]

Actually, "in proportion as reason increases among mankind" the historical record already exhibits the diminution of "the destructive demons of the human race" and "the progress of arts and inventions," under the aegis of natural laws which prescribe not only a "perfection, . . . arising out of the mode of action of the powers" of any particular thing or limited system of such things but also such holistic regulations as the subservience of "all the destructive Powers in Nature . . . to the Consummation of the Whole." Natural laws founded, moreover, the permanent welfare of the human race on human reason as the "*one principle* . . . which endeavors to produce unity out of multiplicity, order out of disorder and out of a variety of powers and designs one symmetrical and durably beautiful whole"; they prescribe the necessity that reason and justice "gain more Footing among Men in the Course of Time," since "Times connect themselves together, in virtue of their nature, and with them the child of Time, the race of mankind." They prescribe too the "intrinsic necessity," based on the transcendent principle that "a wise Goodness disposes the Fate of Mankind," that "everything that can take place upon Earth must take place upon it, provided that it happens according to rules that carry their perfection within themselves." Thus the orderly progression of the human race is "Nature's universal plan. . . . Guided by this clue, I wander through the labyrinth of history, and everywhere perceive divine harmonious order." History fulfills its function of teaching us "to act according to God's eternal laws" only when it is so guided, and although Herder does not present it as such the faith in a rational order that does not yet exist but is coming to exist is the source of this guidance for him. "Human reason . . . invents before she can apply. . . . There is nothing enthusiastical in the hope that, wherever men dwell, at some future period will dwell men rational, just, and happy: happy, not through the means of their own reason alone, but of the common reason of their whole fraternal race. . . . Of what kind the modern cultivation of Europe could be is evident . . . : a universal, reciprocating formation of all ranks and nations was not then to be thought of; and when will it be? Reason, however, and the effective joint activity of mankind, keep on their unwearied course; and it may even be deemed a good sign, when the best fruits ripen not prematurely."[47]

Not only Herder's overall design, moreover, but even the force which links the various stages of his developing individualities bear the signs of an extrahistorical origin. The organic pattern of birth, growth, and decline which Herder adjudged to be the process of all particular things in nature and of all individual nations in history has an ancient pedigree, but there is evidence that far from giving the analogy a direct historical form Herder applied it to history by way of the vitalist doctrine he found in contemporary natural science. Thus he insisted that there was what he called variously "a living organic power," "this vital power," and "the vital principle," with which " all the powers of nature are connected" and which creates, maintains, and is responsible for the degeneration of all natural things and national forms of people in time.[48] Whether eighteenth-century vitalism was biological in origin, as it was for Lamarck, or whether it was a central tenet in the philosophy of nature, as it was for Diderot and Goethe, it is clear that as a force which permeated, organized, and unified natural phenomena through space and time the vitalist spirit entered into Herder's historism as the principle of national coherence fully grown in a nonhistorical matrix.[49]

When they are considered from our point of view in tandem, the place of Vico's and Herder's historism in the eighteenth century is not so eccentric as might sometimes appear. For if it is the case at least that Vico is noted for his distinctive epistemology through his identification of truth with "what we made ourselves" and thus with history, and if it is equally the case that both Vico and Herder founded modern historism by positing the ultimacy of national individualities and the autonomy of their developing stages through time, it is also true that they both emphasized the general organic pattern of the stages through which all these individualities coincided in developing; the common genetic character of this pattern which stressed the overriding importance of the primitive, mythical stage; and the role of Providence in guaranteeing the human unity toward which the historical individualities, because of their independence, might not converge on their own.

It is the case too that the two writers were complementary in the location of this pattern: whereas Vico made it the prime content of a "new science" which comprehended the study of man's whole life, with history as its chief dimension and instrument, Herder hypostatized the essential historical nature of this pattern by ensconcing it in his masterwork, his *Ideas Toward a Philosophy of History*. Hence both men were committed to an implicit belief in the rationality of history, and while they opposed the rationalism that would make this derivative from the reason which was thought to inform other kinds of reality Herder demonstrated explicitly that history was the model for the kind of thinking that Vico extended beyond history to all the humanities. Because of their overt hostility to rationalism, there was little danger of confusing the two kinds of rationality in the eighteenth century, but we shall have to bear in mind, to clear up future confusions, the combination of similarity and dissimilarity in the relationship between the kind of rationality that extended over history and nonhistory from the direction of nonhistory and the kind of rationality that extended over history and nonhistory from the direction of history.

The second variant of the historistic tradition—that is, the variant which maintained a plurality of principles for the various kinds of reality, including an isolated historical reason to account for the coherence of the past—goes back most obviously to the special combination of philosophy and history in David Hume. Even if Hume's identification of religion as "a species of philosophy" and his life-long interest in the subject of religion vitiate the simple old notion which had him replace philosophy by history, and make it appear as if the overt turn from the one to the other was more of a prudential than an authentic conversion, the fact remains that intellectually he counted on history to supply the coherence that he had derived from philosophy. Whereas he had demonstrated in *A Treatise of Human Nature* that coherence belongs not to external nature but to the human mind, he came to rely upon human history "to discover the constant and universal principles of human nature" which he could publicly demonstrate in no other way.[50] Hence the moral goal of history, "a most improving part of knowledge" written by "true friends of virtue" may well have sounded in unison with his enlightened friends, but its function with him was radically different from theirs: where they used the junction of history and morality to celebrate the service of history to the universal principles of morals, Hume used it to celebrate the historical basis of morals.[51] For him the coherence in morals, as in knowledge, was derived from a concrete experience to which history provided the principles.

But if Hume's principles, as well as his career, brought the notion of a distinctive historical coherence into bold relief, he was not exempt either from the equally characteristic tendency of the historists to borrow from outside of history the essence of the coherence they claimed to find in history. Thus he echoed the sentiments of his enlightened friends when he held a good part of history's value to consist in the circumstance that it "affords materials to most of the sciences."[52] He was explicit, moreover, about the roots of the primary historical pattern in moral philosophy, for he saw unchanging principles of human nature running through history; he grounded them in the philosophical connection of human with uniform natural principles and of effects with regular causes; he deemed the chief purpose of history to be their elucidation; and, perhaps most revealing of all, he typified what was distinctive in the philosophical approach of eighteenth-century historians by demonstrating the historical congeniality of the philosophically grounded principle of human coherence. Thus he insisted that the idea of a constant human nature—"that there is a great uniformity among the actions of men, in all nations and ages, and that human nature remains still the same, in [its principles and operations, that mankind are so much the same, in] all times and places, that history informs us of nothing new or strange in this particular"—is derived from the philosophical congruity of our judgments concerning natural and social coherence.[53] "As the *union* betwixt motives and actions has the same constancy, as that in any natural operations, so its influence on the understanding is the same, in *determining* us to infer the existence of one from that of another." For "whether we consider mankind according to the difference of sexes, ages, governments, or methods of education, the same uniformity and regular operation of natural principles are discernible. Like causes still produce like effects; in the same manner as in the mutual action of the elements and powers of nature. . . . In judging of the actions of men we must proceed upon the same maxims, as when we reason concerning external objects. When any phenomena are constantly and invariably conjoin'd together, they acquire such a connection in the imagination, that it passes from one to the other, without any doubt or hesitation. . . . Nothing but an absolute necessity can oblige an historian to break the order of time, and in his *narration* to give precedence to an event, which was in *reality* posterior to another."[54]

Hume's notion that the connectedness of events—and particularly the kind of connectedness that was classifiable in terms of cause and effect, i.e., motive and action—was epistemologically rather than ontologically based may have been idiosyncratic, but both his belief in the transcendent validity of universal human principles and his confidence in the compatibility of these principles with their empirical deployment in the particular events of history were representative of the philosophical historians in general and earned him the sobriquet of "the good David" among the philosophes. Hence Hume's assumption that the permanent principles of human nature, formally anchored though they may be in the structure of the human mind, were yet substantively knowable only in the particular history they transcended—that, indeed, history's "chief use is only to discover the constant and universal principles of human nature, by . . . furnishing us with materials, from which we may form our observations, and become acquainted with the regular springs of human action and behavior."[55] Historical reasoning, indeed, was for Hume a subset of the kind of probabilistic inference from factual experience generally which he admitted had not "the good fortune to receive . . . sanction" from the other philosophers, but which he himself found philosophically respectable.[56] Hume was thus linked with the rationalist philosophical historians of his century when he assumed the kind of implicit structure in history that was at once derivative from valid philosophy or science and knowable only as the otherwise invisible bond among the historical facts with which it was consistent.

Thus history and the philosophy of history in the early modern period of Western culture sustain the conception of a period ending with the eighteenth century, witnessing the dominance of classical order with its implication that "history and science will become separated from each other." In universal historians like Walter Raleigh and Jacques-Bénigne Bossuet the divine providential patterning of events remained obvious despite the Divinity's humanistic modulation into a kind of puppeteer controlling the events of earthly history with gossamer strings.[57] The seventeenth-century secular philosophers who wrote history were even more obviously rationalistic in this sense.[58] As has been noted above, Hobbes in his lay histories applied the doctrines of human nature and government derived from his political theory. Spinoza's and Leibniz's approaches to history would be incomprehensible without reference, respectively, to their rationalistic philosophy and to their ethnographic, juristic, and monadic principles.[59] And Pierre Bayle, finally, has been adjudged a climactic seventeenth-century figure whose religious piety permeated his critical history and gave it what body and consistency it had.[60]

It is generally agreed now that what was most distinctive in eighteenth-century historiography was characterized by two related developments: the convergence of the scholarly and the general traditions of history, and the consequent emergence of an amalgam which applied critical standards to the connections as well as the facts of history. In its best exemplars this amalgam produced a combination of secularized, historizable scheme and methodically ascertained fact under the aegis of what is generally labeled "philosophical history." Now it is important to understand the precise bearing of this convergence and its resulting amalgam, because confusion about them has spawned both the older underestimation and the compensatory later overestimation of historicity during the eighteenth century. The convergence of the scholarly and general modes of historical literature meant an advance from the mutual segregation that had characterized their prior relationship, but it did not yet mean the intimate union that would characterize the writing of history in the ninteenth century. Thus on the one hand the best of the general historians—including both what the French and English authoritatively called "philosophical historians" and what the Germans more covertly and politically called "pragmatic historians"—were acquainted with and at least made use of scholarly and antiquarian work in their historical *magna opera*.[61] Indeed, an important group of the German pragmatic historians—notably the Göttingen school but also Justus Möser, the famous historian of Osnabrück—not only applied the scholarly results of antiquarians but themselves contributed to the genre.[62]

On the other hand there always remained a perceptible seam between the two kinds of history in the eighteenth century. The fissure was obvious in the customary scorn which the philosophical historians heaped upon what they considered the pedantry and what we respect as the erudition of the antiquarian mode of history; but it was more indicative, if more shaded, in the equally prevalent insistence of the general historians, from Voltaire through Grimm to such a consummate historian as Gibbon, that the historian "must write as a philosopher," for it was precisely in the connectedness of history—in the emphasis of the philosophical historians on the search for "the human causes" of events—that the philosophy was invested.[63] The gap between a philosophical coherence and a historical factuality was most visible in the cases of failed complementarity, and the lamentable gulf between promise and performance in such ambitious pragmatic historians as the founder of the Göttingen school, Johann Christoph Gatterer, while the claimant to the first coherent and reliable national history of Germany, Justus Möser, exemplifies the continuing conjoint independence of general and scholarly history. Gatterer sketched no less than eight programmatic surveys of a universal history that would be based on a "system of events," featuring their "inner connection" in general and the relationship between "causes and effects" in particular; but he also helped to develop the auxiliary disciplines such as diplomatics, geography, genealogy, and paleography, which seventeenth-century scholars like the Maurists had founded to advance the critical science of factual history, and like them, he concerned himself with the problem of "verification" (*Evidenz*) in history.[64] In his universal histories, moreover, he obviously failed to integrate these different levels of historizing, for his general statements on "the universal nexus of things" and his unintegrated charts of global facts sat side-by-side with little modulation.[65] Möser did better, as befit his narrower, national focus, but for him too the destiny of the "common landed-property-owners" which was supposed to furnish the common theme of a variegated but unified German history turned out, on execution, to be split into objects of specific research into the history of a particular state within the Empire.[66]

But if the relations between general and learned history, at once mutually relevant and mutually distinct, help to define the limits of eighteenth-century historiography, the precise nature of the coherent themes that were the sinews of the general history defines the character of what connection there was. The structure of philosophical history, in short, stemmed from the peculiar eighteenth-century view of what philosophy was. From our point of view the philosophe may have been a man of letters rather than a philosopher properly so-called, but this was not the contemporary view of eighteenth-century men. For them the philosophe was indeed a philosopher, and if he was marked rather by

his love of "moral truth" and his knowledge of "the duties of man"—
by what is "essential to the conduct of life"—than by his metaphysics
or his philosophy of nature, then this characterization defined rather
than invalidated his philosophy.[67] Thus while the philosophers of the
seventeenth century and the philosophes of the eighteenth may have
shared the belief in persistent principles of human nature, where the
seventeenth-century thinkers tended to connect them with metaphysics
and detach them from history, eighteenth-century thinkers tended, in
contrast, to divorce them from the metaphysics they denied and to
orient them toward the actualities of human behavior in which they
were expressed.

Now it is a truism of traditional historiographical commentary that
the philosophical history characteristic of the eighteenth century was
unhistorical in the constancy, the universality, and the logicality of its
human principles, and this judgment is both substantiated and extenu-
ated by the recognition that in the eighteenth century, as ever in the
Western tradition, there were principles of historical coherence that
were suprahistorical in their grounding. What subjected the philosophical historians to an especially negative subsequent review was not only
their failure to acknowledge the transcendent derivation of their principles, but also the congeniality of their extrahistorical principles to
historical facts, a congeniality that made the nonhistorical dimension of
these principles especially egregious.

But in fact that the philosophical historians applied to history constant conceptual linkages which were not themselves historical.
Voltaire, for example, wrote little about principles of historical coherence, but analysis of the histories that he wrote shows indubitably
the application of a philosophical theory of causation which helped to
distinguish his work, with its claim to dwell on "that which deserves the
attention of all time, which paints the spirit and customs of men, which
may serve for instruction and to counsel the love of virtue, of the arts
and of the fatherland," from "minute details" which he deplored in
unphilosophical history.[68] Thus the philosophical historians of the
eighteenth century—Voltaire, Robertson, Gibbon, but definitely not
Hume—all asserted a new kind of rational structure behind the apparent chaos of historical events and identified this structure with the
consistent organization of nature, man, society, or any other conceivable collective reality in this the only accessible world. For enlightened
historians who inherited Descartes' confidence that "those long chains
of reasoning, simple and easy as they are, of which geometricians make
use in order to arrive at the most difficult demonstrations, had caused
me to imagine that all those things which fall under the cognizance of

man might very likely be mutually related in the same fashion," but who applied it to history as he did not; and who therefore believed, along with Voltaire, that "Nature being everywhere the same, men must necessarily have adopted the same truths, and fallen into the same errors" and that "God has implanted in us a principle of reason that is universal": for such historians there was no bar to invoking the substance of doctrines about nature for the interpretation of the acts stemming from human nature or to utilizing rational assumptions about the uniformity of nature for the historical criticism of witnesses to claimed miracles and other natural irrationalities.[69]

The connection between the Enlightenment's exemplary theory of history and its assumption of an extrahistorical uniformity in nature that was relevant to history was overt in Bolingbroke, Voltaire's mentor, who made the connection in the same letter as he gave his famous definition of history as "philosophy teaching by examples how to conduct ourselves in all the situations of private and public life." For he based this definition on history's function of providing an accessible education in that philosophy: "There are certain general principles, and rules of life and conduct which must always be true, because they are conformable to the invariable nature of things. He who studies history as he would study philosophy will soon distinguish and collect them, and by doing so will soon form to himself a general system of ethics and politics on the surest foundations, on the trial of those principles and rules in all ages, and on the confirmation of them by universal experience." It should be noted, parenthetically, that Bolingbroke distinguished history from and subordinated it to "experience."[70] We would remark, more essentially, that the skepticism about the past through which Bolingbroke also represented the characteristic historiography of the Enlightenment and which expressed itself in the thread of critical reason, negatively connecting the more credulous aspects of that past, had its roots in a philosophical Pyrrhonism that lay outside of history.

The most transparent of the eighteenth-century philosophical historians in this transcendent respect was undoubtedly Condorcet, who subordinated history to social science, which, in turn, he identified with social mathematics, and Kant, who subordinated history to natural and moral philosophy. Thus a close analysis of the Marquis de Condorcet's celebrated *Esquisse d'un tableau historique des progrès de l'esprit humain* makes it clear that its notorious doctrine of an inevitable progress was guaranteed not by historical laws but by principles of social mathematics expressed in the general laws governing the activities and the progress of human nature. Condorcet saw the whole history of mankind as a combination of intellectual activities "to further the progress of human reason," and he identified this rational progress with the unitary advance of science, extolling the historical harmony for the future as much as for the past of the species. "The sole foundation for belief in the natural sciences is the idea that the general laws governing the phenomena of the universe, whether they are known or unknown, are necessary and constant; and why should this principle be less true for the development of the intellectual and moral faculties of man than for the other operations of nature?" Hence, "the human species has become what the necessary development of human faculties demanded that it become." The same "general laws" govern the phenomena of nature, "the development of faculties of the individual," "the progress of the human mind," and, consequently, the pattern of history. For "the history of man . . . is linked by an uninterrupted chain of facts and observations; . . . the picture of the march and progress of the human mind" that gave history its coherence was not itself, for Condorcet, historical—indeed, it has been called "meta-historical" by his most authoritative commentator.[71] Condorcet himself assigned the elucidation of its developmental laws to "the true subject of philosophy" and characterized the method of getting at "those general truths" which were founded on human psychology as "this metaphysical method." History, then, simply afforded the empirical evidence of the applications of and erroneous departures from these social scientific laws. History was thus both subservient and congenial to them.

Not only the philosophical historians like Condorcet but eighteenth-century philosophers of history like Immanuel Kant specified the suprahistorical basis of historical coherence. However idiosyncratic Kant's specific concept of a regulative principle may have been as the source of historical connectedness, the general resort to an extra-historical stability for the purpose was archetypical. Kant's famed distinction between "the mutual antagonism," "confusion and chaos of individual subjects" on the one hand and the harmonious progress of the human race toward a just civil constitution on the other was based on his more fundamental distinction between "the disordered play of human affairs" treated by a "merely empirical history" and the "regular . . . ,uniform, continuous course . . . of world history" when it is considered "in the large" by "a philosophical mind" from the perspective of "constant natural laws" which provides "an *a priori* guide" toward "a completed rational end."[72] Thus Kant assigned the connection of historical things to an explicitly philosophical principle, in contrast to the unorganized facts of empirical history, but when he insisted that this principle of philosophical teleology was articulated in an analogy with natural laws and thus with the coherence tailored to the linkage of physical phenomena, he was demonstrating too the affinity of the philosophical principle to the historical facts it ordered. History, in both its rationalistic and its historistic forms, expressed fundamental principles whose primary validity lay beyond history and lent to history the pattern this temporal medium indubitably sported during these centuries.

3

THE HISTORY OF NINETEENTH-CENTURY HISTORICAL COHERENCE

The nineteenth century witnessed the triumph of history and has probably been the most historically minded of Western eras. The most authoritative of its philosophers devised doctrines of change and development that were at least analogous to history. Historians wrote large and integrated works of literature in the grand manner. The receptivity of the cultivated public for historical products that illuminated exotic times and places as well as for those that expanded knowledge of the present by presenting the continuous context of the past reached an all-time high. The search for patterns within history was all the more intensely pursued, for whether history was deemed a most appropriate field for the application of dynamic principles, or the only appropriate field for the discovery of patterns paradigmatic of all reality, or an autonomous field whose coherence was presumably independent of extrahistorical reality, nineteenth-century philosophers of history, theorists of history, and historians retained the constant principles of their early-modern predecessors. Although the shift of these principles to the form of a kinetic, absolute, or covert scaffolding enabled the nineteenth-century paragons of historicity to look with overt contumely upon these predecessors in any case, the most characteristic philosophers and historians in the nineteenth century perpetuated alternative approaches of rationalists and historists and the transcendent tendencies common to both.

As the pervasive rule of the evolutionary idea indicates, the mobilization of the stable concepts which traditionally provided the connections among historical events always postulated a constant substratum which perpetuated an extrahistorical grounding for its apparently historized coherence. The nineteenth century may well have witnessed the first divergence between the philosophy of history and historiography—certainly the mutual aversion of philosophers of history and historical practitioners which is so prominent today finds its precedent in the nineteenth century—for the fact remains that the nineteenth-century philosophy of history exposed the extrahistorical derivation of the various concepts of historical coherence which always had been an implicit truth of historical practice. The reciprocal repulsion of history and the philosophy of history in the nineteenth century manifested the different location of those grounds for the two genres. For philosophy of history the ground lay in the realm of philosophy—obviously—and of science.[1] For the practice of history the ground lay in the realm of politics. Nineteenth-century philosophy of history made explicit a general dimension of time that was distinct from history and that modulated the application of timeless categories to the specific time of history.

The two dominant philosophers of history in the nineteenth century were undoubtedly the rationalists Hegel and Comte, since the first provided the authoritative model for all who predicated an ideal dialectical connectedness in their historical schemes while the second provided the authoritative model for all those who predicated an evolutionary scientific connectedness in their historical schemes. Both combined a transcendence of and a congeniality to history in ways that were clearly perceptible. They buttressed the continuum between historical and extrahistorical reason by temporalizing extrahistorical reason to which historical reason was indissolubly linked.

The more grandiose of these schemes—and the one that was probably the most influential of the entire century—was Hegel's, and it is with justice that the introduction to his lectures on *The Philosophy of History* has been entitled *Reason in History,* since Hegel himself identified "the philosophical history of the world"—the kind of history which he acknowledged himself to be investigating—with the triumph of reason in history. "The only thought which philosophy brings with it is the idea of reason—the idea that reason governs the world, and that world history is therefore a rational process."[2] Moreover, his deliberate refusal to give a formal definition to this reason in history—he characterized it formally as "substance and infinite power," "a general design," the "ultimate end of everything" and "the agent which realizes and implements this end," "the spirit and the course of its development"—was obviously in the service of presenting reason simply as the perspective on the universal rather than the particular in history. For "reason . . . cannot concern itself with particular and finite ends, but only with the absolute. . . . It deals not with individual situations but with a universal thought which runs throughout the whole. This universal element is not to be found in the world of contingent phenomena; it is the unity behind the multitude of particulars."[3] What Hegel makes explicit, then, is what was implied in all of the rationality attributed to history up until then and ever since then—that reason in history stood for coherent pattern or the connectedness of history; and he made explicit too the assumption of his whole panrationalistic genre that this coherent pattern was continuous with the rational structure of reality outside history. He maintained that the rational process which could be inferred from "the result" of history was brought into history by philosophy. The rational reality that philosophy demonstrated became a necessary assumption for history.[4]

What distinguished Hegel from his predecessors and constituted his originality in the attribution of reason to history were the three features of his rationality which smoothed the continuity between the eternity of absolute structure and the mutability of history, guaranteeing that the same reason would be the sinew of both.

First, his dialectical reason had movement, time, and history built into its very being as one of its two essential dimensions. This bidimensionality of reason featured both an absolute core which moved logically, out of historical time, and a phenomenal form which moved historically, within socialized time. The most obvious expression of this bifurcated reason was developmental—reason's movement from its absolute substance to its circumstantial form. The self-determination of reason through its acknowledgment as developmental, and thereby reason's rationalization of its particular objects, was at the heart of the dialectic. Hegel expressed this process variously as the inherent drive of reason from the inner spirit to the outer manifestation of spirit—"the genuine truth is the prodigious transfer of the inner into the outer, the building of reason into the real world, and this has been the task of the world during the whole course of its history"[5]—and as the translation of reason from "potentiality into actuality both in the natural universe and in the spiritual world."[6]

In his masterwork, *The Phenomenology of Mind,* Hegel fused these various expressions in his demonstration that "the inner necessity" of philosophy, which inhered in its "systematic" or logical character, was "the same as" its "external necessity," which entailed its "gradual development" through time. To be dual is thus both in reason's essence—at once logical and historical—and in reason's experience—it recapitulates systematically the stages it goes through developmentally. "Spirit is alone Reality. It is the inner being of the world . . . it assumes objective, determinate form, and enters into relations with itself—it is externality . . . ; yet in this determination, and in its otherness, it is still one with itself. . . . Science lays before us the morphogenetic process of this cultural development in all its detailed fullness and necessity, and at the same time it shows it to be something that has already sunk into the mind as a moment of its being and become a possession of mind. . . . Existence has no more to be changed into the form of what is inherent and implicit, but only the implicit— . . . already present as recollection—into the form of what is explicit, of what is objective to self. . . . Time . . . is the notion itself in the form of existence."[7]

The second way in which Hegel mediated between absolute Being and contingent history was to insert a transitional kind of nonhistorical time between them. Indeed, he operated on the basis of express distinctions between the logic of the dialectic, the time of the dialectic, and the reality of coherent history. Much philosophical argument has been expended on the alternatives of a logical or historical interpretation of his phenomenological spirit,[8] but surely it approaches Hegel's own intention more nearly to see in the history of consciousness which undoubtedly forms one dimension of his *Phenomenology of Spirit* an investment of the dialectical process in a nonhistorical kind of time that is compatible with the purely logical movement of the dialectic in a way that historical time can never be. The deliberate consonance of the systematic and the temporal aspects of the same dialectical truth— Hegel distinguished them as complementary "inner" and "outer" necessities respectively—was a prominent feature of the *Phenomenology*'s famous preface:

The inner necessity that knowledge should be science lies in its very nature; and the adequate and sufficient explanation for this lies simply and solely in the systematic exposition of the philosophy itself. The external necessity, however, insofar as this is apprehended in a universal way, and apart from the accident of the personal element and the particular occasioning influences affecting the individual, is the same as the internal: it lies in the form and shape in which the process of time presents the existence of its moments. To show that the time process does raise philosophy to the level of scientific system would, therefore, be the only true justification of the attempts which aim at proving that philosophy must assume this character; because the temporal process would thus bring out and lay bare the necessity of it, nay more, would at the same time be carrying out that very aim itself.[9]

Although Hegel sometimes called the temporal dimension of dialectical consciousness "history"—he insisted that in penetrating the forms of every moment in time "the universal mind at work in the world has had the patience . . . to take upon itself the prodigious labor of the world's history"—he did not usually call it so, and in general it is clear that for him the temporal process of consciousness was something different from the temporal process of history. For one thing, the temporal process of consciousness was a process of "universal spirit" or at most of "the universal individual." On the other hand, the sphere of particular existence, "with a content in its contingent and arbitrary aspects, features that have no necessity," he tended rather, from the perspective of the phenomenological consciousness, to align with the timeless systematic side of this consciousness, since "the particular individual" merely recapitulates the dialectical process which "the universal spirit" has undergone through "the long reaches of time's extent." Moreover, this sphere Hegel himself more characteristically assigned to "the purely historical aspect" of "historical truths." "In modern times . . . an individual finds the abstract form ready made. . . . Hence nowadays the task consists not so much in getting the individual clear of the stage of sensuous immediacy, . . . but rather the very opposite: it consists in actualizing the universal."[10] From this perspective, indeed, the logical and the temporal aspects of spiritual consciousness are more than alternative views of a single dialectical process: they are dovetailed as essential constituents of the process. Particular individuals become part of the temporal process only insofar as they are the stuff through which the universal spirit determines itself, and this temporal process in turn subserves the spirit's drive to self-knowledge which is itself beyond time. In Hegel's summary formulation: "Time . . . appears as spirit's destiny and necessity, where spirit is not yet complete within itself; it is the necessity compelling spirit to enrich the share self-consciousness has in consciousness, . . . to make manifest what is at first within— i.e., to vindicate it for spirit's certainty of self."[11] Thus the relationship of the time of consciousness to the logical unfolding of the Absolute Spirit's implications in consciousness is but one more in the long list of opposites that Hegel's dialectic claimed to reconcile.

But if the dialectical forms of reason had an inherent tendency to develop from an absolute spiritual core out of time into so many manifestations of spirit in time, the reverse was also true for Hegel: the particular deeds of actual men in the human past had a structure which oriented history toward the realization of conscious progress. Unquestionably, however, a gap subsisted between the heterogeneity of historical events and the uniform integration of rational structure, and Hegel filled this gap with the famous, if ambiguous, notion of "the cunning of reason," which functioned as a third mediatory device. This idea itself had a long history, highlighted at the beginning of the eighteenth century by Bernard de Mandeville's moral formula, "private vices, public benefits," and at the century's end by Kant's hypothetical philosophy of history which acknowledged the prevalence of what is "complicated and accidental in individuals" and therefore of "this senseless march of human events" in "true empirical history," but which yet insisted that "individual human beings" also "work to promote that which they would care little for if they knew about it," and that the philosopher could thus view this empirical history "from another standpoint"—that is, as a progressive process dominated by certain rational principles and directed toward a definite "end of nature."[12]

Now Hegel did more than to transfer this bridge between the particularity of individual interests and passions and the universality of reason from the sphere of philosophical observation to an inference from real history, although he surely accomplished this when he prefaced his discussion of the cunning of reason with the proposition that "the universal arises out of the particular and determinate and its negation. . . . Particular interests contend with one another, and some are destroyed in the process. But it is from this very conflict and destruction of particular things that the universal emerges, and it remains unscathed itself. . . . It is what we may call the cunning of reason that it sets the passions to work in its service, so that the agents by which it gives itself existence must pay the penalty and suffer the loss."[13]

The time of history was therefore for Hegel a different matter from time in general, for the internal relations of history as a kind of actual reality were distinct from the internal relations of the dialectical consciousness through which it was known. As Hegel declared at the end of the *Phenomenology,* when "Spirit . . . gives its [own] embodiment over to Recollection," it attains a "new stage of existence, a new world, and a new embodiment or mode of Spirit."[14] Hence the dialectical duality of logical and temporal process was accompanied by the dialectical duality between the temporal process of Spirit and the historical embodiment of Spirit, imperfectly mediated by the cunning of reason. In various contexts Hegel always affirmed both sides of the latter duality and, despite his own devices, the incompleteness of the linkage between them.

Even in *Reason in History* (the introductory section of his lectures on the philosophy of history), philosophical in its orientation as it was, Hegel posited the empirical a posteriori autonomy of history. After insisting that he *"need not . . . make any . . . claims upon your faith* [in reason]," he went on to underline the empirical basis of his historical rationalism. *"That the history of the world is a rational process . . . must be the result of our study of history. But we must be sure to take history as it is; in other words, we must proceed historically and empirically."*[15]

And yet Hegel emphasized even more strongly, albeit with apparent inconsistency, that the rational—i.e., coherent—interpretation of history was not merely a result but a necessary condition of history, both in the sense of history as a kind of knowledge and in the sense of history as a kind of reality. Thus he repeatedly maintained that as a branch of knowledge history must start from as well as end with the conviction that rational process was primary in history. His own development recapitulated this precedence of the a priori in philosophy over the a posteriori of history in his philosophy of history, for he started from a philosophical framework for history and subsequently filled it with empirical content. He laid the epistemological basis for this requirement in the *Phenomenology*, where in the very same context which justified "history" as "the recollection" of autonomous minds "from the side of their free existence appearing in the form of contingency," he stipulated that in recollection spirit has "conserved" the results of its original experience, that hence in its historical phase spirit, "apparently starting solely from itself, yet at the same time . . . commences at a higher level," and that therefore true history is intellectually comprehended history.[16]

In the *Philosophy of Right* of 1821, which contained the first sketch of his philosophy of history and adumbrated the philosophical emphasis of his initial lectures on this subject during 1822 and 1823, the general acknowledgment of duality was definitely weighted on the side of the internally necessary development of mind. His equable introduction of the historical section in the *Philosophy of Right* ran, "In world history the element in which the universal mind exists . . . is the actuality of mind in the whole compass of its internality and externality alike," but he immediately went on to give a decidedly one-sided gloss on this proposition in the light of the "absolute universality" of world history, subordinating the particular acts of history to the intellectual development of general spirit. "The particular . . . is present only as ideal. . . . Since mind is implicitly and actually reason, and reason is explicit to itself in mind as knowledge, world history is the necessary development, out of the concept of mind's freedom alone, of the moments of reason and so of the self-consciousness and freedom of mind. This development is the interpretation and actualization of universal mind. The history of mind is its own act. . . . In history its act is to gain consciousness of itself as mind, to apprehend itself in the interpretation of itself to itself." And Hegel went on explicitly to insist that whatever "the specific worth and significance" of the particular acts of individual nations, states, and persons: "world history, however, is above the point of view from which these things matter." From the perspective of world history each of these individualities becomes "a necessary moment in the Idea of the world mind. . . . The concrete Ideas, the minds of the nations, have their truth and their destiny in the concrete Idea which is absolute universality, i.e., in the world mind. Around its throne

they stand as the executors of its actualization and as signs and ora-
ments of its grandeur."[17]

When Hegel came to lecture on the philosophy of history as such, the
larger autonomy which he conceded to empirical history in this format
did not prevent him from insisting on the philsophical role of rational
pattern as a necessary assumption of such history.[18] "Even the ordinary, run-of-the-mill historian who believes and professes . . . that he
is dedicated to the facts, is by no means passive in his thinking; he brings
his categories with him, and they influence this vision of the data he has
before him. . . . Whoever looks at the world rationally will find that it
in turn assumes a rational aspect; the two exist in a reciprocal relationship."[19]

But in these very lectures Hegel admitted, frankly, despite all his
devices, that empirical "subjective" particularity and rational process
did not always dovetail in history, and he thereby indicated their separate orbits. "That the union of the universal substance, which exists in
and for itself, with the particular and the subjective, is the sole truth, is a
speculative proposition which is dealt with in this general form by logic.
But in the actual process of world history . . . we find that the subjective element or consciousness is [not] yet in a position to know the true
nature of the ultimate end of history, the concept of spirit. . . . Although the subjective consciousness is still unaware of it, the universal
substance is nevertheless present in its particular ends and realizes itself
through them."[20] Thus time and again Hegel insisted on the empirical
"inadequacy" of "our principle . . . that reason governs the world and
has always done so," together with its "religious equivalent in the
doctrine of a ruling providence," on the grounds that usually these
principles are made to lack "determinate application."[21] Thus repeatedly Hegel noted the discrepancies between the tenets and the facts and
articulated the historically flawed tenets speculatively.

But more important was Hegel's conviction that the dominion of
reason (and of its correlative providential faith) in world history could
be perceived "in its determinate form" through the proper approach to
history itself, and that "a reconciliation" was therefore possible between rational process and empirical facts.[22] It was the dual assumption of this distinction and reconcilability that especially marked the
Hegelian legacy to the historiography of the nineteenth century. For
what the notion did was to legitimate two levels of history, one fortuitous, one rational, the fortuitous one secondary, the rational one
primary, but despite their mutual independence both connected with
each other and both empirically grounded in the facts of history.

Hegel's famous declaration that "what is rational is actual and what is actual is rational" is now generally interpreted in its correct sense of referring to an essential level of intelligible reality behind the confusing vagaries of existence. Nor did he refrain from applying this distinction between actuality and existence to history. "If we say that universal reason is fulfilled," he wrote in connection with his analysis of world history, "this has of course nothing to do with individual empirical instances; the latter may fare either well or badly, as the case may be, for the concept has authorized the forces of contingency and particularity to exercise their vast influence in the empirical sphere. . . . But, to return to the true ideal, the Idea of reason itself, philosophy should help us to understand that the actual world is as it ought to be. It shows us that the rational will, the concrete good is indeed all-powerful, and that this absolute power translates itself into reality."[23]

What is perhaps not so well known is that the context of the proposition stresses the participation of rationality in the one and only world of time and space and the discoverability of rationality only from that world. "Since philosophy is the exploration of the rational, it is for that very reason the apprehension of the present and the actual, not the erection of a beyond, supposed to exist, God knows where. . . . The great thing is to apprehend in the show of the temporal and the transient the substance which is immanent and the eternal which is present."[24]

A second lesser-known contextual qualification of the distinctiveness of historical actuality as compared with historical existence was Hegel's rational processing of existence itself—despite its admitted inclusion of dead particularity and contingency—to make it continous both epistemologically and metaphysically with the actuality that was wholly to be interpreted as the realization of reason. Thus he agreed that existence is not simply a temporal particular but rather an idea, a species, "a specific universality" with a built-in power of self-initiated process, and therefore that it is itself a kind of rationality, representing realized spirit alongside the evanescent forms of spiritual death. While continuing to admit the recalcitrant dimension of particularity he also insisted on its partial rationalness. Religion and ethics, as intrinsically universal essences, have by definition (and hence in the true sense) the quality of being present in the individual soul, even if they do not develop to the fullest extent in it. "As a general rule, we must take it as established that whatever in the world can justly claim glory and nobility is nevertheless subject to something even higher than itself. The right of the world spirit transcends all particular rights; it shares in the latter itself, but only to a limited extent, for although these lesser rights may partake of its substance, they are at the same time fraught with particularity. . . . In simple abstract terms, the means it [ie., the world spirit] employs is the activity of individual subjects in which reason is present as their inherent substantial essence."[25]

Hence Hegel believed increasingly in the presence of a bridge between existence and actuality, just as he certainly and persistently believed in the identity of actuality and reason. "The only appropriate and worthy method of philosophical investigation," he said correspondingly, "is to take up history at that point where rationality begins to manifest itself in worldly existence—i.e., not where it is still a mere potentiality in itself but where it is in a position to express itself in consciousness, volition, and action."[26]

The relationship between the two sides of existence—the side pointed toward rational actuality in history and absolute spirit outside it and the side pointed toward multifarious caprice in the original materials of history was basically a tensile one that would trouble the general historians of the nineteenth century. Hegel himself camouflaged the tension nominally with his doctrine of the cunning of reason and operationally with his focus on the Janus-faced "state," the particular acts of whose governors were epitomized in the rational progress from the freedom of One through the freedom of Some to the freedom of "man as such."[27] Hence when Hegel asked, "How, then, is it possible for the universal or the rational to determine anything whatsoever in history?" and gave as his synoptic answer the declaration that "the pure light of this divine Idea, which is no mere ideal, dispels the illusion that the world is a collection of senseless and foolish occurrences," because men's passions, particular and self-interested as they usually are, can be viewed as the only "effective motive force behind actions whose significance is universal," we can only conclude that he was committing a calculated ambiguity between the phenomenal existence which was the material of history and the underlying actuality which was the equally historical structure of realized reason.[28]

But it must be owned that for Hegel, as for the other nineteenth-century systematic philosophers of history whom he exemplified, the prominence which was given to the coherent motif in human history far outshone acknowledgment of the ambiguous relationship subsisting between rational continuity and factual diversity, as befit the origins of historical coherence in the valuable absolute realm above history. Even in the main body of Hegel's lectures on world history, which had much more to do, as its presumably empirical subject matter required, with the factual data of the oriental, classical, and modern European cultures under discussion, he not only explicated from the start the generally coherent process which conferred unity on each culture and linked the succession of cultures in a rational chain but he expressly proclaimed the primacy of his concern with this process and identified it with the role of philosophy in history.

These are the principal phrases of that form in which the principle of freedom has realized itself—for the History of the World is nothing but the development of the idea of Freedom. . . . We have confined ourselves to the consideration of that progress of the Idea . . . and have been obliged to forgo the pleasure of giving a detailed picture of the prosperity, the periods of glory that have distinguished the career of peoples, the beauty and grandeur of the character of individuals, and the interest attaching to their fate in weal or woe. Philosophy concerns itself only with the glory of the Idea mirroring itself in the History of the World. Philosophy escapes from the wary strife of passions that agitate the surface of society into the calm region of contemplation.[29]

Hegel's was the most influential of the idealist philosophies of history in the nineteenth century, but it was far from being the only one. Romantic litterateurs such as the Schlegel brothers (August Wilhelm and Friedrich) and romantic philosophers such as Friedrich von Schelling also developed philosophies of history along idealist lines, and if their lack of a mediatory reason, in either its logical or temporal form, made for an infinitely cruder approach to history than Hegel's it confirmed all the more emphatically the extrahistorical derivation of coherence in the idealist conception of history, seeing in individual historical truth a reliable way to penetrate the divinity which manifested itself immediately in such truths on the model of Fichte's "divine idea of the world."[30] Other romantics—like Schelling—tended to ignore specific history in favor of absolute, transcendent principle.[31] In both cases, however, the romantic philosophers of history identified the connectedness of the historical process with a reality that was itself outside history and even outside of time. To underline the absoluteness of this reality, the romantics called it God, not, like Hegel, to dignify a secular universal but rather to signify the entire otherworldliness, the complete lack of a temporal equivalent definitive of the divine principle.

Thus even Friedrich Schlegel, whose respect for "historical science and research" was manifest in his identification of his "philosophy of history" (in his book of that title) with the "science of history," asserting that "history cannot be separated from facts, and depends entirely on reality; and the philosophy of history, as it is the spirit of the idea of history, must be deduced from the real historical events, from the faithful record and lively narration of facts," insisted that "the religious spirit and views" pervade "the combined efforts of historical learning and philosophical speculation," and that, consequently, the philosophy of history exhibits a "progress of mankind" in which "a divine Hand and conducting Providence are clearly discernible."[32] Indeed, he characterized the historical process in general as "the progressive restoration in humanity of the effaced image of God, according to the gradation of Grace in the various periods of the world, from the revelation given at the beginning, down to the middle revelation of redemption and love, the coming of Christ, and from that to the final consummation." Nor was he any less explicit in associating this providential interpretation of history with that which was coherent in history. His interest, he declared in the context of this interpretation, was in "the one connected whole of history," in "the knowledge of the general destinies of mankind," a knowledge which entailed the maintenance of "these general destinies, and every object connected with them, steadily in view, without losing ourselves in the details of special inquiries and particular facts." Thus the coherence in history must, at one and the same time, start from the "faith in Primitive Revelation, and in the glorious consummation of Christian love"—"the only thing we must here pre-suppose, and from which all our historical deductions must be taken"—and without "some decided predilection." It must conform exclusively to "the clear arrangement" which will yield "the great events and general results" of "the different nations, and particular periods of the world."[33]

The pattern of history for Schelling was even more emphatically supernatural, as his definition of history as "a successively developing revelation of God" indicates. "God . . . reveals himself progressively," he wrote in the same vein. "In his history man gives a proof of the existence of God, but a proof that can be furnished only by the completed course of history."[34] Schelling's own intellectual career confirmed the transcendental bias of his philosophy—or, more precisely, his theology—of history, for he came to stress history more and more, pari passu with his ever intensified systematization of his philosophy, as he strove to fit recalcitrant existence into his theosophical framework. In his unfinished masterpiece on *The Ages of the World* Schelling characterized history as the sphere in which man's "principle which is outside and above the world" dialectically engages the countering "external principle," as a "higher" with an "inferior" principle to produce the progressive union of "super-sensory ideas" with "physical force and life," and conversely confronts "nature" with "the visible embodiment of the highest concepts." In this historical engagement the first, or divine, principle furnishes the coherence, while the natural principle, as such, stands for "internal disorder, . . . random movement without sense or purpose." "The

integration in human life is dissoluble, in divine life indissoluble."
Schelling characterized his whole conception of the world's history as
starting from "only the eternal life of the divinity; the authentic history which we have resolved to describe, the narration of that succession
of free actions through which God has determined to reveal himself
from all eternity," can occur only on the basis of this conception of
God—"on grasping that unity in God which is at once duality, or
conversely that duality which is at once unity."[35]

Since history is thus essentially a cosmic drama, it follows that historical time is subsumed under eternity. As "the synthesis of the
supreme spiritual life with the natural" God can be known only in the
past, and since it is God's past it is an "eternal past," in which eternity
"is not that which excludes time but contains time (eternal time), subordinated to itself. . . . Succession in God is real, and yet it is not one that
passes in time. . . . There is a succession in eternity itself, which includes a kind of time; it is no empty (abstract) eternity, but rather
contains time, subdued, in itself." For the subordinate natural principle
requires that there be a past, and therefore a history; but since "the
being of God can never become, but rather simply is from eternity,"
there must be "an eternal past" just as there is "an eternal present."[36]

It follows that "if we want to travel the pure road of historical, that is
scientific, presentation" we must start from God and his eternal past.
This means, in practice, that the historian must grasp the coherent
internality of things and can never be content with the mere recital of
externals. "What would all history be, if an inner sense did not come to
its aid? What is true of so many who indeed know most of every
occurrence but understand not the slightest thing about authentic history. . . . Everything remains incomprehensible to man before it becomes
internal for him, that is, before it is led to the most internal level of his
nature, which for him is, as it were, the vital witness of all truth."
Consequently, too, the destiny of the individual man is paradigmatic
for the history of humanity. "The events of human life from the depths
to its highest perfection must be in accord with the events of general life.
It is certain that whoever can write the history of his own life in its
fundamentals has thereby also grasped the epitome of the history of the
universe."[37]

Positivism was the arch-rival of idealism, in all its varieties, for the
intellectual allegiance of nineteenth-century philosophers and scientists, and the fact that both of these disjunctive approaches to reality not
only included philosophies of history as a central feature of their respective doctrines but that these philosophies of history were homologous
serves to underline what was common in the assumptions about history

for the characteristic writers, including historians, of the nineteenth century. For positivists as well as for idealists the universal factors which conferred coherence on the multifarious actions of men in the past as in the present were factors that were rooted in a stable divine, natural, or human reality underlying the reality of history and that had a historizable dimension, usually in the form of a general development, built into them.

Auguste Comte, founder of positivism, was also the most categorical formulator of its attitude toward history. He is notorious both for his "law of the three periods" (he also called it, alternatively, the "law of the three states," an alternative which faithfully reflected its hybrid philosophico-historical character), a law which, purporting to find in the succession from the theological through the metaphysical to the positive states "the natural laws by which the advance of the human mind proceeds," seemed limited to intellectual history, and for his aversion to standard history and historians, which seemed to confirm his limitation of history.[38] Actually, however, his law of the three periods was a corollary of a more fundamental law that was both more universal and more explicitly historical than its more famous derivative. Comte's attitude toward history can be correspondingly specified: he expressly approved of historical coherence; it was the factual history in which practicing empirical historians specialized that drew his ire.

Comte's basic law, which he termed optionally "the fundamental law of human development," "the theory of the natural progress of human society," or "my fundamental theory of human evolution, illustrated by the history of human progress," was general in its logical, its functional, and its extensive senses. He referred to it as a "sociological" i.e., scientific—or a "philosophical" law, for it was the principle of "social dynamics," one of the two essential conditions of the human race (the other was "social statics"), and as such it was necessary, total—i.e., it comprehended all the functions of man's organized life—and pan-human in its scope. Thus when "we regard, as a whole, the movement of humanity, from the earliest periods till now, we shall find that the various steps are connected in a determinate order," that is, in a "necessary succession" which prescribed that "the chief progress of each period, and even of each generation, was a necessary result of the immediately preceding state." The necessity which governs historical progress stems from its being "subject to invariable laws," which govern the changes—i.e., the "growth"—of "Humanity," that new "Great Being" which has replaced God as the "central point" of all life.[39]

Obviously a history that could fit these specifications had to be a

distinctive kind of history indeed. This history was always philosophical, but as Comte aged it became ever more schematised. In his *Cours
de la philosophie positive* of the 1830s, Comte claimed to present the
actual "history of mankind" as the kind of human reality to which his
"great sociological conception" of "the law of human development"
could be applied to provide the "interpretation" and thereby to acquire
"verification." Correspondingly, he required a history that would be
pre-treated—i.e., "restricted"—to focus on "the most advanced social
development" and on "the commonest facts," to the deliberate disregard of "exceptional events and minute details," in a procedure that
would be consonant with the scientific "search for the general laws of
society" and its habitual grasp of "the most general phenomena" to this
end. History, then, as he frankly admitted at this stage, must be "abstract," and he expressly separated "the abstract history of humanity"
from the "concrete," giving it his imprimatur because only so could he
estimate "the rational character" of each historical period, exhibit "its
filiation to the preceding, and its tendency to prepare for the following,
so as to realize by degrees the positive concatenation whose principle
has been already established." By the time of his survey, *A General
View of Positivism*, which he published in 1848, history had become
the indispensable ally of philosophy as the factual adjunct of the coherence it supplied. "We cannot understand the connexion of our
conceptions except by studying the succession of the phases through
which they pass. And on the other hand, but for the existence of such a
connexion it would be impossible to explain the historical phases. So
we see that for all sound thinkers, History and Philosophy are inseparable."[40]

As the revolutionary years immediately preceding the mid-nine-
teenth-century passed into the reaction of the 1850s, Comte underwent
an analogous development and from his original balancing of progress
and order committed himself ever more to the preponderance of social
order. The historiographical corollary of this political emphasis was a
definite priority of philosophy over history in the study of human reality
and of the schematic over the factual within history in the depiction of
human evolution. Comte himself admitted the connection between the
more conservative politics and the more philosophical history in the
Système de politique positive which he published between 1852 and
1854. Conceding that, contrary to his expectation of increasing the
historical details and proofs, "the reader will find that the general
coordination has become more intensive and more complete, while the
special expositions are less developed" in the present work as compared
with "the historical part" of his earlier treatise on the positivist philoso-

phy. On the ground that he "appreciated better the true conditions of the philosophic regimen," Comte now labeled his entire consideration of "social dynamics" or "human progress" the "philosophy of history" rather than history as such; and he argued explicitly that just as progress should be "subordinated to order" so the historical laws of evolution "would remain too empirical" and "consecrate instability" were historical "movement" not "subordinated to existence"—that is, to the "static foundations" represented especially by "the corresponding laws of human nature" and conferring on "historical conceptions . . . a coherence they could not otherwise acquire."[41]

But let us, finally, be clear about what Comte's self-confessed development toward an ever more pronounced systematization did and did not do to his concept of history. What it did do was to expand the role of philosophy in its relationship to history and of coherence in its relationship to factuality within history. What it did not do was to alter the connection between the evolutionary philosophy and historical coherence vis-à-vis the connection between historical method and historical detail, connections which were constant in his thinking. The summary which he gave of the historical sections in his earlier *Course of the Positive Philosophy,* published between 1830 and 1842, while he was still presumably maintaining some kind of equilibrium between scientific philosophy and actual history, may stand as the classic formulation of this positivistic constancy:

Always guided by the logical principle . . . on the general extension of the positive method to the rational study of social phenomena we have gradually applied my fundamental law of human evolution, at once mental and social, to the whole of the past, . . . a law consisting in the necessary and universal passage of humanity through three successive states. . . . The judicious use of this exclusive law has permitted us to explain, in a manner truly scientific, all the great phases of history, considered as the principal consecutive stages of this invariable development . . . : whence results, for the first time, the familiar conception of a homogeneous and continuous linkage in the whole sequence of former ages. . . . The historical elaboration was designed here to consist above all in appreciating precisely the characteristic mode of participation by each of three consecutive ages in the general destiny [*destination*] of humanity.[42]

Between such avowed philosophers of history as Hegel and Comte and the practicing historians who detached history from philosophy and established it as an independent branch of knowledge in the nineteenth century was an intermediate level of historical theorists who were at once more earthly and more empirical than their doctrinaire mentors. Correspondingly, these theorists thought in terms of history rather than the philosophy of history, but they nonetheless addressed themselves to historical coherence and derived its principles from a constant nature and logic outside of history. Their emphasis upon the mediatory function of experience in history revealed explicitly the assumptions which the practitioners, amateur and professional alike, tended to ignore or to mask. The two most influential of these intermediate theorists were Marx and Engels in the Hegelian mode and John Stuart Mill in the Comtean. All three exemplars developed schemas that were less transcendent, more actual, and therefore more inherently historical than those of the systematizers who were their mentors, and yet these too depended for their connections on structures by which mind and world were organized and for which science underwrote the validity.

Marx and Engels adopted the Hegelian pattern of two independent but related levels of history along with the logic of the dialectic that guaranteed both the independence and the mutual relation of the two levels. But because they rejected the bridging devices that had enabled Hegel to mask the ambiguity attending his subscription to both rational process and particular diversity they had to struggle with this ambiguity all their lives. First, they avoided the literal ascription of reason to the intelligible structure of the past because of reason's association with the consciousness whose primacy they denied, and with this avoidance they had to do without the devices of actualizing dynamism and of a meaningful "cunning" with which Hegel graced his principle of reason. Second, they refused to see in the state the mediatory agency which Hegel interposed between the subjective individual and a cosmic reason. Hence the problem of the connection between history and metahistory, which Hegel resolved, at least verbally, with his philosophy of dialectical reason, turned for Marx and Engels into the more persistently tensile problem of the connection between law and fact in science.

The historiographical position of Marx and Engles may thus be described as that of a rationality without reason, since they applied the dialectic to human history as "the real part of natural history," emerging with a primary historical process that was rational in the sense that it was lawful, integrated, and universal but that had nothing to do with either a human or metaphysical principle of reason and was accessible only through the empirical activities from which it was in part inferred and which were in part deduced from it.[43] This relocation of the dialectic by Marx and Engels, together with the end of ambiguity that was the implication of the relocation, meant that the relations between the two levels of history—the primary and the derivative, or the lawful and the contingent—at different times adopted both of two extreme postures: either they brooked no problems or they raised insoluble problems. In general, the relations between the basic and the incidental levels of history were unproblematical when the history was negative—that is, of man's alienated, divided, and exploited experience—and they were irreducibly paradoxical when the history was positive—that is, of man's progress toward the communist revolution. History was therefore most pervasively capable of rational explanation when the historical process was at its most overtly irrational, while it was least capable of a rational explanation that would cover both underlying structure and superstructural events when the conditions for the realization of rational historical process seemed at their maximal capability. This fundamental distinction in the views of Marx and Engels on historical rationality undercut, moreover, the more familiar distinction between the early evocation of humanistic integration and the later adversion to natural laws as the alternative sinews of history.[44]

The young Marx—that is, the Marx of the *Economic and Philosophical Manuscripts* of 1844 and *The German Ideology* of 1845— was preoccupied with distinguishing his naturalism from the idealism of Hegel and with demonstrating the appropriateness of the dialectic to a history of man who did without the hypostatization of reason either within or without his own consciousness. Thus he denied the independent reality of reason either as the dominant force of human consciousness or as a transcendent power beyond human consciousness, and he insisted that history must be the natural history of the whole man, even if this approach did mean the destruction of philosophy. "Consciousness can never be anything but conscious existence, and the existence of men is their actual life process," he wrote critically. "When reality is depicted, philosophy as an independent branch of activity loses its medium of existence. At the best its place can only be taken by a summing-up of the most general results, abstractions which arise from the observation of the historical development of men. Viewed apart from real history, these abstractions have in themselves no value whatsoever." Reason, in this view, is literally the "efflux" of men's "material behavior." "Each new class which puts itself in the place of one ruling before it is compelled . . . to represent its interest as the common interest of all the members of society, put in an ideal form; it will give its ideas the form of universality, and represent them as the only rational, universally valid ones."[45] But although "the production of material life itself" is not only the first historical act but also a fundamental condition of all history," and although the history of man "must always be studied and treated in relation to the history of industry and exchange," this history still shows a dialectical pattern that should be formally familiar to us: the human past has been dominated by the divisions, the contradictions, and the self-interestedness that ae the natural products of alienation and by the steps toward universal organization that represent man's historical tendency to recover his integrity. Both in the *Economic and Philosophical Manuscripts* of 1844 and in *The German Ideology* of 1845 (as in the later *Communist Manifesto* of 1848, written, like the earlier works, before the revolution from which Marx and Engels expected so much), first Marx alone and then Marx and Engels together kept to this general, anthropological, schematic level of rational history.

But perhaps even more important was the other historiographical feature of these works. The historical part of these sketches was concerned primarily with the stage of man's alienation, while the positive recovery from it was a matter not of the human past but of action for the future. The crucial aspect of alienation was that in it empirical fragmentation and rational process coincided. As Marx and Engels wrote in *The German Ideology:* "This estrangement . . . can, of course, only be abolished given two practical premises. . . . In history up to the present it is certainly an empirical fact that separate individuals have, with the broadening of their activity into world-historical activity, become more and more enslaved under a power alien to them." The coming communist revolution was also an empirical fact, but it was obviously one of a different kind. "But it is just as empirically established that, by the overthrow of the existing society by the communist revolution . . . , this power, which so baffles the German theoreticians, will be dissolved; and then the liberation of each single individual will be accomplished in the measure in which history becomes transformed into world-history."[46] Would it be too much to infer that it was to this problematical present and constructive phase of human "history" that Marx and Engels were referring when they confessed that "our difficulties begin only when we set about the observation and the arrangement . . . of our historical material, whether of a past epoch or of the present"?[47]

In the young Marx and Engels, then, the multileveled articulation of society, reducible roughly to the problematic two-tiered relationship between infrastructure and superstructure, was a faithful translation of the relationship between the coherent and the particularized levels of history. Both in Marx's own terms and in the concepts which have been imputed to him, rational history took place on the substructural level of man's continuously developing productive forces, while empirical history occurred on the level of the superstructure, with the particular unpredictability of its false consciousness. For the young Marx, the philosophical origins of the fundamental continuity in history were patent. In both *The Economic and Philosophical Manuscripts* of 1844 and *The German Ideology* of 1845 history was indeed nominally justified as an empirical pursuit, with its patterns ascertainable only through a posteriori inference.[48] But if this empiricism was the approach to history as a kind of knowledge, as a structural kind of philosophical anthropology which made the historical process the medium for the alienation and subsequent integration of human nature, obviously an a posteriori inference dominated Marx's approach to history as a dimension of social life. The derivative function of lived history is especially transparent in *The Economic and Philosophical Manuscripts,* where it is always presented as the human dimension of a natural development toward wholeness.

Communism is the *positive* abolition of . . . human self-alienation, and thus the real *appropriation* of *human* nature through and for man. It is, therefore, the return which assimilates all the wealth of previous development . . . It is the solution of the riddle of history and knows itself to be this solution. . . . The history of *industry* . . . is an *open* book of the *human faculties,* and a human *psychology* which can be sensuously apprehended. This history has not so far been conceived in relation to human *nature,* but only from a superficial utilitarian point of view. . . . *Industry* is the actual historical relationship of nature, and thus of natural science, to man. . . . One basis for life and another for science is *a priori* a falsehood. Nature, as it develops in human history, is the act of genesis of human society, is the *actual* nature of man; thus nature, as it develops through industry, though in an *alienated* form, is truly *anthropological* nature. The whole of history is a preparation for "man" to become an object of *sense* perception, and for the development of human needs (the needs of man as such). History itself is a *real* part of *natural history,* of the development of nature into man. Natural science will one day incorporate the science of man, just as the science of man will incorporate natural science; there will be a *single* science.[49]

By 1846, Marx had joined forces with Engels and jointly they dropped the overt philosophical scaffolding which was still evident in Marx's thinking of 1844, thereby preparing themselves for the "most comprehensive statement of historical materialism" set forth especially in the first, unpublished section of their *German Ideology.* In this statement they stressed both the exclusively empirical nature of history and the historical identity of universal, integrating factors within that history; thereby they exposed the procedure through which nineteenth-century historians internalized extrahistorical sources of coherence.

Because of its bent against the primacy of consciousness in Hegel and the Young Hegelians and its association of philosophical integration in history with that primacy, the *German Ideology* stressed the counter-vailing primacy of man's material activities—defined in philosophical equivalence with "the production of life, both of one's own labor and of fresh life in procreation"—as the essence of "the real basis of history" which is prior to consciousness. But it associated the individual variegation of historical empiricism with these activities, and it relegated the linear unity of the process to the writing of history "according to an extraneous standard." The older, unauthentic history, according to Marx and Engels, achieved its unity by excluding "the total living sensuous activity of the individuals composing [the sensuous world]," thereby banning "the relation of man to nature" from history, and establishing the unhistorical abstraction "man" to replace the abstraction "God" as the integrating force in history. Using an argument as applicable to Marx's earlier position as to their contemporary rivals, Marx and Engels now seemed to reject the notion of an extrahistorical unity:

The individuals, who are no longer subject to the division of labour, have been conceived by the philosophers as an ideal, under the name "man." They have conceived the whole process . . . as the evolutionary process of "man," so that at every historical stage "man" was substituted for the individuals and shown as the motive force of history. The whole process was thus conceived as a process of the self-estrangement of "man."[50]

Obversely, it was with "the real individuals," "split up and in opposition to one another," alienated from the community and even from their own deeds, hostile to members of other classes but isolated too within their own class from both their classmates and the class as such, with which Marx and Engels claimed their history was concerned. From this point of view, "history is nothing but the succession of the separate generations, each of which exploits the materials, the forms of capital, the productive forces handed down to it by all preceding ones, and thus on the one hand continues the traditional activity in completely changed circumstances and, on the other, modifies the old circumstances with a completely changed activity."[51]

Ostensibly Marx and Engels discovered a coherence within the historical process that was as historically empirical as the separate activities of disunited individuals and classes: this coherence consisted in the process of universalization exhibited within history itself. For this history evinced the development of productive forces and of the social relations which were dependent on them into an actual, demonstrable coherence. Thus the "universal development of productive forces" establishes "a *universal* intercourse between men . . . and finally has put *world-historical*, empirically universal individuals in place of local ones. . . . The further the separate spheres, which interact on one another, extend in the course of this development, . . . the more history becomes world-history."[52] Now, however much the contents of the universal forces identified by nineteenth-century historians may have differed, by the later years of the century it was undoubtedly the global expansion of Western culture in its many facets that gave the historians keys to actual coherences which stretched through the past. The difficult question, perhaps answerable in the relatively transparent operations of Marx and Engels, is whether these coherences had roots in the more enduring realities outside the historical process, roots that were in some measure conserved.

What complicates the problem in the case of Marx and Engels, despite the insights permitted by their articulateness and their development from one genre to another—Marx, from philosophy through history to economics, and Engels, from economics through history to philosophy—is the inapplicability both of their own claim to the primacy of empirical history and of others' imputation to them of an absolute and unhistorical doctrine. The fact is that the coherence of the historical process that was presented by Marx, with assistance and elucidation by Engels, did have connections with constant positions which they held to be outside of history; but these were positions to which they gave authentic embodiment in universalizing agents within the historical process. It was this double relationship that enabled Marx and Engels to be paradigmatic for later historians of nineteenth-century historiography in a way they never were to their contemporary nineteenth-century historiographers. They have been paradigmatic because they exhibit two kinds of extrahistorical roots of coherence, one philosophico-scientific in nature that explicates what is nonhistorical in the coherent historical process and the other political that joins Marx and Engels to the kind of coherence that was common to practicing historians of the nineteenth century and that, by its association in Marx and Engels with the philosophico-scientific framework, stresses the extrahistorical derivation of the political premise in history.

The clue to the origin of historical coherence outside of history lies in the location of the coherence within history, for the location is such as to make it point beyond itself. It is well known that the continuity of the

Marxist historical process and its development into an actually universal stage rests on the primacy of constantly expanding productive
forces, but what may not be so well remembered is the essentialness of
this continuity and universalism to economic growth. For in *The German Ideology* the "universal development of productive forces" did not
simply pit these productive forces against an antithetical individualism
in social relations and political institutions, since the separation between the productive forces and the individuals reaches only through
the penultimate stage in the development of those forces and yields to a
more fundamental lineup between the ultimate universal productive
forces together with the individuals who control them on the one side
and the penultimate universal productive forces together with the individuals who are controlled by them on the other. Thus "the difference
between the individual as a person and what is accidental to him, is not
a conceptual difference but an historical fact. . . . The communal relationship into which the individuals of a class entered . . . was always a
community to which these individuals belonged only as average individuals, only insofar as they lived within the conditions of existence of
their class—a relationship in which they participated not as individuals
but as members of a class. With the community of revolutionary pro-
letarians, on the other hand, who take their conditions of existence and
those of all members of society under their control, it is just the reverse:
it is as individuals that the individuals participate in it. It is just this
combination of individuals (assuming the advanced stage of modern
productive forces, of course) which puts the conditions of the free
development and movement of individuals under their control—conditions which were previously abandoned to chance and had won a
separate existence over against the separate individuals just because of
their separation as individuals."[53]

What was primary, then, was not so much the development of the
productive forces in themselves as the historical development of a coherence that found its most congenial embodiment in productive forces.
The interpretation of history was less a matter of recognizing the primacy of productive forces within history than of applying principles of
coherence from outside of history. These principles of coherence were
not explicated by Marx and Engels in *The German Ideology,* but they
do appear in later philosophical and economic analyses by Engels and
Marx respectively.

What led Marx and Engels to spell out the coherent process in
history which they had merely assumed heretofore was, first, the series
of events around mid-century which rendered problematical the mutual
conformity of the historical reality represented by fundamental co-

herent process and the historical reality represented by the empirical contemporary facts of men's concrete circumstances and activities; and, second, the turn from an implied philosophy to an explicit science as the intellectual aegis of their thinking. Certainly Marx demonstrated clearly how problematical the relations between process and events seemed to him in the French revolution of 1848, when he showed himself to be only too aware of the discrepancies between the underlying rational process of socioeconomic development and the actual political course of the revolution. He admitted how much "in historical struggles must one separate the phrases and fancies of the parties from their real organism and their real interests, their conception of themselves from their reality," not so much to debunk the former as to emphasize the differences between the two levels of history. And his wry observation that in France each class does "what normally" the class above it "would have to do" threw into bold relief his notion that the underlying reality of the revolution was a level of history untouched by the events of the revolution, which were expressions of "pre-revolutionary traditional appendages."[54] Clearly the overt history of this revolution, like the details of his anthropological history of man and like Engels's unproblematical account of the German revolution in 1848 and 1849, made sense only negatively, as a superstructural level corresponding to the alienated stage in the rational history of man.

The later Marx was not nearly so leery of recognizing the rationality in his underlying process of historical reality. Now he defined his relationship to Hegel in terms of his discovery of "the rational kernel within the mystical shell," and he characterized his own dialectical history as the "rational form" which "includes in its comprehension . . . of the existing stage of things, at the same time also, the recognition of the negation of that state."[55] This rational structure of history was continuous with the lawfulness of natural science, to which it was joined by the logic of the dialectic. It is well known that the later Engels articulated this association in his *Dialectics of Nature,* the uncompleted and unpublished book which he wrote, as he said, precisely to show that "in nature the same dialectical laws of movement are carried out in the confusion of its countless changes, as also govern the apparent contingency of events in history. . . . It is, therefore, from the history of nature and human society that the laws of dialectics are abstracted. For they are nothing but the most general laws of these two aspects of historical development, as well as of thought itself."[56] Engels's chief concern, here as in the *Anti-Dühring* which he was writing about the same time—in the 70s of the nineteenth century—was clearly with nature and natural science, "with showing that the dialectical laws are

CHAPTER THREE

really laws of development of nature, and therefore are valid also for theoretical natural science."[57] It is not coincidental that during this very period when Engels was stressing the dialectical pattern which linked the lawfulness of nature and history he was also underlining the empirical basis of this pattern—"it is no longer a question . . . of inventing interconnections from out of our brains, but of discovering them in the facts"[58]—and the interactive compatibility of the superstructural historical facts with this pattern. With the rational economic process of history securely anchored to nature and the dialectic, everything worked.

As if to demonstrate the inadequacy of his own contention that nature and history were convertible and were governed by common internal laws, Engels characterized these laws as laws of the dialectic and dwelt upon their origins in a logical realm that transcended nature and history alike. He made it abundantly clear that "the laws of dialectics," as he called the principles of dialectical logic, were the only valid residues left from philosophy, that their function was to provide connections among divergent particulars, and that their application to both history and nature was in the service of establishing coherence in both of those realms. Since Engels tried to show both that the dialectic supplied the pattern to historical reality and that as a derivation from historical reality it was itself an entirely historical coherence, it is not surprising to find that he vacillated between the acknowledgment of the extrahistorical validity of the dialectic and the emphasis upon its historicity.

On the one hand, then, Engels defined "the fundamental laws of dialectical thinking" as a kind of logic that was the antithesis of metaphysical logic not only in its attunement to the true movement rather than the artificial stability of things but more importantly in its demonstration of "the internal connections in this motion and development." Indeed, the essential function of the dialectic was its provision of a coherence in contrast to "the task of natural science and historical research," which, like metaphysics, have bequeathed to us "the habit of observing natural objects and natural processes in their isolation, detached from the whole vast interconnection of things." It is precisely this habit which dialectics corrects, for it "grasps things and their image, ideas, essentially in their interconnection, in their sequence, their movement, their birth and death. . . .An exact representation of the universe, of its evolution and that of mankind, as well as the reflection of this evolution in the human mind, can therefore only be built up in a dialectical way, taking constantly into account the general actions and reactions of becoming and ceasing to be, or progressive or retrogressive changes."[59] When he was in this gear, he analyzed dialectics as an approach not distinctively historical, since it applied to the laws of motion wherever they might be found—that is, in nature and thought as well as in history. "Amid the welter of innumerable changes taking place in nature, the same dialectical laws of motion are in operation as those which in history govern the apparent fortuitousness of events; the same laws as those which similarly form the thread running through the history of the development of human thought."[60] Dialectics accordingly retains the philosophical root it originally had in its Hegelian mystical form, and insofar as philosophy shrinks, as it is doomed to do, it will be replaced not by history as such but by science in general as the seat of the dialectic. In Engels's candid formulation: "Only when natural and historical science has adopted dialectics will all the philosophical rubbish—outside the pure theory of thought—be superfluous, disappearing in positive science."[61] And even when science becomes predominant, dialectics will retain something of its philosophical—i.e., transcendent—origins. Through dialectics, Engels wrote in terms that could apply to his conception of history as easily as they could to his conception of natural science, "philosophy takes its revenge posthumously on natural science for the latter having deserted it."[62] "What still independently survives of all former philosophy is the science of thought and its laws—formal logic and dialectics. Everything else is merged in the positive science of Nature and History."[63]

If Engels seemed equally intent on demonstrating the historicity of coherence—on demonstrating, that is, the empirical, a posteriori inference of dialectical patterns from the facts of history—this intention was muddied by his alternation between two different paths of demonstration. He was most unambiguous when he associated dialectics with historical relativism—i.e., with "the historical outlook" which abjures finality and absolute truth—and consistently argued that dialectics was essentially a generalization from history, with nature and human society considered two subsets of history. "It is, therefore, from the history of nature and human society that the laws of dialectics are abstracted."[64]

But his second way of asserting the historicity of dialectics was more equivocal: while insisting just as strongly on the empirical character of the Marxist dialectic, he now treated inference of the dialectic from the facts of history as merely one of the valid modes of such generalizations; and he paid more attention, if anything, to the induction of these laws from the evanescent phenomena of nature than to the induction of these laws from the analogous and equivalent disorderly facts of history. At times he set forth this complementary relationship in categorical terms:

"In this work [the *Anti-Dühring*] dialectics is conceived as the science of the most general laws of *all* motion. Therein is included that their laws must be equally valid for motion in nature and human history and for the motion of thought. Such a law can be recognized in two of the three spheres, indeed even in all three, without the metaphysical philistine being aware that it is the same law that he has come to know."[65] When he wrote from this dualistic perspective he would see Hegel's mistake in "the fact that these [dialectical] laws are foisted on nature *and* history as laws of thought, and not deduced from *them*"; and although he went on to advance the corresponding affirmative proposition that "the dialectics of the brain is only the reflection of the forms of motion of the real world, *both* of nature *and* of history" his emphasis was on nature as "the test of dialectics" and on his concern "only with showing that the dialectical laws are really laws of development of nature."[66]

Now it is clear that both these sets of inconsistencies—the equal assertion of the apriority and the aposteriority of the dialectic vis-à-vis the real world and the equal assertion of the exclusively historical composition of that real world vis-à-vis both its natural and historical components—were only apparent in Engels, for he referred to all these positions indiscriminately in the same contexts. It seems advisable, therefore, to impute to Engels a distinction which he did not himself formally make but which explains the continuity of these putative opposite tenets in his own mind. The distinction is one which has already been found appropriate to the interpretation of Hegel.[67] What Engels rejected in Hegel was the idea of a dynamic nontemporal reason and logic to match. What he accepted from Hegel was the idea of a dialectic that was temporal but not necessarily historical as well as of its implication of a dialectic that was invested in history as a historical principle of coherence. And just as Hegel failed to distinguish explicitly between a temporal dialectics that was a priori to history but continuous with it and a historical dialectics that was visible only as an inference from the events of history, so did Engels. Even more than Hegel, however, Engels exhibited the concatenation, which was implicity prevalent for historians of the nineteenth century, of a developmental scheme that was within time but above history with a connectedness of events that was within both time and history.

Engels was notorious for his interest in the physical and biological sciences, and his appropriation of their stress on the dynamics of energetics and natural selection for the support of the dialectical reason in Marxist history was perhaps to have been expected. But what makes it of significance beyond Engels's penchant for intellectual troubleshooting was the presence of an analogous tendency in the later Marx. Where Engels elaborated on the philosophical implications of the original Marxian coherence of history, Marx himself was developing its economic base both within and without the confines of history; and the way in which he did this showed not only the joint scientific interest that was a substantive counterpart of their personal collaboration but also the invisible philosophical scaffolding that was unequally shared by them and cradled their scientific interpretation of history.

The manuscript of 1857–58 which has been published as the *Grundrisse* modulated Marx's shift from the primacy of philosophy and politics in the 40s to the primacy of economics evident in the first volume of *Capital* (1867). In the *Grundrisse* Marx established two crucial positions in the relationship of economics to history: first he accomplished the substitution of economic for philosophical categories to denote the continuity which would link the primary reality outside of history with the coherent continuity within history; and second, he achieved the principled independence of economics from history.

The rationale of Marx's transfer from philosophical to economic categories for the provision of a coherent thread through history inhered in his subscription, common to his philosophical and his economic periods, to the primacy of "production." In the *German Ideology* he (aided by Engels) had made man's production of his life the driving force of the anthropological dialectic; in the *Grundrisse* he made production analogously the driving force of the economic dialectic. "Whenever we speak of production, then," he wrote in a faint reversion to an earlier generality, "what is meant is always . . . production by social individuals. . . . All epochs of production have certain common traits, common characteristics. *Production in general* is an abstraction, but a rational abstraction insofar as it really brings out and fixes the common element and thus saves us repetition. Still, this *general* category, this common element sifted out by comparison, is itself segmented many times over and splits into different determinations." Production is thus not only a dialectical whole through time; it also commands a substantive dialectical process within economics. "Whether production and consumption are viewed as the activity of one or of many individuals, they appear in any case as moments of one process, in which production is the real point of departure and hence also the predominant moment. . . . Production, distribution, exchange, and consumption . . . all form the members of a totality, distinctions within a unity. Production predominates not only over itself . . . but over the other moments as well. The process always returns to production to begin anew."[68] The relationship between these moments and the production that determines them is in some measure a historical one. Those economists are wrong, admonished Marx, "who portray production as an eternal truth while banishing history to the realm of distribution" and to the realms of similar moments, for "by the process of production itself they [these moments] are transformed from natural into historic determinants, and if they appear to one epoch as natural presuppositions of production, they were its historic product for another." Such questions thus "reduce themselves in the last analysis to the role played by general-historical relations in production, and their relation to the movement of history generally."[69]

And yet Marx was also careful, in this same manuscript of the *Grundrisse,* to indicate the analytical, suprahistorical dimension of economics in general and of production in particular. "Production, distribution, exchange, and consumption form a regular syllogism," he wrote, to symbolize the logical coherence of economic categories which in any specific period lie partially outside of history. "Production is the generality, distribution and exchange the particularity, and consumption the singularity in which the whole is joined together." Already in the *Grundrisse,* moreover, he adumbrated a fundamental thesis of *Capital,* to the effect that the economic science appropriate to the analysis of bourgeois society was independent of the historical movement of the productive forces in the economy. "It would . . . be unfeasible and wrong," he wrote in a declaration of economic independence, "to let the economic categories follow one another in the same sequence as that in which they were historically decisive. Their sequence is determined, rather, by their relation to one another in modern bourgeois society, which is precisely the opposite of that which seems to be their natural order or which corresponds to historical development."[70]

The role of history in *Capital* evinces a patent ambiguity precisely because Marx's economic categories were at once analytical and historical in character, with the result that what is problematical and even antithetical in the relations of economics and history for us was not such for him. The discrepancy between Marx and us tends to disappear once we realize that his economic categories supplied the coherence to his historical facts in an osmotic way that was standard for the whole tradition of Western historiography.

Marx's combination of rational economic science with empirical economic history appeared not only in his physical juxtaposition of analytical and historical sections but also in his propositions of principle. Certainly he thought of economics as a science—that is, as an approach to a selected reality for the purpose of eliciting the laws which governed its particular phenomena. This approach was evident not only in the analogies with the physical sciences which he characteristically drew but directly in his penchant for "exact analysis of the process" which "demands that we should, for a time, disregard all phenomena that hide the play of its inner mechanism"—i.e., that we should inquire into "the natural laws of capitalist production," into "their tendencies working with iron necessity toward inevitable results."[71] He claimed, therefore, a perspective "from which the evolution of the economic formation of society is viewed as a process of natural history" and from which "a law," such as that regulating the division of labor or capitalist accumulation, "acts with the irresistible authority of a law of Nature."[72] On this tack he defined the "tendency to develop the productive forces absolutely" in terms of "the productive activities of human beings in general . . . , independent of societies, lifted above all societies, being the common attribute of unsocial man as well as of man with any form of society and a general expression and assertion of life."[73] He characterized the tendency, in short, as an economic tendency outside of particularized history, and to get at it one should penetrate beneath the phenomena—when they are not disregarded—"to their hidden substratum," which here, as in nature, "must be discovered by science."[74]

But Marx also represented this process as being inherently and necessarily historical. Especially when he was castigating the propensity of bourgeois economists, deluded by the "fetishes" of the capitalist system, to hypostatize the particular tendencies of their own era by erecting them into timeless categories, Marx stressed the transitional historical character of this system and its era. Thus an economic law of the capitalist system is "metamorphosed by economists into a pretended law of Nature," and really refers to a "relation" which "has no natural basis, neither is its social basis one that is common to all historical periods. It is clearly the result of a past historical development, the product of many economic revolutions, of the extinction of a whole series of older forms of social production." When he was in this overtly communist posture, moreover, he specifically stressed the historical character of the forms taken by the process of production. "The view which regards only distribution relations as historical, but not production relations," he stated categorically, "is . . . solely the view of the initial, but still handicapped criticism of bourgeois economy. . . . To the extent that the labor-process is solely a process between man and Nature, its simple elements remain common to all social forms of development. But each specific historical form of this process further develops its material foundations and social forms."[75] Indeed, whenever Marx was conscious of his dialectical method as "in its essence critical and revolutionary" he saw it regarding "every historically developed social form as in fluid movement" and taking "into account its transient nature as well as its momentary existence."[76]

Now the substantive distinctions that Marx made to establish the compatibility of the analytical and the historical dimensions of his economics are clear enough. The basic categories, such as productive forces, or "the process of production" as such, and "division of labor in the society at large," apply to all societies and are therefore not historical, while the "forms" or "relations" of production and the specific mode of "division of labor in the workshop" are particular historical developments produced by specific economic systems at certain times for definite periods. Undoubtedly the substantive distinction between the forces and the relations of production was effective in providing coherence within the Marxist system: indeed, he could make of "the contradictions and antagonisms between the distribution relations, and thus the specific historical form of their corresponding production relations, on the one hand, and the productive forces, . . . on the other hand" the overt issue of the crises that power the movement of history in general.[77] But the distinction also involved a formal procedure that was equally synthetic, albeit much more covert: the extrahistorical economic categories supplied the general categories which made the historical relations and forms intelligible and coherent. Hence Engels could argue that "on the basis of this [analyzed] surplus value he [Marx] . . . for the first time drew up an outline of the history of capitalist accumulation and an exposition of its historical tendency," thereby acknowledging the priority of economic concepts over integrated history.

And thus too Marx could distinguish between two levels of history, investing his fundamental economic categories in the continuous historical process of productive forces and assigning the particular social forms of production and their appropriate distribution relations to the level of de facto incoherence, explicable only in terms of their relationship to the more basic process. He could therefore maintain that "whatever the form of the process of production in a society, it must be a continuous process, must continue to go periodically through the same phases," and he could frankly distinguish between the fundamental productive forces of "Modern Industry" which, "by its very nature, . . . necessitates variation of labor, fluency of function, universal mobility of the laborer," and "its capitalistic form," which "reproduces the old division of labor with its ossified particularisation." Hence "this absolute contradiction between the technical necessities of Modern Industry, and the social character inherent in its capitalistic form" can only be resolved by the "revolution" which secures the domination of the coherent productive process now represented by Modern Industry—a revolution wherein "Modern Industry . . . compels society, under the penalty of death," to recognize "as a fundamental law of production, . . . fitness of the laborer for varied work, consequently the greatest possible development of his varied aptitudes."[78]

The occasional reference to "revolution" in *Capital* raises the question of the role of political principle in the Marxist theory of history. Unquestionably, as Marx and Engels aged, the place of politics in their doctrine became more and more implicit. The supreme categories in the later works of both were economic and philosophical, and political principle tended to be translated into cognates of these categories—that is, the revolution was acknowledged in the overt principles of movement and of contradiction. But in their early work Marx and Engels (like Herbert Spencer) made their political program an explicit part of their historical theory, and from this overtly political phase it is clear that the political appeal had a synthesizing function which no intra-historical factor could exercise. "Universal dependence, this natural form of the world-historical cooperation of individuals," wrote Marx and Engels in *The German Ideology* after demonstrating the diffractive estrangements of class struggles which must accompany this natural form, "will be transformed by [the] communist revolution into the control and conscious mastery of these powers, which, born of the action of men on one another, have till now overawed and governed men as powers completely alien to them." They went on, moreover, to stipulate even more emphatically the indispensability of revolutionary politics to the integration of history. For this integration could be effected only through "the appropriation of a totality of instruments of production," and this appropriation, in turn, "can only be effected through a union, which by the character of the proletariat itself can only be a universal one, and through a revolution, in which . . . there develops the universal character and energy of the proletariat. . . . Communism . . . turns existing conditions into conditions of unity."[79]

In politics as in philosophy, moreover, the ultimate Marxist response to the circumstantial disappointments of the mid-nineteenth century was to harden their notion of the inevitability of the communist revolution and of the coherent historical process that led to it.[80] No wonder that *The Civil War in France,* the contemporary history that Marx wrote while working on *Capital,* manifests a much greater mastery of the presumptive structural process of history over its experienced facts than his earlier historical works did. When he concluded that "working men's Paris, with its Commune, will be forever celebrated as the glorious harbinger of a new society," he was sealing his reading of the uprising of 1871 in terms of the underlying rational process which he deemed to be making for social revolution. For Marx, the event of the Commune made history and philosophy cohere.

What Marx and Engels did to Hegel for the understanding of history John Stuart Mill did to Comte—that is, he naturalized and hence more emphatically historized the temporal and only indirectly historical processes propounded by the master and made political principle a more essential ingredient of coherent history. Where Comte had little patience with the empirical discipline of history as such, Mill accepted it, under the rubric of "the science of history." This he validated as an essential step in the linked hierarchy that extended from history, which treats of "the collective series of social phenomena, in other words, the course of history"; through the "philosophy of history," which infers "empirical laws"—i.e., actual rather than necessary uniformities—governing "the order of succession . . . among the different states of society and civilization which history presents to us"; to "a general science of society" which establishes "deduction *a priori*" in the form of "the psychological and ethological laws . . . of human nature" on which the empirical laws of social progress must depend.[81] Mill's whole enterprise, indeed, was designed to prove "the consilience of deduction *a priori* with historical evidence, . . . the subjection of historical facts to scientific laws," and he was not loath to admit that if the facts adduced by the specific discipline of history are susceptible to general laws, since the empirical sequence of events evinces "a certain degree of uniformity in the progressive development of the species and of its works," still the actual ascertainment of all the "general laws" to which the phenomena of history are subject, both of the empirical and the deductive varieties, was a matter for philosophy in the guise of general sociology. In Mill's frank formulation: "History . . . does, when judiciously examined, afford Empirical Laws of Society. And the problem of general sociology is to ascertain these, and connect them with the laws of human nature."[82]

Mill's advance beyond Comte in the affirmation of history lay not only in the emphatic logic of induction which authenticated both facts and empirical laws in contrast to Comte's depreciation of mere facts and his lack of mediatory principle between the general facts he did admit and the necessary natural laws of human society he hypostatized; it lay also in the liberal politics which, by reason of its inherent mobility, performed an integrative developmental role within history far better

than Comte's authoritarianism, with its ultimately transcendent religious ground. Mill insisted that "there was some one element" in man
which was "the prime agent of the social movement, . . . the central
chain, to each successive link of which the corresponding links of all the
other progressions being appended, the succession of the facts would by
this alone be presented in a kind of spontaneous order," and that this
one cohesive element, at once "deduced from the laws of human
nature" and "in entire accordance with the general facts of history," is
"the state of the speculative faculties of mankind"—that is, its "intellectual convictions," including "human opinions."[83] But this centrality
of intellectual opinion in the developmental process of human history
entails the essentiality of "the liberty of thought and expression" in
history, for "free discussion" is necessary to the mental progress of
man, and on this "the order of human progression in all respects will
mainly depend."[84] The preeminence of thought and opinion in both
Mill's politics and his history made his politics the source of the most
coherent strand in his historical schema.

But the voluminous historical studies which have helped to earn for
the nineteenth century its distinction as "the great age of history" made
up a corpus of writing in many ways quite different from the substantive philosophies of history for which the century has become equally if
more pejoratively reputed.[85] Certainly, the long-established gulf between philosophical and learned history, which had been somewhat
narrowed during the eighteenth century, continued to converge despite
protestations to the contrary. These protests were motivated in part by
the extension of illustrative philosophical history into general history
on the one side, and the parallel extension of learned into scientific
history on the other, with the consequent increase of the tension between the two genres: increased in part by the conscious hostility which
surfaced between philosophers or litterateurs (like Spencer and Carlyle)
who scorned what they took to be the pedantry and triviality of scientific history, and scientific historians (like Ranke) who rejected the
apriority of the philosophers of history; and in part by the cumulative
divisions, among historically minded writers, which overlapped and
exacerbated the differentiation between the theory and the practice of
history. Nineteenth-century historians were polarized between ama-
teurs and professionals, romanticists and empiricists, generalists and
specialists, and they were fragmented into national historiographical
schools which were at best indifferent and at worst inimical to the
historical ideas of their national competitors.

H. Thomas Buckle exemplifies this hostility. The chilly reception
accorded Buckle showed how untypical was his advocacy, embodied in

the *History of Civilization in England,* of the direct application of positivistic natural science and philosophy to history. For his openly acknowledged belief in "mental laws," different from but analogous to natural laws, as "the ultimate basis of the history of Europe," and his equally open characterization of the historian as one who "is imbued with that spirit of science which teaches, as an article of faith, the doctrine of uniform sequence; in other words, the doctrine that certain events having already happened, certain other events corresponding to them will also happen," Buckle has been consensually labelled "a historical sociologist whose main interest was in the development of general historical laws" rather than "a historian of England."[86]

And yet, from the perspective of the coherence in the histories that were coherent there was a common feature in nineteenth-century historiography that was shared by all its parties—but most overtly by the large number of distinguished historians who, precisely because of their candor, we may call rationalist. Political beliefs and doctrines provided channels of practicality for philosophers of history, threads of continuity within the work of single historical practitioners, and bonds of communication among the works of several practitioners. Politics thus became an avenue of theoretical imposition for practicing historians who otherwise eschewed theoretical impositions and an implicit tie to philosophical historians who otherwise rejected factual history as a mere chaotic compilation of incomparable events.

Even in a mind as rigid as Buckle's there was a descrepancy between the historical generalizations he professed and the historical anecdotes in which he liked to indulge, and among other philosophically inclined historians, more characteristic of their age, the relationship between philosophy and history went beyond the categories of consistency and inconsistency to one of mutual indifference. Thus Hippolyte Taine, who was trained in philosophy, lastingly influenced by Spinoza, Condorcet, and Hegel, labeled a Comtean positivist, and author of a philosophical treatise (*De l'ntelligence*) as well as of a monumental history (*Les Origines de la France contemporaine*), developed his theory of history in different places and along different lines from his actual history. Taine's historical theory insisted upon the essential unity of every historical epoch on the grounds that "mankind is not a collection of objects lying next to one another but a machine of functionally interrelated parts," that human civilization and its changes are therefore caused by combinations of "race, environment, and occasion" (*race, milieu, moment*), and that therefore "history is a science, analogous to physiology and zoology." All this referred back to his early philosophical perception of "the great firm network by which all things and all ideas are tied together." This theory appeared in this correspondence and in the prefaces of such peripherally historical works as his collection of *Essais de critique et d'histoire* and his *Histoire de la littérature anglaise.*[87]

The great work in which Taine invested his serious historical endeavors and which remains the basis of his fame as a historian, on the other hand, was held together by principles of quite a different order. As its title indicates, the *Origins of Contemporary France* was persistently motivated by Taine's overt desire to understand the politics and society of his own country in his own time and by his unexpressed commitment to political conservatism. He was frank about the presentist interest in France's politics that dominated the purpose of his history. "The social and political forms into which a people enter and *remain* . . . are determined by its character and its past," he wrote in this historical preface. "All should be molded on the living features for which they were designed; otherwise, they will break and fall to pieces. Hence it is that, if we succeed in finding our constitution, it will come to use only through a study of ourselves. . . . What is contemporary France? . . . . Hence it is that, in striving to comprehend our actual situation, we constantly revert back to the terrible and fruitful crisis by which the Ancient Regime produced the Revolution, and the Revolution the Modern Regime. . . . If, indeed, I had any motive in undertaking this work, it was to seek for political principles."[88] Although Taine insisted on his own detachment—that, far from political partisanship, "to describe with exactitude . . . is my sole object," like "a naturalist" regarding "my subject the same as the metamorphosis of an insect"—the counter-revolutionary bias for which his history has become notorious actually played the constructive role of integrating what might well otherwise have decomposed into a string of social details, dramatic incidents, and different *milieux* and *moments.* Taine somewhat disingenuously declared that the one political principle to which he had attained in his history was that "*human society, and especially a modern society, is a vast and complicated thing*";[89] but what he did not declare was that the way he made sense of it was by converting the historical assumption of conservation into the additional political principle of conservatism. It was from this coherent perspective that Taine's treatment of the revolution, which he considered to be a combination of social "disintegration" by the needy masses and of the "dictatorship of evil and low passions" by the fanatical "crocodiles" who led them, dominated the analysis of the Ancient Regime that prepared it and of the Modern Regime that failed to overcome its despotism and its divisions. It is, indeed, because of the prominence enjoyed by his coherent political perspective that the richness and vitality of the detailed social descriptions of the French people and institutions during the old regime but especially during the nineteenth century have suffered from the neglect which has been their lot.[90]

Most nineteenth-century historians did not indulge even in the problematic philosophy of history of a Taine; but they shared his reliance on extrahistorical political principles for a covert coherence, and in this respect no single political tendency enjoyed a monopoly. Certainly Taine was not alone as a politically conservative historian, as the striking example of Ranke attests, but it must be owned that the thematic grid of politically liberal historians was more obtrusive and therefore more easily identifiable.

The nineteenth-century historians who were most candid about the political ground of their histories were the constitutional nationalists to whom the labels of "Prussian school" and "political school" have been affixed in acknowledgment not only of choice of favored subject matter but commitment to a preeminent thread of continuity. In the case of the Prussian school, whose leading lights were Droysen, Sybel, and Treitschke, the centrality of the Prussian state in their political as in their historical considerations automatically guaranteed that in their desired blend of politics and history the politics, while openly serving as the purpose of the history, would also function as its abiding theme. For Prussia was to the historians of this school both the political agent of German unification and, in Droysen's words, "a veritable hub and matrix of history."[91] Thus when Droysen shifted from the cosmopolitan idealism and liberal nationalism which had dominated his approach to history before 1848 to the realistic Prussian patriotism which preoccupied him thereafter, the history of the Prussian state became the incarnation of the religious, moral, and developmental themes which a mixture of classical humanism and historized Hegelianism had borne before. Not only was the Prussian mission the main cement of the sprawling *Geschichte der preussischen Politik* on which he worked for some thirty years from 1855 on, but in the reflections on history—the *Historik*—which were of the same vintage as his Prussian history, he combined the idea of "research into the continuity" of human activities and endeavors with the rejection of "impartiality" as "a kind of impotent [literally, eunuchistic] objectivity, with the recognition of the state as the final and most comprehensive" of the moral organisms which were the empirical forms of man's ethical life, and with the persistent notice of politics as a necessary concern of the historian. "Historical study is the basis of political improvement and education. The statesman is the practical

historian."[92] Neither Sybel nor Treitschke was as idealistically or pro-
grammatically minded as the older Droysen, but they shared all the
more univocally the latter's blend of principled political edification in
history, empiricism in historical method, and the consequent use of the
historical Prussian state as the central organizing core of their
works.[93]

The French analogue of the Prussian school of historians has been
denominated, correspondingly, the "political school," a rubric that
refers especially to the characteristic posture of a Guizot, a Mignet, and
a Thiers, "whose object was rather to explain than to narrate" and
whose chosen historical agency tended to be overarching institutions
like the state rather than particular individuals. In his historical writing
Guizot ever stressed the tendencies, inner ideas, the coherent perspectives manifested by the trends which govern events. He insisted that far
from immersing himself in the partialities of the past—in his language,
far from approaching the past with the attitude of "one-sidedness"
(*Einseitigkeit*)—the historian should set himself up as a judge of its
total bearing. Consequently, he denied advocacy of either the ancient
regime or the revolution, declaring instead the necessity for justifying
both in the light of their necessary harmony. Hence he strove always for
a historical *juste milieu* as a principle of comprehension, writing the
histories of the two Frances and of the European middle class as the
prime representatives of the thematic European liberty in which he was
essentially interested.[94]

Thus in his published lectures on *The History of Civilization in
Europe* Guizot noted the indelible character of variety and struggle that
pervades modern European civilization in contrast to "the unity," the
"solitary dominant principle" that features the premodern, extra-Euro-
pean civilizations; but he rationalized even this substantive quality of
modern diversity into a pattern of its own. Not only did he note that "a
certain unity pervades the civilization of the various European states;
that, notwithstanding infinite diversities of time, place, and circumstance, this civilization takes its first rise in facts almost wholly similar,
proceeds everywhere on the same principles, and tends to produce well
nigh everywhere analogous results"; but he insisted that "the relation
of events to each other, the connection which united them, their causes
and their effects are as much historical facts as any other, so that
"European civilization has entered, if we may so speak, into the eternal
truth, into the plan of Providence; it progresses according to the intention of God."[95] The search for connections he called, indeed, "the
immortal part of history." He acknowledged "the necessity for generalization and rational result," and he claimed for himself the charge to

study "the dominant ideas," "the generally adopted principles of the past."⁹⁶

Guizot's programmatic keynoting of coherent history was genuine, for it was borne out by the actual patterns in his historical writing. But his justification of his focus on France and on the bourgeoisie was disingenuous, for he gave intellectual reasons for what seems to be a political motivation. He justified his concentration on France with the argument that he would be able to go into greater detail in the historical treatment of "one of the principal European nations in which it [the history of civilization] has been developed" than of European civilization as such and with the assumption that French civilization "has reproduced more faithfully than any other the general type and fundamental idea of civilization."⁹⁷

Again, he discursively qualified his theoretical identification of the bourgeois "destiny" with the self-governing French nation of the nineteenth century by adducing two related historical limitations of it. His picture of the historical diversity of the bourgeoisie between its inferior status in the twelfth century and its superior status in the nineteenth was dignified into a counterproposition by his historical principle that every "bond" which unites and harmonizes historical facts "exists in the facts themselves" rather than in any philosophical or political "hypothesis."⁹⁸

And yet Guizot actually used the French connection and the bourgeois emphasis in a way that betrayed the political orientation of the putatively philosophical doctrines that informed his analytical lectures and held together his descriptive and narrative historical accounts. He called the general views which distinguished authentic history from "a heap of inconclusive, incoherent, and unconnected facts," the "philosophy of history," and he exalted philosophy of history as a coming science.⁹⁹ As for the covert politics, Fustel de Coulanges would astutely judge, in a blanket characterization which included Guizot, that "for the last fifty years [he propounded the judgment in 1872] our historians have been men of a party. However sincere they were, or however impartial they thought they were, they followed one or other of the political opinions which divided us. . . . Writing the history of France was a way of working for a party and fighting an adversary." And a later authority on Guizot has opined with equal generality that "in nineteenth-century France it was never possible to leave politics behind."¹⁰⁰ In unquestionable confirmation of these subsequent assessments, Guizot's own ancillary historical works—especially the *History of England* and the *History of the Origin of Representative Government in Europe*—make clear in their articulation the derivation of his historical themes from his overriding political concern with the establishment in France of a moderate liberty under law and under the tutelage of the responsible middle class. Thus he dwelt on the "great . . . analogy" between English and French developments, and he justified his consideration of the English past with his acknowledgment that a properly institutionalized "liberty was born, and increased in growth in that country more than any other," although he confessed his teleological confidence that "it has developed in England less universally, less equally, and less reasonably . . . than we are permitted to believe will be the case at the present day in our own country."[101] It has been said of Guizot that "he philosophized about history rather than produced a philosophy of history" or even endorsed "a philosophical approach to history,"[102] and this indirection catches the attitudes of the whole political school.

Perhaps nothing is as indicative of the immediately political and ultimately philosophical derivation of the coherences in nineteenth-century historiography as the celebrated status that has been accorded to those like Jules Michelet, Lord Acton, George Bancroft, John Motley, and, to a lesser extent, Georg Gervinus, who are exalted for having written history in the grand manner, who are not classified in any "political" school but who actually embody a democratic doctrine serving at once thematic historical and active political purposes. One set of the myriad apparent contradictions that are regularly discovered in Michelet seems particularly relevant for our purpose, and its resolution goes far to explain the political mediation of a seemingly antithetical critical history and transcendent philosophy in the nineteenth century. The contradiction has to do with Michelet's simultaneous belief in the incessant vital movement of history and in the validity of moral themes beyond history. In the language of a recent commentator on Michelet, the latter's themes each have "two roots: an historical root and an existential root. That is why historical criticism cannot reach Michelet without having first established his thematics."[103] On the one hand, there is Michelet's unobtrusive archival work and his corresponding evocation of the dramatic incident, the incidental emotion, the passion for the irrational in Vico. On the other hand, there is Michelet's insistence upon continuity, repetition, and even verbal constancy in history, his penchant for woven networks of historical objects and themes, his convergence of a homogeneous nature and history through the moralization of nature, his emphasis on the unity of France, his quest for philosophy in history. What joined these two facets of Michelet the historian was his democratic politics, at once historically articulated and theoretically doctrinal.

Thus his *History of the French Revolution* (1847–53) was written unabashedly in "the spirit of the Revolution," which, he avowed, "contains the secret of all bygone times." The Revolution and its precedent Enlightenment arose, in his account of them, under the aegis of an eternal "Right and Justice," for they "did not seek to add to this certain principle one derived from dubious history." The historical agent was similarly a constant entity throughout time—"the people," whose rights and liberties were thereby vindicated against the antithetical principle of Christianity and its oppressive lay allies.[104] Michelet's was an approach which permitted him to participate vicariously with the revolutionary figures and masses in the events of the eighteenth century's anticlerical crusade and of the Revolution's tumultuous events and at the same time to use his history as a buttress in fighting the doctrinal fight of his political present. So he castigated the contemporary liberal party because they "have evinced of late . . . symptoms of an inward evil," and particularly because "they have proved false to their friend—nay, to their own father, the great eighteenth century."[105]

Lord Acton, would-be author of what has probably been the most famous history that was never written—the History of Liberty—reflects an analogous combination of critical research into the facts and eternal libertarian principle, but in him the demonstration worked by default. Through all of his adult life Acton was torn between his dogged belief in the heterogeneous factual basis of history and his commitment to a general tendency—progressive, liberal, religious, indeed providential—in history. Of his participation in the detailed, critical methodical history which sponsored the development of what had been a literary genre into a scientific profession during the nineteenth century there can be little doubt. His inveterate habits of archival research, the conscientious attention which he paid to the recalcitrant variegation of the ineluctable facts of the human past, his ultimate appointment to the Regius Professorship of Modern History in the august and conservative Cambridge University, his early castigation of Buckle for ignoring "individual acts" and "personal doings" and his later acknowledgment of his age as "the documentary age," a quality which for him made "our branch of study . . . progressive"—all these activities and tenets bespeak his concern with the duly authenticated particulars of the historical record.[106]

And yet he also looked for "abiding issues" and looked to history, as he said, because it "rescues us from the temporary and transient." Along these lines he not only asserted the generalization that "the first of human concerns is religion, and it is the salient feature of the modern centuries," but he frankly confessed his general belief that the "constancy of progress, of progress in the direction of organized and assured freedom, is the characteristic fact of Modern History, and its tribute to the theory of Providence." Thus this history demonstrates "that the wisdom of divine rule appears not in the perfection but in the improvement of the world.[107] It was an open scandel that the disjunction between the actualities of history, which show that "the supreme conquests of society are won more often by violence than by lenient arts," and the liberalizing destiny of history inhibited Acton from prosecuting the large-scale history of liberty which he projected from an early age. "I know not," he admitted at one point, "whether it will ever fall within my sphere of duty to trace the slow progress of that idea [of liberty] through the checkered scenes of our history."[108] For him the idea of liberty was a human constant, the root of the equally constant idea of religion and itself "the unity, the only unity, of the history of the world, and the one principle of a philosophy of history." As he aged, he tended more and more to moralize this intellectual principle and therewith to hypostatize it into an absolute idea essentially separate from and antithetical to the ebb and flow of actual authoritarian history. Thus in a late lecture he maintained "that achieved liberty is the one ethical result that rests on the converging and combined conditions of advancing civilization." With the conversion of historical unity into private morality and his detachment of morality from historical Catholicism, the extrahistorical derivation of Acton's sense of the coherence in history becomes obvious.[109]

A convincing confirmation of the transcendent origins incumbent upon this eighteenth-century democratic faith exalted into a political and moral principle was its appearance in the very different circumstances of a Germany mired in the reaction of the 1850s. Georg Gervinus admitted that his decision to publish separately a historical introduction to a general history of his century which would be devoted to the articulation of this principle stemmed from his desire "to re-establish the much-shaken faith of men in our future, to restore the much-diminished faith in the present," by "considering as a whole the powerful strokes with which Providence writes."[110] While insisting that what he wrote was free of system and emerged "spontaneously from the historical events themselves," he also maintained that "the plant of actuality . . . appears here in its typical-simple lawfulness," that he sought "the meaning and the inner sense of the events," that "a single constant tendency amounts to a 'law,' " both for the history of Europe and of humanity as a whole, which prescribes "a regular progress from the spiritual and civil freedom of individuals to that of the many" for peoples in the process of political organization. Hence for Gervinus the advance of "democratic principles" and the character of the popular movements which bore them not only demonstrated "the Providential character, . . . the irresistibility, . . . the lawful course" of the historically rooted movements of his contemporary age but were themselves dogmas originating beyond the realm of the history that putatively generated them. Thus the metaphor he devised for them, "as if the powers of fate had the immediate effect of giving form and body to an historical idea," was more than a figure of speech. His plea that "the emancipation of all who are oppressed and miserable is the mission of the century," to which the contribution of "all history" has been "its tendency for many centuries toward the greater equality of men and conditions," was clearly an article of political faith around which the pattern of his history was organized.[111]

The oft-remarked democratic ideology of the American "romantic school" of historians becomes comprehensible in this larger context. John Lothrop Motley, German-trained American historian of Europe, may stand for us as the mediator between the democratic beliefs of Europe and those of the United States. In his primary concern with the revolt and independence of the Netherlands during the early modern period, he blended the democratic outlook that characterized the main line of American historiography in the nineteenth century with the substantive libertarianism that was perceived at the same time as the integrated theme in the development of European civilization. The result was to underline the external references of this putatively historical theme in a more obvious way than through the analysis of the components going into the work of liberal European historians. Motley himself testified to the connection in a synoptic passage from his history of the Dutch revolt: "The maintenance of the right of the little provinces of Holland and Zeeland in the sixteenth, by Holland and England united in the seventeenth, and by the United States of America in the eighteenth centuries, forms but a single chapter in the great volume of human fate; for the so-called revolutions of Holland, England, and America, are all links of one chain."[112] Nor was he reticent about identifying the tendency of his historical chain. It is, he indicated, the expression of a cosmic law, which governs "all bodies political as inexorably as Kepler's law controls the motion of planets. The law is Progress; the result Democracy."[113] America is thus "on the point to which other peoples are moving."[114] Nor did he mask the extrahistorical basis of this integrated historical process. For it was in

94

the context of defining this process that he declared: "The lessons of history and the fate of free states can never be sufficiently pondered by those upon whom so large and heavy a responsibility for the maintenance of rational human freedom rests."[115] For Motley, the democratic faith was certainly the purpose and probably the foundation of historical study.

The democratic theme which served Motley as the juncture of European history and American politics was expounded in its western-hemisphere applications positively by George Bancroft and negatively by his friend and fellow New Englander, William H. Prescott—two prime representatives of the nineteenth-century American school of amateur romantic or "literary" historians. The antithetical correlations which comparatively inform the work of the two contemporaries underline the transcendent ties of historical coherence when it is found in nineteenth-century historiography. Where Prescott combined a distrust of the union of history and politics with a choice of antidemocratic— i.e., Latin American—topics, with a preference for literary, narrative, and descriptive, over philosophical, thematic, and analytical approaches, and with an inability to merge the two in his climactic but unfinished history of the reign of Philip II, Bancroft juxtaposed careers as a Democratic politician and American colonial historian throughout his mature life and joined this choice for the compatibility of political principle and historical study with the insistence that human history was indeed dominated by the continuous progress toward democratic freedom and that the task of the historian was to reveal and trace it.[116]

Thus Bancroft prescribed for the historian the duty "to write the changes in humanity," by treating "events in connection with each other, . . . observing the general principles by which that succession is controlled," considering them frankly in the deductive light of "the *discovery*, the *diffusion*, and the *application* of truth in the histories of men and nations." Moreover, he explicitly equated this truth with the necessary providential progress of political freedom. "When history is viewed from this point, it is found that humanity is steadily advancing, that the advance of liberty and justice is certain."[117] His own historical work faithfully executed these general formulas. He dwelt on the colonial period of American history because he felt that "the spirit of the colonies demanded freedom from the beginning," but he prosecuted this theme under the universal assumption that "the United States of America constitute an essential portion of a great political system, embracing all the civilized nations of the earth. . . . They have the precedence in the practice and the defense of the equal rights of man."[118] He expounded the purpose of his history, then, in the most general terms, as following "the steps by which a favoring Providence, calling our institutions into being, . . . has conducted the country to its present happiness and glory."[119] Since he thought to have found in his history "the idea of right, . . . the vestiges of moral law, . . . the reality of justice," all of which he deemed to be parts of God's design extensible into the future,[120] the religious, ethical, and political seat of the libertarian connectedness Bancroft found in history was patent.

Thus for the German and the French, for the British and the Americans, a given author's preference for political history gave practical expression to what was ostensibly a philosophical position. Extra-historical principles of rationality were relied upon again and again to enhance the coherence of traditional narrative, frequently to accomplish a political end. Examples of reliance upon an extrahistorical rationality to derive an allegedly historical coherence span the spectrum of nineteenth-century political history. Albeit for the most part unintentionally, Hegel was restored again and again throughout the century by these efforts of political historians. Reliance upon an extrahistorical reason made the historizing of political positions both easy and authoritative.

For many on the Continent the practicality of this change from traditional historism to the *modus operandi* of the Hegelian philosophy of history was of a piece with the shift from the French model of constitutionalism to the Prussian model of administration. For the Frenchman Comte (although history was not a science for Comte, it should have been) the practicality of his system made the just constitution the determining factor in history as well as the final goal of history; but this practicality was wedded to what has become known as the Atlantic community. In either case, the whole Hegel was never restored. The Hegel who worked in the context of the ripening fruit of Enlightenment in Germany and who specified a self-rationalizing world-spirit as a proper reference for historical inquiry was never restored. Political historians after Hegel worked only in the context of "national models," without reference to the Hegelian universal. And Germany's political historians worked only in the context of "national spirit," itself all too often divorced from natural scientific experience and allied for better or worse with the example of the ancients. In Germany these intellectual conditions led straight to the non-national conceptions of the state associated with Heidegger and Gadamer, and they contributed to the more general conditions which allowed for the rise of the Third Reich. Elsewhere, the proponents of the "national models" schools of practice persisted simply in the pattern of competitive and potentially explosive coexistence to which they were accustomed.

As these examples infer, however, what was crucial was that the historizing of philosophical positions as political ones went typically from the philosophical to the political without passing through the social, that is, without passing through the realm of potential qualifications wherein the consequences of the position taken would eventually be felt by everyone. All too easily politics stood without qualification for the whole of history while it was the social that comprised the field of individual conception and the ground for realizing the historical enterprise. The tendency to temporalize and make homologous non-historical and historical time and subjects within the confines of empirical research and epistemological principle easily could and often did generalize the social beyond the scope of its genuine historicity. The social was made to rest either in an experience and time too distant to be wholly relevant to contemporary problems or was grounded by a principle too intransigent to facilitate the historizing of a changed future. But then really no one has solved this problem.

The rationalist variant of historical coherence is only one side of the story, however. The nineteenth century also saw the triumph of the opposing tradition, the historistic, or auto-rational, view of history which tended to favor rather the writing of history than the theorizing about history and which, therefore, despite the intellectual eminence of its forebears and progeny, was itself far less transparent and provocative than its rationalist contemporary. These historists set greater store by the narrative and genetic modes of coherence that were traditionally history's own; but ultimately if unadmittedly they too found such internal modes of coherence unsatisfactory, and like the rationalists they resorted to borrowing concepts and patterns from outside history. Whether they adopted the variant of historism or chose the one which persisted in espousing an extrahistorical reality that was indifferent to history, and whether they admitted it or not, these historians still relied upon concepts and patterns from without history to aid in establishing coherence within history.

This final stage in the nineteenth-century history of historical criticism and critical coherence was ushered in by the scientific history of that century. It is associated with the names of Niebuhr and Ranke in Germany and Fustel de Coulanges in France. The continuity of this historical approach with the whole tradition of critical history is undeniable, and the most quoted propositions of the factual and objective emphasis embodied in the tradition come from these nineteenth-century proponents of the tradition. Ranke flatly asserted that, based on the principle that all knowledge "is documentary," "strict presentation of the facts . . . is unquestionably the supreme law, for historical research is oriented by its very nature to the particular," and he declared his intention "to show only what actually happened [*wie es eigentlich gewesen*]." Fustel de Coulanges declared that "history is and should be a science," and he claimed that "only the patient study of the literature and the documents which each century has left behind . . . allows our mind to free itself sufficiently from our immediate concerns and every kind of partisanship so that it can depict with some exactitude the life of men of times gone by. . . . Long and careful study of the particular is . . . the only way that can lead to some general outlook."[121] This tradition existed as counterpoint to the Hegelian synthesis of the bifurcated reason of the enlightened individual.

But if the scientific history of the nineteenth century was thus obviously continuous with the long tradition of a critical approach to the facts of history, it contributed nonetheless a distinctive dimension to this tradition—a dimension which essentially transmits the tradition into our own day. Whereas the older, early historical criticism looked for a literal truth in the report conveyed by the documents and methodically vetted the documents for error, fraud, interpolation, or other extraneous matter that might distort the faithful translation of past reality in the reports, the increment added by the scientific historians of the nineteenth century saw in those same reports mere indications, or symbols, of a past reality which had to be reconstructed from the traces left in the documents and, after Ranke, in other kinds of sources. Niebuhr made the relationship explicit: "The critic might be content with the excision of fiction, the destruction of fraud: he only seeks to expose a specious history. . . .But the historian demands something positive: he must discover at least with some probability . . . meaning and structure where assuredly these once existed and where they could be discovered through some traces. . . . "[122]

There are two kinds of scientific history: irreducible human facts and natural scientific facts. The first was personified in Hegel, who added the passion to reason and therefore established particularity as part of his system. The second was personified by Buckle. The first was later called the Ranke renaissance. For Ranke what history delivered was "a holy hieroglyph," which it was the task of the historians to "decipher." Historical facts were to him but external appearances which must be plumbed for their underlying essence or spirit: "History opens to us not the realm of fleeting appearance alone but also that of eternal spirit. . . . In events there is more than what appears on the surface; there is the content to be researched—the idea." Hence in the famous slogan which identified valid history with "what actually happened," the "actually" referred not to the literal transcription of past facts but to the reconstitution of a vanished past.[123]

Even Fustel de Coulanges, the member of the triumvirate who applied the tradition of Cartesian doubt and the positivistic approach of the nineteenth century most expressly to scientific history, contributed to the figurative modernization of the critical historical method. Certainly, he inherited the documentary scholarly attitude associated with the Ecole des Chartes and the Société de l'Histoire de France, with their dedication to "purely scientific history, objective and disinterested erudition"; and certainly he put repeated stress on the invalid anachronism of reading "the modern spirit" back into the "inimitable" character of ancient times. Yet he, too, insisted that the duly ascertained facts of history were but the outer shells of the truth to which the historian must penetrate. "History does not study material facts and institutions alone; its true object of study is the human mind: it should aspire to know what this mind has believed, thought, and felt in the different ages of the life of the human race." "Science does not reside in the documents, but in the intelligence which knows and understands the diverse documents. . . . History is composed of a multitude of small facts; but the little fact, in itself, is not history." "Convinced that the external and visible laws which appear among men are only the signs and symptoms of moral facts which originate in our souls, . . . I thought I could see that between beliefs and institutions there is such a close bond that the one explains the other."[124] So did the empirical history of the nineteenth century believe: most characteristically it used the principles of historical criticism to depict a contemporaneous past reality that was only fossilized in the extant documents.

Moreover, in the same measure as the extrahistorical derivation of the patterns exhibited in history was open for the schools of political and liberal historians, that derivation was masked for the noted empirical historians whose claim to be the founding fathers of modern scientific historiography lay precisely in their overt inductions of general connections from the facts of history themselves. Ranke, Burckhardt, Fustel de Coulanges—those great names in the early history of history as an independent branch of knowledge—were remarkable for their stress on and their insistence upon the necessary coherence as well as the essential historicity of this coherence because of its derivation from the critically established data distinctive of historical study. And these two emphases proved in time to be incompatible. Because of their critical approach to the data of history, they could sustain their demand for general historical patterns only by connecting those patterns with the validity of principles taken from outside history and hence held independently of its data.

That these historians required coherence from history is beyond cavil. For Ranke coherence was "most of all . . . the connectedness of history in the large," in the "holy hieroglyph" that was to be deciphered by the historian.[125] Ranke insisted upon this even before he insisted upon the requirement of that coherence's a posteriority. "The historian should keep his eyes open for general truth, not by thinking it out beforehand like the philosopher but by letting himself be shown, during his consideration of the particular, the course which the development of the world has taken in general."[126]

Burckhardt was even more hostile to specialist scholars, calling them derisively "capricorn-beetles." Burckhardt admitted that he turned to history to satisfy his "respect for the universal." He sought in history, "the *recurrent, constant,* and *typical* as echoing in us and intelligible through us," and was aware of the past as a "spiritual *continuum* which forms a part of our spiritual heritage."[127] But he was also more sensitive than Ranke to "the mutable" and "the multitudinous" in human affairs. Burckhardt considered the character of "historical life" as something "rolling on in a thousand forms, complex, in all manner of disguises." Thus he insisted that the historian must never separate the desired general truths from the knowable particulars. He asserted that "the task of history" was to show the "twin aspects, distinct yet identical," of spiritual life whereby at once "it appears as change, as the contingent," while at the same time evincing the "aspect by which it partakes of immortality." The student of history, therefore, must be able to "discern and feel the general in the particular." He must be able to present the "small and single detail as symbol of a whole and large view," for "any specialized knowledge of facts possesses, in addition to its value as knowledge or thought in a particular field, a universal or historical value, in that it illuminates one phase of the changeful spirit of man, yet, placed in the right connection, it testifies at the same time to the continuity and immortality of that spirit."[128]

Fustel de Coulanges, finally, rigorous methodologist of objective factual history though he was, and even though he repeated stridently the necessity of understanding past eras in their own terms rather than in contemporary terms, thereby implying a discontinuity between the insulated past and the infectious present, was also insistent upon the fundamental connectedness of history. Although he warned that because "the object studied by history is infinitely complex, . . . a long and scrupulous observation of detail is the only way which can lead to any view of the whole," it was precisely in this view of the whole that he was most interested. Fustel never tired of warning that "history is composed of a multitude of small facts; but the little fact, in itself, is not history," because for him history had to include "the connections between facts" and even "research into general laws." He announced the purpose of his magnum opus to be "to describe" at once the ancient institutions of France and "to mark their linkage." He emphasized "the continuity of things and their slow modification." He defined history as "the science of origins, links, developments, and transformations." Fustel denied that history is "the accumulation of all kinds of events produced by the past." He characterized history as "the science of human societies" and even pronounced it to be synonymous with "sociology." Usually, Fustel maintained the compatibility of the coherent and the critical functions of history by insisting that the historian could integrate the facts within the past, as when he maintained the primacy of the religious impulse through all the social relations of *The Ancient City*. But at times his stress on continuity was such as to lead him beyond the distinctiveness of the past that was his usual emphasis and to make him admit that a connection between past and present was a condition of historical knowledge. At such times he conceded that "the past never completely dies for man. . . . He always preserves it within him. For, take him at any epoch, and he is the product, the epitome, of all the earlier epochs."[129]

Clearly, in one of these instances were the patterns which these professional historians found within the past as historically immanent as they claimed, although it is certainly true that the staggering reputations which they have enjoyed with later historians attest to their relative success in historizing themes which originated in their extra-historical commitments.[130] Thus in his prime Ranke asserted the connectedness of history to inhere more in the actual material of the human past than in the historian's thematic imputation; but our own retrospective analysis can trace his assertion of historical connectedness as much to his own prior religious and classical concerns as to the comprehensiveness of his historical perceptions. Ranke defined world history in Western terms precisely because he saw an objective continuity in the history of Western civilization—"hitherto spiritual development has always progressed in the western nations"—and he saw in the successive issues of religious versus political domination in medieval Christianity and monarchy versus popular sovereignty in the modern states of Europe the linked themes binding together the whole past of the West. "On the opposition of the particular and the general all European history is based," he declared synecdochically, and he confirmed the unitary thrust of this constant theme by assigning to the

Christian church and to the sovereign prince successively the historical mission of mediating between the parties to this chronic conflict and thereby creating harmony in the culture.[131]

Yet, however successful Ranke was in temporalizing the universal pattern he sought through all humanity, it is clear that the origins of his passion for historical unity lay outside the sphere of history, in his search for the constant values associated with his version of philosophy, with his explicit religious belief, and with his persistent literary classicism. The humanity he sought to synthesize was "men's divine nature," the most explicit investment he made of God's harmonious but invisible being in the visible varieties of men's action, and to this translation of Christian piety into history he joined his concern for the modern application of the moral integrity and the civic virtue he found best exemplified in the ancient Greeks and Romans.[132] These extra-historical drives, moreover, invested though they primarily were in their inimitable historical format, continued in being for him as such, acting like so many enduring founts for his historical coherence. Most dubious in this respect was his philosophical drive, for his early enthusiasm for Kant and Fichte was progressively replaced by his animus against the historical philosophies of Hegel and Schelling, and this animus was sometimes expressed as a rejection of philosophy per se in favor of history. Actually, however, Ranke retained his philosophical interests and simply modulated them to be more consistent with his own empirical approach to history. Not only did he insist in general on how "ridiculous" it is to say "that I lack philosophical or religious interest, . . . since it is precisely this and this alone which has driven me to history," but he maintained always that history "is not a denial but a fulfillment of philosophy."[133] As for religion alone, even as an old man he avowed "an absorption in divine things" and clung more "unshakably" than ever to his "faith in Providence" as "the sum of all faith."[134] Nor was his addiction to the independent value of classical humanism any less permanent. As an octogenarian he celebrated this value both within history in the form of an ancient Greek culture "toward which all humanity must strive" and independently of history in the shape of "the ancient classics," which gave him now, as always, great edificatory pleasure.[135]

Ranke dabbled in theory sufficiently and wrote enough history in the grand manner to provide the historistic tradition of historical reason with its academic and public respectability for decades to come. This he achieved essentially by blending the two variants of the tradition, making the connections within the historical process the only accessible manifestations of the Divinity, who was the prime, but inscrutable, reality outside the historical process. Because of the dual function of his historism, establishing a distinctive historical reason at once within and without history itself, Ranke represents both those historians like Burckhardt and Spengler—whose historicity was expressed at least as much in their historically conditioned philosophies as in the actualities of the history that they wrote—and those like Georg Waitz and Numa Fustel de Coulanges, who could focus on the historical process because of its principled separation from the other kinds of realities and values. Ranke accomplished this feat by specifying the comprehensible embodiment of his divinely ordained historical connectedness to inhere in the activities of states as so many "ideas of God" and in the universal themes represented by the successive course of Christian institutions and the worldwide confrontation of monarchy and revolution.[136] Hence, depending on the perspective from which his words and works were viewed, Ranke could authorize a historistic theory which made history the only access to human and divine reality and a historistic practice which perceived the general coherence within history of properly authenticated facts whatever the ultimate position of the historian on the other dimensions of human and divine reality.

Of his heirs among the historical theorists who were historists of the first—or extensive—kind, Burckhardt may be singled out here for the dependence upon historical tradition and upon the historical synthesis of the aesthetic expressions within any cultural period as the only avenues, amid the conditions of cultural discontinuity and aesthetic individuality, to the preservation of the conservative values he held dear. Burckhardt's view of the human past may have been far more pessimistic and disjointed than Ranke's and his outside commitments were surely far less religious and philosophical, but in his own way he was at least as much beholden as his German mentor to aesthetic and political concerns for the substance of the general historical truths he found so important in that past. Precisely because he was so conscious of the disharmonies and varieties in the world of humanity, he could not glean the integration he found so necessary to understanding them either from any conceptual concatenation or from the usual historical coherences based on genesis and change. The general truths in which he was interested were grounded rather in the composition of particulars within one age and in the "genuine parallels, . . . identities and kinships" which define the relationships "between successive times and peoples," and for this composition and these parallels he was dependent on what a recent commentator has happily called his "visual-pictorial quality," a quality obviously derived from his aesthetic perception.[137] The thrust of this quality was embodied in Burckhardt's promise to present "the detail and the particular as symbol of a whole and a large pattern." He insisted that "the beautiful may certainly be exalted above time and its changes," and he celebrated poetry in particular as history's creditor for "insight into the nature of mankind as a whole." He concluded that poetry, for the historical observer, is the "image of the eternal in its temporal and national expression." In general, "art becomes aware of its high status as a power and force *in itself*, requiring from life only occasions and fleeting contacts." Diachronically, moreover, the one interperiodic connection that he allowed had its source in his political (in the broadest sense), as well as his aesthetic, faith. For he believed, conservatively, in tradition and constancy rather than in liberal progress and development. "Let us remember all that we owe to the past as a spiritual *continuum* which forms part of our supreme spiritual heritage," he wrote, and he allowed his conviction of the indispensability of this preservation to suspend his normal assertion of cultural discontinuity between the ages of man.[138]

Fustel de Coulanges exemplified most dramatically the group of nineteenth-century historians whose extrahistorical roots of historical coherence were masked by their indifference to the principles of extrahistorical reality. As we have seen, this group had precedents among such historical thinkers and historians of the early modern period as Bacon, Hume, Vico, and Herder; but if Ranke and Burckhardt resembled these forebears in their transparent conviction that history was the only comprehensible manifestation of an extrahistorical reality otherwise inaccessible, Fustel de Coulanges represented the ambiguous side of the same group, predecessors and approximate contemporaries alike, in the explicit emphasis he gave to the essentially historical character of his coherences at the expense of any possible extrahistorical connections. In his commitments to the genetic principle and to the belief in massive human development, Fustel de Coulanges seemed to announce distinctively historical patterns that were consistent with his dogmas of historical objectivity and historiographical detachment— dogmas which implied the exclusion of the historian's extrahistorical tenets from his study of history—but his failure to admit the role of such tenets in his history has not prevented them from being imputed to him.

In the first place, his protest that history was an idiosyncratic kind of science did not stop his approach to it from partaking of the universal uniformitarian character which he derived from his admitted use of the philosophical Cartesian doubt that "I applied to history" and which was so pervasive in his positivistic and scientistic environment. Not only were his positivistic assumptions manifest in his endorsement of research into "general laws," but his historical work on *The Ancient City* featured a synthetic drive that went far beyond what his material required. He held that religion was the actual centripetal force which held together the various economic, social, political, and juridical attitudes and institutions of the ancient municipalities, both within the single city and "according to an almost uniform pattern" among the cities; that the apparently variegated development of the cities was actually derivative from the uniform development of their religion; and that the end of the ancient city was geared to the end of its primitive religious belief. "We have written," he concluded, "the history of a belief. It was established, and human society was constituted. It was modified, and society underwent a series of revolutions. It disappeared, and society changed its character."[139]

In the second place, there is evidence—disputed though it be—that in fact Fustel de Coulanges found the major thesis of his masterwork, *Histoire des institutions politiques de l'ancienne France,* in the patriotic politics from which he was so careful to separate history theoretically. The thesis for which he became notorious in that work was the priority of the Romans over the Germans in determining the character of ancient Gaul and of Gallo-Roman over Teutonic influence in determining the character of medieval France. His diatribe, after the Franco-Prussian war of 1870, identifying the historiographical positions of German historians with the distortions of a misplaced patriotism and the historiographical positions of the French historians with a defensive objectivity in their approach to history, betrayed his association of the historical detachment he required so unconditionally with a Francophilic position whose roots lay outside of history.[140]

This association, at once so marked and so ambiguous in Fustel de Coulanges, indicates two characteristics of the historistic tendency which he represented. First, the nineteenth-century historists are more important for their critical than for their coherent innovations in the history of history. Second, insofar as they were concerned with coherent patterns—and, as we have seen, they certainly were so concerned—the historists made the historical dimension so prominent in their conception of human reality that a necessary ambivalence was built into the patterns which they recognized in the manifestations of that reality. Commentators have quarrelled about the internal historicity or the extrahistorical provenance of those patterns because the historists themselves made little distinction between the two arenas. The factual historization of all knowable reality by historists of the nineteenth century prepared the way for the theoretical recognition of that historization by historicists at the end of that century, and with this recognition the problem of the foundations underlying patterning in history which had been previously camouflaged now became inescapable.

4
HISTORICISM

The crisis which, in the decades spanning the turn to our own century, beset both philosophers of history and historian theorists who were concerned about the methodology of their discipline was essentially the destabilization of the extrahistorical principles which had served as the source of historical coherence. Both in the form of an openly acknowledged realm wherein could be located the secure fulcrum with which to move the world and in the form of an assumed realm of constant truth which tacitly underlay the patterns which historists insisted on finding in history, the human, and at times even the natural, reality outside of history was now deemed to be subjected to the same unremitting flux and relativism that governed the historical world. Indeed, reality outside history no longer held a comparative advantage for the seating of principles of coherence. Thus it seems most convenient to select this historization of all reality around the turn of our century as the dominant meaning of that variously defined term "historicism" and to distinguish it from both the nineteenth century subjection of this reality to laws of development (confusingly labelled historicism by Karl Popper),[1] which is better denominated rationalistic, and the nineteenth-century identification of this reality with unknowable absolute principle, better denominated historistic. In our usage, then, historicism is the late, extreme, and philosophical stage of historism which came into increasing currency as a term from 1900 on and was associated with philosophers of cultural crisis and with historians who acknowledged and responded to the cultural crisis by ignoring the traditional values outside of history and insisting on social-scientific or philosophical derivation of coherent values for history that were compatible with history. But it is necessary that a twofold distinction in our terminology be drawn and remembered throughout. We must distinguish between historism and historicism in this context, seeing historicism as the particular movement of historism which rose to preeminence during the early decades of our century, with the further qualification that between both of these terms and the term historicity rests the difference between those who—in ways more traditional than they either knew or admitted—derived historical patterns from outside of history and those who—in ways more obscure than they knew or claimed—derived historical patterns from within the historical process itself, as Chapter 5 will make plain.

Historicity signifies a movement within history itself sometimes referred to as historical theory and of which the nineteenth-century historian Ranke was a paragon. Spawned during that ever-increasingly scientifically-minded century, the movement opposed itself to philosophy of history. Where the philosophy of history emphasized the negotiation of history with that which is outside of history, historical theory or historicity emphasized the negotiation of what was internal to history with history proper. This situation made for the two hybrid forms of historism common to the nineteenth century, rationalist and historist, as was covered in the preceding chapter. As we have seen, nineteenth-century historists tried to avoid reaching outside the confines of their discipline to establish its coherence, although, ultimately, they did not wholly succeed. Thus the Ranke of the *Ideenlehre* emphasized both historism and the philosophy of history while the scientific Ranke combined historism with historicity to emphasize historicity. In the scientific Ranke this emphasis went so far as his stressing that every historical epoch is unrelated to the next: historicity in the extreme, indeed.

But by the second half of the century, Ranke's historism and notion of historicity already had become outmoded. Positivism had proved itself the dominant philosophy, the dominant humanism, if you will, of the century's second half. Only future events could prove sufficient to dislodge it from its eminent domain. Once science saw that nature possessed no comparative advantage over history in the establishment of coherence or in providing a standpoint in the absolute, that requisite event had transpired. The dominance of positivism was now thrown into question and persisted only with an attending note of anachronism. Historicism arose to supplant this fallen dominance with a new approach to human reality. The need was to impart coherence to the apparently incoherent discourse of nature or history; either one gave cause for the rise of historicism. It was to this crisis that historicism was a reply.

As a term "historicism" extended back to the beginning of the nineteenth century, was used pejoratively thereafter, and attained the currency and respectability of its present meaning only after World War I. As a movement historicism betokened the recognition of universal flux and had a countervailing ambition to overcome it. It dominated historical thinking around the turn of the century. In the philosophy of history, which became an overriding concern for philosophers (and theologians) of pre–World War I vintage, historicism presided over the crucial shift of attention from the actuality of history to the knowledge of history—in philosophical terms, from historical

metaphysics to historical epistemology. In part, this shift was a product of the insight that far from the morally beneficial or at least
morally neutral pattern formerly thought to have been exhibited by
the actual processes of human history, this process demonstrated a
continuous pattern that was malevolent to humankind. Certainly the
tendency of German philosophical sociology went in this direction:
Ferdinand Tönnies' scheme of society's development from organic
community to mechanistic society was the backdrop for Georg Simmel's notion of culture's inherent drive toward calcification, and this
notion served in turn as the context for Weber's influential idea of
rationalization as the summary direction of human history. All these
thinkers and still more denied any substantive necessity for this re-
gress, but they affirmed it as an empirical continuity nonetheless. Historicism always insisted upon the present's relation to the past and
that this relation was embedded in factual history.

But an even greater part of the philosophical shift from process to
epistemology in the location of history's coherence was conditioned by
the growing acceptance of the absence of any pattern in the substantive
historical process, by the inclination for defining history more as the
historian's reconstruction of the past than as the past itself which would
be less and less sought after for its own sake, and by the consequent
growing insistence upon the discovery of historical coherence in the
historian's own way of knowing the past. The professional as well as
the self-confessed philosophers who espoused historicism in this sense
of the extreme development from historism as over and against nineteenth-century rationalism, and who maintained the ultimate and
irreducible changeableness and individuality of all human affairs were
represented most prominently by Croce, Collingwood, Dilthey,
Rickert, Troeltsch, Ortega y Gasset, and Oswald Spengler. The basic
tenets of historicism were upheld as well by certain prominent figures of
the age who were closer to the rationalist philosophers, although they
made their reputations in another field, as with the philosophical sociologists Georg Simmel, Max Weber, Emil Durkheim, and Karl
Mannheim, as well as with the neo-Marxists of the Frankfurt School,
Herbert Marcuse, Walter Benjamin, and Theodor Adorno. Only the
philosophers of cultural crisis will be dealt with in this chapter.

More obviously than any other development in the early twentieth
century, for both philosophers and historians historicism manifested a
profound shift in Western thinking, for in and of itself it publicized a
massive double crisis in the conception of history. Historicism's emphasis on pervasive flux and consequent multiplicity not only undermined
the notion of historical coherence in both variants of the older historism

but also dissolved the stability of the general laws and principles, whether constant or developmental, that were so important to the older rational views of history. The shift of attention from the historical process to the ways of knowing it becomes explicable along the lines of the two most representative solutions to the problem of historical relativism that were advanced by the philosophical historicists.

First, for the bulk of the historicists the unrelieved fragmentation and mutability of all human reality meant that coherent principle could be sought only in the universal principles, whether transcendent or immanent, which made it possible for the historian to know that reality. For this group the exaltation of historiography over history had to do with the logic, the values, the faith or spirit that enabled the historian to invest even "the singular vicissitude of history" with coherent meaning, to assert, in Croce's notorious phrase, that "all true history is contemporary history."[2] For Croce, who in this respect did not change his mind under the successive impacts of world war and fascism, history was defined by its vitality. The "relationship of history to life is to be conceived as its relationship to unity," with both qualities now bestowed upon history by the historian, who invests it with "a unity of a perfectly logical kind." Thereby he makes history "the identity of the universal and the individual." Hence the only pattern in history is that which is provided by the spirit of the historian. History shows no continuity of progress or even of development, and yet it is rational because of the positive attitude of the historian who makes it "intelligible and capable of comprehension only insofar as the rational is represented and understood . . . as though the irrational were . . . not merely the shadow projected by the rational, the negative aspect of its reality," but as an integral aspect of what history explains.[3] Croce defined the unity in history—or, as he explicitly called it, the "coherence"—as "mental," "philosophical," "moral," that is, as a kind of rationality that was necessarily imported into history from the outside through the mind of the living historian.[4]

Croce insisted upon "the identity of philosophy and history" and that this identity must be understood to work both ways. In this view the place of philosophy has been usurped by "philosophy insofar as it is history." Croce meant to affirm "the whole conception of life as essentially and unalterably change and movement" and to deny "metaphysical" and "transcendental philosophy"; but he also maintained the reverse—that is, "history insofar as it is philosophy"—and attributed to the philosophical and moral dimension in history (he strictly correlated morality and philosophy in this medium) the unity which consituted its defining vitality.[5] Thus he expressly characterized "the writing of history" to be "simply a logical judgement of the only true kind; it is the bringing of the individual under the universal, the intuition under the category."[6] History depends therefore on what the consciousness of the historian brings to it; it "should get beyond life as it is lived, in order to present it as knowledge." Or, as he phrased it in his activist period: "It is the act of comprehending and understanding induced by the requirements of practical life."[7] His strictures against the application of transcendental, philosophical, and religious categories to history were designed to exalt not so much the process of history as the immanent "spirit" which was infused into history by the historian.

Hence Croce's arguments against all forms of closed integration in history—whether it was the idea of progress or the notion of historical necessity or any kind of teleological interpretation—were directed not only against the traditional approach which he associated with "philosophy of history," but—and this bespoke the collapse of philosophy into history as well as the nature of historicism—against anything masquerading as intrahistorical pattern as well. Thus by the same token Croce rejected the idea of "universal history."[8] He proceeded to deny the validity of universals as the inherent historical connectedness of things in favor of their validity as the historian's inevitable classification of particulars under them. He expressed this supersession of inherent historical coherence between events by the historian's imposition of universal categories on events: "The denial of universal history does not mean the denial of the universal in history. . . . That specific particular and finite thing is determined, in its particularity and finitude, by thought, and it is therefore known at the same time as the universal: the universal in this particular form. . . . History is thought, and as such it is thought of the universal, of the universal in its concreteness, and therefore always particularly determined. There is no fact, be it ever so small, that can be conceived (realized or qualified) otherwise than as a universal."[9]

Yet most certainly Croce did not deny the existence of connections in history. He opposed Ranke's dictum that every historical epoch was independent of every other one on the ground that "every act stands altogether in relation to itself and altogether in relation to something else, it is both a point of repose and a stepping-stone, and if it were not so it would be impossible to conceive the self-surpassing growth of history or progress which is a concept without which no history is thinkable."[10] But unquestionably the historicism to which he subscribed (*storicismo*) was, in his own terms, "the very category of logic; it is logicality in its full acceptation, the logicality of the concrete universal";[11] that is, it was applied primarily to the individual and elucidated the universal grounds of the individual, with the connections in history being considered from the point of view of the individuals who were connected. Thus he criticized Ranke for focusing on the historical particulars and on the universal connections of these particulars—that is, on "the particular for its own sake" and on "the reciprocal activity of peoples"—rather than on "the unity of the spirit" which considers particulars in the light of the universal and in which "the coherence of history" really lies.[12] What we might call this vertical connectedness of the individual in history has as one of its dimensions "the eternal life." This dimension "we already possess and experience in every action" and it therefore guarantees the partial extrahistoricality of the historiographical spirit.[13] Were it otherwise, this connectedness would form an intrahistorical pattern of the sort Croce sought to deny.

Thus Croce becomes a model for all those early twentieth-century historicists and philosophers of cultural crisis who, after insisting on the exclusive reality of a single historical realm defined by incessant flow and change, put so much of their effort into the establishment of a coherent order amidst the flow and, hoist by their own petard, at once reflecting and defining the crisis which they worked to resolve, still had recourse to a realm outside of history—albeit seemingly not outside of historized reality—when establishing principles of coherence. Like Croce, they tended to find those principles in the cognitive procedures of the historian who worked in the present. Under these conditions wherein the historian's thought in and of itself made him historical, it was both logical and easy to understand how philosophy had collapsed into history, just as it was equally logical and easy to comprehend that the historian had gained new responsibilities as an intellectual.

The twentieth-century philosopher with whom the name of Croce has been most frequently associated is R. G. Collingwood, if only because Collingwood eventually came also to identify philosophy with history; and even if Collingwood's own protestations of independence are endorsed, his development exhibits more clearly than Croce's the seams between extrahistorical and historical coherence in contemporary idealism that have been so ambiguous in Croce's tighter integration of the realms. According to his authoritative editors, even when Collingwood thought that he had merged philosophy and history, "philosophy would . . . seem to have resisted absorption into history at the very time when its absorption was being proclaimed."[14] Collingwood retained the distinction which he originally proclaimed between the kind of philosophical truth which was universal and valid for all thought and the kind of historical truth which proceeds through the interpretation of evidence to the relative truth of human actions done in the past, despite his late notion that the first kind of truth was derivative from the second. The mediatory idea between these two conceptions was Collingwood's notion that far from being the fundamental constant in all thought philosophical truth was primarily oriented toward discovering this universal in its analysis of historical thought specifically.

Thus his classic *Idea of History* is actually a compilation which reflects both stages of his thinking without apparent contradiction. The bulk of the *Idea of History* is predicated on its introductory discrimination between the historian's apprehension of the past as "thought of the first degree" and the philosopher's thought about historical thought as "thought of the second degree," and was therefore continuous with the conclusion of the *Idea of Nature* in which Collingwood affirmed that history was not only *the* alternative form of thought to natural science but was actually prior to it and hence the only alternative to philosophy. In Collingwood's own terms, "natural science as a form of thought . . . depends on historical thought for its existence. . . . 'We go from the idea of nature to the idea of history.' "[15] The kind of coherence that is represented by scientific law is consequently inappropriate for history. Valid historical coherence takes the form of intellectual development or staging, and it is philosophy that supplies this coherence. Since "it is only in the historical process, the process of thoughts, that thought exists at all; and it is only in so far as this process is known for a process of thoughts that it is one . . . an inquiry into the nature of historical thinking is among the tasks which philosophy may legitimately undertake."[16] The touchstone of historical truth, for Collingwood, is not fidelity to the facts, for the historian's "web of imaginative construction, . . . far from relying for its validity upon the support of given facts, . . . actually serves as the touchstone by which we decide whether alleged facts are genuine," and this web is the product of a philosophical idea—innate in Cartesian terms and a priori in Kantian—"which is clear, rational and universal."[17]

If the subject matter of history is defined as Collingwood defined it, as the historian's conscious reenactment of past thought, then this subject matter involves not only the individuality but also "the universality of an event or character." It involves, that is, that which in the past enables it to be known in the present, namely, its possession of "a significance valid for all men at all times," which enables the historian's thought to arrest the succession of states that is consciousness so as to apprehend that consciousness "in its general structure."[18] That this thought is ultimately philosophical—whether it be autonomous or subordinated to its location in history—is guaranteed for Collingwood by its being necessarily rational. "Irrational elements are the blind forces and activities in us which are part of human life as it consciously experiences itself, but are not parts of the historical process. . . . They are the basis of our rational life as it consciously experiences itself, but are not parts of the historical process. . . . They are the basis of our rational life, though no part of it. Our reason discovers them, but in studying them it is not studying itself. . . . Its own task [is] the self-conscious creation of its own historical life."[19] The extrahistorical connotations of this historical rationality, so visible in Collingwood, go far toward elucidating the long and influential career in the twentieth century of the notion of a knowable historical coherence that is dependent upon the necessarily rational criteria of historical truth. Historicism allows for the thinker to be rationalist and historist both, equally and simultaneously or in expression of a preference.

One of the leading intellectual preconditions of this osmotic derivation of historical coherence on the part of early twentieth-century historicists was the miscarriage of Wilhelm Dilthey's agonized attempt to discover a distinctively historical reason. Dilthey always felt that historical experience must be the basis of all knowledge, but he also felt strongly that in its original state this experience was so unstructured that only the categories of the knowing subject could furnish the form which was necessary to understand it. He admitted the result to be "an apparently insuperable contradiction" between "the finitude of every historical phenomenon"—the historical "relativity of every kind of human conception of the coherence of things"—on the one hand, and "the striving of philosophy for a generally valid kind of knowledge" on the other. "I seek," he said, in other words on another occasion, "for the specific disciplines of man, society, and history a basis and a coherence in experience, independently of metaphysics."[20] For Dilthey the problem was not so much the establishment of an empirical coherence as such, for he had little trouble throughout his career in demonstrating men's involvement in "the realities which constitute the dynamic unity [*Wirkungszusammenhang*] . . . of our life" or in showing the historical basis of that unity, since the historian is himself implicated in the whole network of "vital relations" which "intersect" in his life.[21] In general, this compatible relationship between history and the historian was an expression of Dilthey's commitment to "ideal realism" (*Idealrealismus*), a position that posited the philosophical derivation of the coherence subsisting among discrete historical events and thus the "mutual penetration of the historical and the philosophical."[22]

For Dilthey, the experience of life "is permeated by mental structures and transpires in sociocultural coherences."[23]

What he did have trouble with was the demonstration of the ultimate individual coherence—that is, the application of general rules directly to the individual, on whom finally rests all historical coherence. In the service of such an individual coherence he resorted transitionally to the structure of what he called a "descriptive" and "comparative" psychology. In the last analysis, however, Dilthey depended on philosophy, and particularly on the regulations of its hermeneutical subdivision, to establish this direct coherence of the individual. He had to conceive of this kind of philosophy as continuous with empirical history—thus philosophy can be viewed as "a culture system," and, as such, it performs the function of "relating [concepts] to all inclusive coherence and grounding them on a final principle." This universalizing function made "philosophy only the most consistent, powerful, comprehensive kind of thinking, . . . separated by no definite frontier from empirical consciousness."[24] But as long as Dilthey held philosophy to be thusly based on history he remained implicated in what he admitted to be "the difficulty . . . of the vicious circle," whereby the only resolution of the paradox was a pluralism which destroyed all coherence whatsoever.[25] In this sense his criterion of "openness to experience" led him to an acceptance of historical variegation that ran counter to his own emphasis upon the immanent unity of experience.[26]

More typical of the historicist philosophers than Wilhelm Dilthey, however, was Heinrich Rickert. Rickert represented the southwest neo-Kantian school in the philosophy of history. As a representative of this school he exercised a specific influence that was both mimetic and provocative upon the theologian Ernst Troeltsch and the historian Friedrich Meinecke. Rickert was one of the philosophers who rationalized most clearly the general shift of attention from philosophical history as the pattern of the historical process to the philosophy of history as the historical theory of knowledge. He linked this shift to the critical approach that moved toward the substance of history and cast doubt on the validity of the older speculative orientation, whether Hegelian or Comtean. By drawing a logical and epistemological distinction, moreover, between natural science and history in terms of the former's attention to the validity of general laws and the latter's concern with the description of the particular and individual things that actually happen, and by limiting the natural-scientific in favor of the historical approach, Rickert established historicism as the dominant mode of knowing reality and established the problem of universal imposition upon the historical enterprise, a problem which he felt called upon to solve.

Rickert insisted that any science, historical as well as natural, must have as its aim "not the confirmation, the description, or the necessary genesis of facts," but the comprehension of means that are connected with "the establishment of a general conception of the world and of life." For history, which necessarily has "transcendent elements" in it, Rickert saw his task as the formulation of a distinctive "historical concept" into which the particular and individual things of which the historical world and historical life were composed could be integrated in a non-naturalistic way.[27] Rickert started by insisting that all historical individualities were causally connected with other historical individualities, and in this notion of "historical coherence," plus the analogous notions of historical teleology and historical development, he found the universals that were compatible with the particulars and the individuals that were the stuff of history. Since the distinctiveness of these historical concepts inheres in their positive relationship to values, and since values are taken from the idea of culture, historical sciences are necessarily historical/cultural sciences, and the interest that Dilthey's paternity earned through his association of history with "the human sciences" (*Geisteswissenschaften*) accrued to Rickert by virtue of his association of history with "the cultural sciences" (*Kulturwissenschaften*). This preference was more than merely verbal—it signified Rickert's preference for "objective" over his notion of Dilthey's "subjective"—i.e., psychological—universality in history, and his disposition to view the distinction between the natural-scientific and historical view of things as a logical distinction in the ways of seeing reality "as a unified whole" rather than a distinction between two kinds of reality.[28]

But because the concepts of coherence, teleology, and development are themselves historically conditioned—i.e., individualized in certain temporal circumstances—and because the universal knowledge of the historical process which would be necessary to generalize these concepts is an impossible demand on the finitude of human knowledge, Rickert had to find another way to generalize these integrating concepts for historical science, and this he found in the idea of generally valid value and in the relating of each individual historical object to it in such a way that the coherence, teleology, and development constituting the connections among such objects were true historical concepts. Since the material of the historical world has an "incalculable multiplicity" and is therefore incapable of being subsumed under historical "laws," historical concepts must link its particular objects to common cultural, universally normative values.[29] Since Rickert characterized these cultural values as not only "transcendent" but "timeless" and assigned them to the discipline of philosophy as constituting the bases of historical judgment, in the final analysis he deemed "the forms of thought" which made "history uniform as a meaningful structure" to be imposed from the outside upon the particularities which constituted the stuff of empirical history.[30]

Be it noted once more, however, that in one crucial formal respect the historicists followed the historiographical tradition whose continuous and progressive substance they rejected: their efforts too—as with Croce and Collingwood—were divided between rationalist and historist tendencies. The philosophers and theologians led by Dilthey, Troeltsch, and their ilk derived universal historical structures from extrahistorical principles drawn from the mind of the historian. This derivation is clear enough in thinkers like Troeltsch and Rickert, but it holds for Dilthey as well, since he traversed the fateful line between historical life and a more stable reality when he sought to root historical worldviews (*Weltanschauungen*) first in a descriptive psychology and then in a philosophical hermeneutics.[31] Rickert repeated these steps in his own way, after the manner of a Kantian.

The general validity that Dilthey and Rickert sought in vain to secure through philosophical science, their beneficiary, Ernst Troeltsch, tried even more desperately to attain through his religious belief. Despite his theological training and his Christian faith, Troeltsch was one of the most transparent representatives of the crisis articulated by historicism. He formulated the ingredients of the crisis in categorical terms, pointing unmistakably toward the problem of historical coherence; and he emphasized those elements so markedly that he was unable to resolve the crisis even though he insisted on their extrahistorical derivation from an absolute realm of values which for him had to constitute any possible resolution. The large volume which he devoted to the problems of historicism—*Der Historismus und seine Probleme*—he dedicated significantly to Dilthey (as well as to Windelband), and in it he summed up the issues, albeit not the solution, that he shared with his erstwhile friend, Max Weber. Here, as elsewhere, Troeltsch defined "the general problem of the age" as the dissolution of all norms under the impact of "the endless turbulence [*Bewegtheit*] of the current of historical life" and thus of "the most fundamental inner convulsion and change in almost all spheres."[32] In a famous phrase, moreover, he insisted that his aim was "to overcome history through history."[33] Denying that the crisis lay in what he called "historical science," what we would call "critical history," and what together he and we agree is "empirical" or "factual history," he not only explicitly located "the crisis" in history's "connectedness" (*Zusammenhang*) but identified this historical connectedness with "worldview" (*Weltanschauung*) and, in general, with "the philosophical elements and relationships in history."[34] For Troeltsch, the problem of coherence in history was a problem not of history but of the philosophy of history, and he minced no words in subsuming philosophy of history under philosophy rather than history or some other intermediate realm. "Philosophy of history is a part of philosophy and consequently is closely tied to all the other parts of philosophy."[35] The crisis of historical coherence has followed from the historization of all life, and therefore the problem it evokes is the problem of "the philosophical assumptions and effects of history": in short, the problem of philosophy—that is, of "spiritual life" in general—has become primarily a problem in the philosophy of history.[36]

Hence the philosophy of history must ground a coherence in history that transcends history itself. An authoritative commentator on early twentieth-century historicism called Troeltsch's historicistic conception of history "Janus-faced" because of his insistence that historicism had both a "good side"—i.e., it spawned a metaphysic, a logic, and an ethic that transcended the anarchy of values—and a "negative side" i.e., it made for a "relativistic skepticism of values."[37] Thus Troeltsch did affirm the presence of a universal in the sense of a common ground and a common goal for all particular striving by individuals. But because for Troeltsch the universals themselves were historically conditioned so that it "is certainly more than doubtful whether they can ever become visible on earth," he remained indecisive about their knowability and indeed about their validity as universals above and across the stream of historical becoming.[38] For history is the locus of a caustic movement, while the mastery of that movement by fixed norms is a matter of a "system of values" which is none other than a "system of ethics," standing over and against history.[39] History is too individualistically oriented to comport with any "systematic historical process" or "teleological construction of a gradual realization of purpose." The function of the philosophy of history can therefore never be wholly objective or factual; it can only be the acquisition of an ideal with which a new cultural unity will be created in the present and in the light of the past. If such a cultural synthesis cannot be created without "a great and broad conceptual coherence" in history, it must be understood to be a coherence connecting past, present, and future and thus must be "a practically and normatively conditioned coherence." This is "the only possible philosophical mastering of historicism," and it marks not the religious completion of historical knowledge but rather religion as the limit of historical knowledge. For Troeltsch any independent coherence on the part of history was impossible. "To grasp the connection between this abidingness in religion and the infinite doings of history . . . goes far beyond all the soluble tasks of any philosophy of history."[40] Certainly we must start from factual research in empirical history, but the resulting individuals of history must be measured by "the general coherence of values" in the observing historian. To relate such a coherence to the historical process itself is to create a vicious circle. For Troeltsch, then, the problem of finding a historical base for the coherence in history was a problem that remained to be solved.[41] As it was, the rationalist orientation of his historicism served merely to confound the religiosity that was so fervently longed for.

Yet a solution was raised to Troeltsch by Karl Heussi, author of an influential little book which he published under the title of *The Crisis of Historicism*.[42] More historically and less philosophically minded than his predecessor, Heussi defined "historicism" more broadly than Troeltsch did as "the enterprise of history for its own sake"—that is, the collection of specific historical facts (the kind of history that we have labeled "critical")—and, consistent with this usage, he specified the symptoms produced by "the crisis of historicism" as those occurring within the historical discipline itself, such as the attenuation of political and military history, the vogue of "reconstructing" or even "revolutionizing" the historical profession (especially in the direction of "neo-romanticism"), and by noting the inroads of both systematic thought and belletristics upon scholarly history.[43] Although a church historian and therefore more authentically historical than Troeltsch, Heussi was nonetheless a theologian, and his insistence that historicism was essentially a movement of the recent past was a means of allowing him to adopt the Troeltschian point of view on the profundity of the crisis. This viewpoint permitted him to sketch a scheme of validating "the connection of systematic thought and history," thus transcending the crisis of historicism while accepting the undeniable individualization and relativization of historical events asserted by the crisis. This Heussi did by affirming a kind of perspectivism—by asserting that history is not reflective of an objective reality but is what the historian makes it. Moreover, he associated the coherent context in which a historian must present his facts with a philosophical orientation which imposes both a logic and a generality upon them, an association that led Heussi to approve the pairing of "history" and "metahistory" in the transcendence of historicism.[44]

José Ortega y Gasset, a member of the famed Spanish intellectual generation of 1898, belonged indeed to a later age than did Croce, Dilthey, and Troeltsch, but his indelible training was in the pre–World War I vintage of German culture, and if he developed substantively from vitalism toward existentialism in his authoritative writing between the wars and in the era after World War II, his basic approach remained constant from his earliest philosophical work in 1914.[45] Early on he called his own philosophy "the metaphysics of vital reason" to signify his constant search for a structure of life that would be transcendent in its relationship to every existing reality and yet that would itself be located within the framework of temporal and spatial reality. Like Dilthey, whom he revered as "the most important thinker of the second half of the nineteenth century," he denied truth to any stable principle that set itself up as superior to the flux of life, including that of natural science, and he assigned to "history," as the reality of "a past . . . active in us *now*," the task of supplying man's only "fixed, pre-established, and given line," of converting itself into the "historical reason" which secures the one kind of continuous, empirical progress of which man is capable. "*Man, in a word, has no nature; what he has is . . . history.*"[46]

Indeed, Ortega even gave an explicit defense of "historicism" for its advocacy of the necessary instability of human life. And yet, despite his exaltation of the ubiquitous "mutability of everything human," his invocation of history as humanity's appropriate science, and his overt emphasis on the "original, autochthonous" basis of "historical reason," Ortega insisted, as his later emphasis upon "historical reason" and his defense of the idea of progress showed, both on the systematic quality of history and on the "transcendent" character of physical reason.[47] Now, although the doctrine of transcendence in Ortega can be traced back to his early formulation of the prime human reality as consisting in "I and my circumstances" and thus to an intrahistorical form of things, a derivation which he later confirmed by labeling his philosophy "perspectivism," the fact is that he lamented the flux of all things as something peculiarly and destructively modern. He also tended to define men's "circumstances" in terms of "certain elemental, basic phenomena that involve human society" and that in actual fact imposed themselves from the outside on the historical process that he theoretically followed from within.[48] Thus both historist and rationalist elements of coherence were stressed in the historicism of Ortega.

A product of the same generation as Ortega but at once shorter-lived and more notorious, Oswald Spengler demonstrated a gap between promise and performance that was even more egregious than his peer's. Like Ortega, a philosopher rather than a historian, but unlike Ortega, not so much a professional as an amateur intellectual whose high point was precisely in the philosophy of history, Spengler, too, identified the necessarily "new philosophy"—that is, the philosophy of the twentieth century—with history, in sharp contrast to the previous identification of philosophical principles with nature; and through "the morphology . . . of the world-as-history"—that is, through the "picture of life" in which the forms and movements of the world are presented "not as things-become, but as things becoming." Thus Spengler promised to present a description of historical processes that had their own principles, and consequently their own intrahistorical coherences.[49]

In the Spenglerian sense, historicism makes of history an autonomous primal reality, with its own concepts (organicism, symbolism, chronology, and destiny), in contradistinction to the familiar concepts (mechanism, system, mathematics, and cause) drawn from the anachronistic imposition of nature upon history. But if Spengler's pretension to subsume philosophy under history, to create a "logic of time" in which time predominated over logic, was not vitiated by his actual prior intention to write a work of politics and the actual later involvement of this work in political theory, certainly it was vitiated by the overweening role of biological pattern in his presumably historical morphology and by his prominent assumption from the philosopher Nietzsche and the novelist Thomas Mann of the distinction between culture and civilization.[50] Spengler's insistence upon a biological determinism that underlay the pattern of history, upon a derivation of coherence every bit as anachronistic as that which he declaimed but failed to recognize, namely, a teleology, proved his undoing. For Spengler exalted his historicism into "the philosophy of the future,"[51] and the future, replete with its own organicism, symbolism, chronology, and destiny vouchsafed his ostracism from the ranks of honored scholars. Here was an instance of historicism consuming its young.

Thus it was that four other figures who have been acclaimed rather for their roles in the origins of modern sociology than of modern history have exercised a longer-lasting and more profound influence on the kind of historical thinking that goes under the common understanding of historicism. The necessarily rational criteria of historical truth were given an apparently more authentic historical form by Georg Simmel, Max Weber, and their progeny. Simmel, Weber, Durkheim, and Mannheim all concerned themselves secondarily with the problem of history, and their resort to sociology as their primary commitment was in good measure attributable to their reaction against the instability of historicism and their search for stable principles to serve as a dam against the flow of history.[52]

Georg Simmel, the intellectual jack-of-all-trades (he wrote in all fields and was called, desperately and vaguely, a "philosopher of culture" or "philosopher of life"), to whom the influential Max Weber confessed a debt of intellectual gratitude, dealt with history both explicitly, in his *Probleme der Geschichtsphilosophie,* and implicitly, in his essays on sociology and on culture—especially in his *Philosophie des Geldes* of 1900, his *Soziologie* of 1908, and his *Philosophische Kultur* of 1911. To all these topics he applied a philosophy which has been aptly described as the "connection of the metaphysical with the historical principle," and in this philosophy the metaphysical principle stood for the Absolute in which Simmel always believed despite his recognition of its fragmentation by history.[53] Simmel's dubious early identification of historicism with historical realism, i.e., the doctrine that history was the objective representation of past events, did not prevent him ultimately from being classified with the historicists he nominally rejected.

Simmel argued against the representational notion of history which exalts the "brute fact," "the chaos of events and the fragmentary data concerning their properties." His work on the philosophy of history, which he published first in 1892 and then in larger and more cogent editions in 1905 and 1907, identified "historicism" with "historical realism" for the purpose of arguing the validity of Kantian universal categories which make historical knowledge possible and thereby "emancipate the self."[54] One of Simmel's best-known students, Bernhard Groethuysen, said of his mentor's relation to the Absolute that for him the biblical assertion held, "I have not seen it, but it was there,"[55] an assertion that pinpointed Simmel's problem of finding a stable knowable investment for his Absolute in a world dominated by historical instability and differentiation. History, according to Simmel, is distinctive in that despite the a priori propositions in the mind which it shares with the knowledge of nature, it produces "realities of incomparable and irreducible individuality."[56]

Nor was this belief in the problematic relationship between the objects and the categories which the historian uses to grasp the objects merely an early and undeveloped notion in Simmel. In his late essays he was still insisting on the discrepancy between the apparent "atomic structure of the event," which leads to its "dissolution into genuine discontinuities," and the "vital continuity" of the "unified forms," which the historian adds to historical events to make them comprehensible. "The structure of all understanding," he wrote in this historical context, "is the internal synthesis of two originally separate elements. Given is an actual phenomenon which is not yet understood as such. And a second element is added from the subject to whom this phenomenon is given, . . . precisely the understanding idea, which as it were penetrates the element that is given and makes it understood."[57] Simmel now saw "historicism" in the relativizing terms which have become its most familiar meaning, and his nominal rejection of it in these terms has earned him the label "counter-relativist."[58] Explicitly rejecting now "the radical historicism" that defines historical understanding in terms of the conditions and stages of an entity's temporal development, Simmel deliberately included "suprahistorical" or "transhistorical" understanding—"timeless symbols as it were"—among the "categories" which the subject brings to bear on "the particular contents" of the past in order to create a "historical stream of development" in which these contents first attain the "reciprocal connections and unified orderliness" that makes them intelligible.[59] Hence even if these propositions are considered to be the universals which inform all knowledge, the relationship between the individual instances to which they are applied and their own universality remains a problem, and it was this problem of the relationship of the universal categories of thought to the heterogeneous objects of experience that spawned Simmel's idea of sociology, among the other devices which he used to bridge the gap.

His way was ever to establish the fundamental distinction between the values called for by the universal categories and the reality dominated by heterogeneous particularity. Thus, first, he established that by reason of "the substantial uniformity of knowledge and its object . . . history becomes quite remote from . . . what we are disposed to designate as reality as such."[60] Second, he deliberately intended the money in his *Philosophy of Money* to function as "simply a means . . . for the presentation of relations that exist between the most superficial, 'realistic' and fortuitous phenomena and the most idealized powers of existence, the most profound currents of individual life and history."[61] But if Simmel considered money entirely from the philosophical and sociological point of view as the symbol of "interaction," that is, as the demonstration of "the possibility . . . of finding in each of life's details the totality of its meaning," the fact is that he also showed the historical development of this interactional concept from its early concrete investments to its later abstract function. In its later manifestations, money thus belonged to "the category of reified social functions," with its status an "ultimate purpose" whose demands "are never fully met by empirical reality." Thus money helped to produce a society in which there are "two epistemological categories"—"the valid purpose of things, brought forth by its inner coherence that assigns each element to its proper place, and our perception of things that signifies their reality for a human subject"—and in which their separation is manifested in the predominance of the purposive and functional "objective culture" of the species over the substantive "subjective culture" of the individual.[62] Thus for Simmel the ordering relationships that made historical sense out of the chaotic events of the past became more abstract as they became more unifying, and with this concept Simmel was admitting that the increasing variety of the concrete past required an ever more importunate visitation of ideals from the outside to constitute an intelligible history.

Since Simmel considered money now (in 1900) to be "entirely a sociological phaneomenon," his notion of its development into a form of abstract interaction among individuals was derivative from the general ideas about sociology which he was developing around the same period.[63] For Simmel saw that "the really practical problem of society is the relation between its forces and forms and the individual's own life" and he developed his notion of scientific sociology as the admittedly "abstract" form of knowledge that groups or "synthesizes" the given individuals into the interactive relations "that tie men together."[64] Thus Simmel defined "general sociology" in terms of its judgment upon historical life from the standpoint of society in order to elicit "the general principles" from the "data" of the past, and if he distinguished "former sociology" from it to concentrate on the study of the societal—in contrast to the individual or historical—forms themselves he also admitted "philosophical sociology" as a legitimate branch of the science to emphasize the external interpretive problems of the discipline in contrast to its "quite different" empirical propositions. The role of Simmel's sociology in imposing conscious philosophical categories upon the variety of historical phenomena in modern times was confirmed by his elaboration of "philosophical sociology" as an intellectual history whose guiding theme was precisely the replacement of commensurable individuals by integral society as the predominant interactive relationship of human life.[65]

But society could not be the final solution for Simmel precisely because the differentiation between what was individualized and what was integral in life overlapped the distinction between the individual and the societal; therefore he could not rest content with so mechanical a distinction as that between the individual and his society. For he was disposed toward a unity born of interaction, not of distinction. He even admitted that whatever perspective the observer chose, whether the standpoint of society, the individual, or the particular object, the result was "a process which *we* inject into reality, an *ex-post-facto* intellectual *transformation* of the immediately given reality" in the service of experiencing "this life as a unity." Consequently he required a discipline that would encompass all these persepctives.[66] He found this ultimately in a philosophy of culture, for he defined culture as a blend of the "subjective soul" and "the objectively spiritual product"—that is, the particular objects viewed as a product of a unifying objective "spirit"— and he identified the process of culture as the procedure on both the subjective and objective levels as the passage from "closed unity through developed multiplicity to developed unity"—a process which synthesized both the individual and the integral principles and the subjective and objective aspects of life.[67] But because Simmel continued to set "the point of unity in us," that is, in the subject, he repeated the failures of sociology in "the tragedy of culture," that is, in its persistent inability to synthesize the subjective and objective realms of culture, and he attested to the climax of this division into "subjective culture" and "objective culture" by recognizing them as "the dissonances of modern life."[68]

The famed pluralism of Max Weber—he was an economist, historian, and sociologist—was overlaid by a persistent philosophical conception which was related to his connections with historicist thinkers such as Dilthey, Troeltsch, and Simmel and which testified to his total acceptance of the individual variegation that they saw in modified ways as the basic human reality as well as to his determination to overcome this variegation with a set of universally valid concepts.[69] His ultimate resort to sociology was, like Simmel's penultimate resort to his new social science, in the service of constructing a set of such stable concepts which would transcend the individuality of historical facts and confer an intelligible rationality upon the study of human affairs, past and present. Whether one adopts the traditional picture of a Weber developing from the distinctive historical emphasis typified by *The Protestant Ethic and the Spirit of Capitalism* (1904–5) to the systematic emphasis of *Wirtschaft und Gesellschaft* in its ultimate version (1922) or the more recent interpretation that posits Weber's persistent combination of the historical and the systematic motifs,[70] the fact remains that for Max Weber the patterning and ordering categories which made history a rational discipline were separate from the empirical, individual stuff of history. It is true, certainly, that both the earlier Weber who joined his systematic interest integrally to a preponderant concern for cultural history and the later Weber who stressed the

CHAPTER FOUR

distinction of his systematic sociological occupation from his individualizing historical one maintained that history includes "causal
analysis and explanation" as the key to the use of historical material in
"the acquisition of general concepts, analogies, and rules of development." In both stages, however, Weber made clear a context that
pointed to the external source of the coherence of these general concepts, analogies, and rules.[71]

The earlier Weber, who developed his historiographical ideas primarily in his critique of the historian Eduard Meyer, distinguished
explicitly between history as a "professional discipline" and history as
a "logical . . . concept." He castigated the first qualification while he
developed the second, and in general adopted the point of view of
"neighboring disciplines," using the occasion of Meyer's work to discuss "common logical questions," in their particular reference to
history.[72] Even at this stage Weber insisted that the causal relationship
had to be thought through "a series of abstractions" which involved the
transposition of the discrete past "facts" constituting ultimate historical reality into the mental knowledge of the historian who changes
existence into causes by imposing general "rules of experience" upon
"what is historically given."[73] It is hardly surprising, then, that Weber
saw a difference of degree rather than of kind between historical and
natural (scientific) explanation, since the former entailed the same kind
of causal and coherent lawfulness for him as the latter. For Weber, the
difference consisted primarily in the intellectuality of the former in
contrast to the actuality of the latter. As if to underline the intellectuality of the historian's operation to get at "historical meaning,"
Weber argued for counterfactuality (called by Weber "judgments of
possibility") as an indispensable part of thought in the establishment of
historical causation.[74]

Weber's best-known historical work, *The Protestant Ethic and the
Spirit of Capitalism* should be interpreted from this perspective of the
imposed intellectuality of historical patterning. Indeed, Weber admitted, as he did with the later essays on "the economic ethic of the world
religions" with which he combined it, that *The Protestant Ethic* was not
a "comprehensive cultural analysis." Rather, it was oriented toward
"the point of view" from which it was written. Like the later essays, it
was a "constructed schema" with "the purpose of being an ideal-
typical means of orientation," of showing the distinctive aspect of
Western cultural development, that is, "the particular individuality of
western . . . rationalism."[75] Weber's decision to combine the earlier
and later essays on comparative religious history and to preface both
with a discussion defending the role of individual uniqueness in "uni-

versal history" betrayed the continuity of external patterning in Weber's conception of history.[76] Even later, when he made clear his preference for "systematic sociology" over history because of the former's comparative advantage in understanding "the coherences and the regularities" in human behavior, he thought of history and sociology in complementary rather than competitive terms. "Sociology, like history, signifies 'pragmatic;' both explain on the basis of rationally intelligible coherences of action."[77] The methodology of an "intelligible sociology" (der verstehenden Soziologie) furnished for Weber a more certain kind of knowledge of the inherent chaos stemming from his principle that "reality pertains only to the concrete, the individual," than did the "hypotheses" to which historical explanations were so often reduced.[78] Thus Weber's addiction to comparative history gave way to his concern for comparative sociology. As he put it toward the end of his life: "Sociology's formation of concepts takes its material, as paradigms, very essentially albeit not exclusively, from the realities of action relevant to the historical point of view. . . . As with every generalizing science the characteristic feature of its abstractions is that its concepts must be relatively hollow of substance vis-à-vis the concrete reality of the historical. What it has to offer in compensation is the univalence of its concepts."[79] For he attributed especially to sociology the formation of " 'pure' ('Ideal') types" into which historical phenomena "can be fitted."[80]

Thus Weber started from the principle, common to the historicists, which considers "the particular individual as the basic unit. . . , the sole bearer of meaningful conduct" and which holds the ultimate values of individuals to be scientifically unknowable because they are incompatible—because, that is, "the various value spheres of the world stand in irreconcilable conflict with one another." Like many of the historicists but more frankly than any other of them, Weber opted for sociology over history precisely because to him it offered larger scope for the establishment of coherences and hence for rational understanding.[81] But if his formal distinction between the historian who treats of individuals and the sociologist who seeks "typal concepts" and general rules is ignored in favor of his analogous treatment, as a "historical sociologist," of individuals and societies, then we may remark upon two of his distinctive contributions to twentieth-century historiography.

In the first place, where other historicists—with the exception of Spengler—perceived no rational pattern in Western history, Weber publicized one that he evidently did not like—"the disenchantment of the world," as he preferred to call it, or "rationalization," as sometimes he labeled it. Scientifically and neutrally as he tried to represent this process, he found it at the very least intellectually, morally, and politically inadequate. It was intellectually inadequate because it was not a dominant enough trend to constitute a "unilinear development"—such competitive principles as the patriarchal and the charismatic remained present and active—and also because the idea of "rationalization" contained too many meanings to be self-explanatory for Western history.[82] It was morally inadequate because its "ethic of responsibility"— that is, of the rational proportioning of means to ends and the equally rational calculation of consequences—had to be supplemented by a now morally doubtful "ethic of absolute ends"[83] and it was politically inadequate because the legal bureaucratization and routinization that was rationalization's public form was inimical to the spontaneity of personality which was thought to be the basis of a true and desirable democracy.[84] Hence it was easy for Weber—and for those who followed him—to turn from this problematical substantive development increasingly to the methodology of dealing with it.

Weber himself elaborated one of the species of methodological rationality that would be as long-lived as his notion of rationalization in the historical process but that would be taken up by very different groups. Most of his prescriptions for eliciting statistical uniformities or causal laws from an unpromising collection of social acts would be sociologically specified; but one was not. When he stipulated that men's rational behavior was the rule, with their irrational behavior being measured by its declination from the rule, and when he encouraged the historian, as well as the sociologist, to construct "causal explanations" through "observed deviations" from "an ideal typical construction of rational action," he set forth a model that would be used by epistemological philosophers of history during the rest of the century.[85] As it would be for the rationalists who followed him (like Collingwood and Morton White), the rational model for Weber was an intrusion of concepts with roots outside of history into history. Whether he related rational conduct to the notion of purpose (*zweckrational soziales Handeln*) or to the notion of value (*wertrational soziales Handeln*), the patterning was part of his sociological definition.[86] Yet Weber might have been a historist but for this strong emphasis upon rational principle. As it was, Weber was either a historical rationalist, displaying a preference for sociological analysis, or a rational historist with a penchant for shoring up our sense of the universal in the face of an advancing relativism. Weber himself, however, could not decide between them.

But Weber, and Simmel before him, were not the only sociologists of pre–World War I vintage who defined independent history in individualistic terms and who imposed social categories upon it in order to make historical life manageable and intelligible. Emile Durkheim's dual approach to history, like that of his predecessor, Auguste Comte, is explicable in these terms. On the one hand, Durkheim seems like the ahistorical social scientist. In this role what Durkheim denied was precisely the connections which claimed to be intrahistorical. Thus he rejected the view that "history has for its object precisely the linking of events in their order of succession," on the ground that "the stages that humanity successively traverses do not engender one another." He admitted the existence of "different historical societies," and he confessed that "we can observe experimentally in the species . . . a series of changes among which a causal bond does not exist." But he insisted that the scientific fact was precisely the causal fact and that the primary fact in this sense was irreducibly sociological—that is, it consisted of the irreducible "social milieu."[87] In other words, Durkheim's well-known insistence upon the independence of social facts and their separation in principle from the facts of individual life, while explicitly directed against the association of sociology and psychology, was equally oriented against the connection of sociology and history by reason of his denial of the interaction between the individual and the collectivity that is at the very heart of history.[88]

The same Durkheim, on the other hand, at times wrote very favorably about history, and apart from the inconsistency which is the lot of every moral being, the explanation of Durkheim's duality may be his approval of history in its critical but not its coherent sense. Much has always been made of Durkheim's appreciation, frankly avowed by him, of his collegiate history teachers, Fustel de Coulanges and Monod.[89] But little has been made of the kind of historians that these two worthies were and of the kind of influence which they exercised on the impressionable young Durkheim. Both were avatars of the rigorous scientific method in history, Fustel through his statements on the obligation of the scholar to historical objectivity—i.e., to the faithful delineation of the facts in the documents—and Monod through his own indebtedness to his mentor, the German medievalist Georg Waitz, for his stress on the details and the specialized bibliography of his favored subject, the institutions of France during the medieval age and the ancien régime. Indeed, Durkheim came to criticize Fustel precisely for the pattern which the latter saw in his *Ancient City*, the pervasive causative role of religious belief.[90]

But on the occasions when Durkheim wrote in explicit recommendation of history, as he did in his prescription that sociologists prosecute historical researches on the genetic principle that to know present-day "social reality . . . it is necessary to know how it has come to be, that is, to have followed in history the manner in which it has been progressively formed,"[91] it was for the more intensive knowledge of the social facts that he advocated it. The process of social change which he invested in his *Division of Labor* and which has been attributed to his covert partiality for history was in fact a pattern of coherent social transformation through time which he felt was the function of sociological analysis and which has not prevented anthropologists like Claude Lévi-Strauss from lumping Durkheim's ultimate defense of ethnography together with history as ancillary sciences providing material for a structural sociology.[92] Certainly, as has been maintained,[93] if Durkheim's final recourse to the problem of primitive religion and his insistence upon the autonomy of "collective consciousness" betrays a certain sympathy with history, his conclusive demonstration, to his own satisfaction (and to Lévi-Strauss's), that " 'society' is the universal and eternal cause of these sensations *sui generis* out of which religious experience is made," it shows definitely the kind of historical process that he ultimately appreciated, the kind of process behind his declaration that "man is a product of history," a sociological history whose primary categories may have had a historical origin but which are known through a method of sociological rather than historical analysis.[94] Yet the problem's origin remained in its end: the subjects of explication for which Durkheim is most renowned, *anomie* and suicide, are both the products of a process that takes man as a whole toward a historical conclusion.

From the generation following that of the founding fathers of modern sociology was Karl Mannheim, another philosopher-sociologist, whose sociology of knowledge went further than the fathers' in accepting the concrete heterogeneity of existence as an inevitable condition of life and of reality and who was therefore all the more tortuous in his construction of coherence upon its basis. Hence his doctrine was notorious for its historical relativism; but Mannheim himself thought of it as a sociological "relationism," thereby shifting the emphasis from the fragmentation that he accepted to the unification he desired.[95] Even more frankly than his forebears in the sociological tradition, therefore, he drew a distinction between, on the one hand, the individualizing history (which he labelled "historicism") that he saw being practiced and which he rejected, and, on the other hand, the generalizing history that, fructified by sociological analysis, he considered normative and which he accepted. In an early article on "historicism" he characterized it as fundamentally "the real bearer of

our Weltanschauung," the successor of the medieval and Enlightenment views of the world, the "inescapable basis of all our thinking and
acting," and he defined this historicism categorically to be the totality
of dynamism, the "all-changing" (*Allwandel*), now the primary principle of life.[96] In this historicistic gear the only stability Mannheim
could find was a perspectivism that assumed historical relativity. And
neither was Mannheim afraid of the moral relativism that this assumption implied, for he believed in the eventual victory of democracy over
its rivals.

But ultimately Mannheim came to consider a generalizing history,
fructified by an analytical sociology, normative and acceptable. In this
gear he denied both abstract sociological doctrines, like those of "formal sociology," and "over-emphasis on concreteness and historicism,"
like that practiced by any unscientific historian who "traces the relationship between events in a unique historical issue."[97] The mistake
which such historians make is "to reconstruct the individual framework of a society, or its individual development without taking universal factors into account." Hence the bases of a single age in social
history constitute "the *principia media* which are in the last analysis
universal forces in a concrete setting."[98] In the final analysis, the division of society between ideologists and utopians, Mannheim's view in
his critical gear, gave way to the desired perspective in which he defined
the "sociological approach to history" as the one that "will see in the
sequence and co-existence of phenomena more than mere accidental
relationships"—indeed that seeks "an ever-widening drive toward a
total conception" of things—i.e., that seeks to view every situation "as
part of a larger whole." Since Mannheim admitted that, in the hands of
the free-floating intellectuals whom he posited, this would be "a sociological technique for diagnosing the culture of an epoch," his
coherent relationships, however applied to historical situations, were
themselves of reconstructive sociological origins and were imposed
upon history for its own good.[99]

Thus it was that a whole series of important thinkers, according to
their wont, followed the lead of Georg Simmel in attempting to accom-
modate and supplant an ever-advancing, ever-more encompassing
historical relativism. What is not so commonly noted in this regard,
however, is that another distinct group of thinkers, who bypassed Simmel in favor of Marx, fit equally well the same historicist mold. Indeed,
the neo-Marxism of the twentieth century has been characteristic of the
nonhistorians who were affected sufficiently by historicism to have
their extrahistorical pattern and its historical application shaken to its
foundation. Such thinkers laid the explicit groundwork for the ambigu-

ity between the external reference of a restored historical pattern and the internal fabrication of such a pattern within history itself. Most revealing of this later group of thinkers has been the neo-Marxism of the Frankfurt school, for this school has been sociological in its main emphasis and thus has continued the concerns of central European culture in the age immediately preceding our own.

At once confirmatory and surprising is the assignment of twentieth-century neo-Marxism to both the rationalist and historistic traditions. But the presence of both traditions in the twentieth-century neo-Marxist conception of history is hardly surprising in view of the dual influence exercised by both Marx and historicism over prominent representatives of the school. What may be surprising are the anomalous commitments of the various tendencies of the various neo-Marxists. Both Lukács and Marcuse belong to the historistic wing of the movement despite their apparent acceptance of the rationalistic Hegel, their perception of rationalization as the dominant tendency of the actual historical process, and their literal espousal of objective, critical, or dialectical reason as the underlying principle of human history. Figures like Adorno and Benjamin, who wrote so decisively about the planlessness of history, denying any demonstrable connection between reason and history or between reason and reality, yet advocated an ahistorical origin for the reason that did enter history. They belong to the rationalist tradition. Max Horkheimer, in the historical as in many other respects, stood with a foot in both camps.

The common experience of the neo-Marxist group was the failure of modern empirical history—and particularly of the proletarian agents of it—to converge with the putatively rational process of objective history in the Marxian format—that is, actually to make the social revolution which that process called for.[100] It was in the diverse reactions to this overriding negative fact that the neo-Marxists divided in their approach to history. For Lukács and Marcuse, who took over the historical but not the independent-spiritual status of reason from Hegel, there are two kinds of reason in history—one empirical and spurious, the other synthetic and authentic—but both testify to the fundamental continuity and intelligibility of the historical process. Indeed, this historistic wing of neo-Marxism is the only significant kind of twentieth-century historical theory, with the exception of such mavericks as Spengler and Toynbee, to stress the pattern in history as it has been lived. For this wing, integral reason—the ultimate reason which is the instrument of men's freedom and of their control of their own destiny—is not the rationality of the historical theorist with the rational possibilities of the society as their articulator. Integral reason joins the rationalization of the oppressive society of the past to the reason of the potentially free society in the present. Indeed, the empirical "technological rationality," as Marcuse called it, served "the logic of domination" and hence was ultimately "irrational," but he associated this kind of irrationality with the fundamental rationality of the historical process: he called the irrational "technological rationality," "the latest transmutation of the Idea of Reason," in order to indicate the capacity of this empirical, alienated irrationality to generate the change to an authentic realization of integral reason and in order to equate the empirical irrationality of the oppressive system with the fundamental reality of alienation in the rational process of human history.[101] "In reality Reason is still Unreason."[102] For Marcuse as for Lukács, the rational structure which he saw as a level of history had been for Marx a logical process which had been imported into history from the outside, and although both Lukács and Marcuse intensified the ambiguity of this structure by historizing Hegel, still it was Hegel's ontological structure of Reason that furnished the roots for the rationality of history in his neo-Marxist successors.

From the standpoint of historical approach Benjamin and Adorno are rationalists who stand apart from the historists of the Marcuse stripe, while Horkheimer shares points of view with both groups. For these rationalists, the disappointment with the working class and the experience of fascism resulted not in an integrated view of the past under the rational category of "reification" but rather in a view of the past as disjointed and meaningless until the interjection of philosophy between the moments of history gives it integrity and meaning. This position can be contrasted with the historists who insisted on the ultimate historical rationality of this apparent irrationality, and it can even be compared with that of Horkheimer, who joined Adorno in the rejection of Hegel's identification of reason and reality and in the general principle that "history *has* no reason" but who, on the other hand, did not share Benjamin's and Adorno's confidence in philosophy. Thus Horkheimer emphasized more than they the historical conditioning of rational critical reason and insisted that even if there was "no justifying meaning" in history that there were "a number of explanatory connections," and he proposed to analyze them in terms of "the rationalization of alienation." For Benjamin, however, "the past can be seized only as an image which flashes up at the instant it can be recognized and is never seen again." When "history is the subject of a structure," its "site" is "time filled by the presence of the now . . . at a moment of danger;" the historian thus "remains man enough . . . to blast open the continuum of history. . . , grasps the constellation which his own era has formed with a definite earlier one, [and] thus establishes the present as 'the time of the now' which is shot through with chips of Messianic time."[103]

Benjamin's disciple, Theodor Adorno, made the same point even more directly, deriving the reason in history from the philosophical interjection of critical theory from the outside into history. History itself "formed no structural whole," he taught. Identifying reason with universality and unreason with particularity, he insisted that "the general reason that comes to prevail is already a reconstructed reason" because "a positivistically advancing historical science has splintered the conception of totality and unbroken continuity," thus making "history . . . the unity of continuity and discontinuity." "The irrationality of the particularly realized *ratio* within the social totality is not extraneous to the *ratio*, . . . rather, it is immanent to it." As an attitude toward reality, the general reason is imposed, "a unity over something"; it installs itself "above something else." For Adorno, "the painful antithesis of nature and history," glossed over by Hegelian rationalism, not only withdraws the universal meaning from the "historic process" as such, but also betokens the gap in history which can be filled by theory.[104] In the words of a recent commentator, "for Adorno, the present did not receive its meaning from history; rather, history received its meaning from the present." As Adorno himself said repeatedly: "History is in the truth; the truth is not in history."[105]

So much for the philosophers, theologians, sociologists, and neo-Marxists who appreciated historicism in the ultimate sense of the mobilization of all reality and sought to impose stability upon the historical process from the outside in the effort to overcome its essential instability. Obviously, as can now be surmised, the dominant thrust of twentieth-century historical theorists and philosophers of whatever stripe has been toward the recognition of the broader contexts which envelop human existence; and, as we shall see, this is true of the historians of the twentieth century as well.[106]

What is frequently overlooked or forgotten, however, is the reason why these various thinkers all looked to the broader contexts of human reality in the first place. They resorted to their various models and principles of coherence, generally each one reliant at some point upon an extrahistorical authority, because of the general perception of cultural crisis, of change as the dominant note of human reality—because of the recognition of the fact that nature is no more privileged than history when it comes to establishing the coherences requisite for critical thought. And this recognition cut across the field of modern Western culture. No one was left unaffected; everyone responded to the generally perceived crisis. This perception of the fact is what occasioned the shift of concern from the reality of the past to the epistemology of history. This shift of attention was not carried out for its own sake alone.

But what is also not commonly enough recognized or admitted is that the models and principles of coherence put forth by this spectrum of thinkers did not wholly succeed in getting the job done. The crisis of Western culture is more or less synonymous with twentieth-century historicity and no one as yet has succeeded fully in resolving it. All of the coherences covered above, regardless of their being weighted toward rationalism or the concrete universal of an intrahistorical pattern, are more indicative of twentieth-century attempts to deal with the crisis than of success in fully resolving it. "Coherent wholes" have been either invested in an insufficiently critical historical reality or they have not been truly whole. They either lack sufficient emphasis on the universal elements of the human condition or they undercut that proposition by relying on an extrahistorical determinism of some kind, or, because of their emphasis upon rationalism or logic or the dialectic of Reason, they fail to allow sufficiently for the heterogeneous nature of reality which they themselves were among the first to recognize as the true totality. The preference for rationalism of some sort allows for the absoluteness of the things or objects under consideration but not for the absoluteness of the forms that the things or objects take, forms that all too quickly vitiate the remnants of any ahistorical principle or system.

What is, I hope, now clear is that the thinking of these philosophers of cultural crisis set the context and put forth the models and principles which have served the historical enterprise in our century. Indeed, they left the historical enterprise in more or less the fourfold division which has been one of the tasks of this narrative to draw out. First, there is the critical history that is defined by the application of facts to ideas of coherence. Second, there is the science of documents, the diplomatics, if you will, of negotiating between the realities of the past and the understanding of the present. Third, there is the idea of recreated history whereby it is thought that the actuality of the past can be reconstructed from surviving documents. And fourth, there is the stress upon the historical coherence of the present, or historicity, which strives to fix both the presence and the absence of the past in the present.

But where the models and principles covered in the history of this fourfold division are still being followed to the letter, it must be confessed that the crisis of culture to which historicism was the dominant response still persists. As we shall see, the ambiguity between the external reference of a restored historical pattern and the internal fabrication of that pattern within history itself is as implicit in the historical writing of our century as it is explicit in the thinking of the historicists. Indeed, in the continuity between the apparently separate poles of the ambiguity is demonstrated the actual external reference behind the putatively internal reference of historism.

5

HISTORIOGRAPHICAL COHERENCE IN
THE TWENTIETH CENTURY

Twentieth-century historiography presents its historian with a problem not previously encountered in this study, namely, with a tremendous pluralism which seems to defy the coherent exposition of twentieth-century historiography. It cannot be recounted, as was here recounted the historiography of the nineteenth century, as following from two models, the Hegelian and the Rankean, where politics acted as the extrahistorical source of coherence for that century's historiography and for its history for the purposes of a later history of historiography. To the contrary, historicism left behind it a pluralism of models and methods, not one or two; and these models and methods are as various as the historians who employ them, and as various as the objects of study to which they are applied.

Where the traditional historian would like to be able to judge that the issue of the divination of coherence in the historian's work comes to substitute for the nineteenth-century reliance upon politics in this regard, he simply cannot. Where the traditional historian would like to be able to judge for the sake of a historically derived source of coherence and for the historical integrity of his profession that twentieth-century historists and auto-rationalists simply retooled the faces of old coins to fit the changed circumstances of their time, retooled the models of Hegel and Ranke now enshrining some theory of historical coherence where the issue of politics had once been, he simply cannot. The evidence of a pluralistic historical practice is simply too great to support such a viewpoint. No singular element of synthetic coherence is present in twentieth-century historiography that successfully links the efforts of a Meinecke or a Toynbee with those of, say, a Foucault.

Yet it remains the hypothesis of this history that historians as seemingly opposite as Meinecke and Foucault nonetheless do belong to a singular history of twentieth-century historical practice. Although twentieth-century historians have faced unevenly the problem met head-on by historicism, the problem of the dissolution of universal values, and thus, in the aftermath of historicism, have responded to the announced crisis in a great variety of ways, these many historians and the many examples of their historical practice still belong to the same posthistoricist time frame, to the same century, and in at least one key respect, to the same historical experience, whether or not they were conscious of having done so. They have all partaken of a common historicity even where they have failed to recognize or have chosen to ignore or have gone too far with the fact that historicism did indeed sound the dominant note of this century's historical experience with its evocation of the modern notion of crisis. This is as true for the century's historical practice as it is for its social and political and economic life.

Thus the traditional historian might do well to lament the fact that the issue of the derivation of coherence in his work has not been taken up across the board by his colleagues, not been made an explicit concern of their work, not been scrupulously defined and rigorously and self-consciously employed on the behalf of a historical science. But this would be merely to lament the failure of our century to have produced a specifically historical reason, long-promised by the profession's idealists, whereby history would be uniformly defined and practiced when in fact no such procrustean bed of historical reason can exist. There are indeed a plurality of histories to be learned and a plurality of historical methods to be practiced and necessarily so something historical that remains beyond the scope of historical reason. No doubt there is yet to come a specifically historical reason, or true historicism, if you will. But in and of itself it will never succeed as a substitute for a pluralistic definition of historical practice. Nonetheless, as this book has been at pains to demonstrate, time has its reasons, and where coherence is wanting, in time, that coherence will be supplied.

So if, in the recounting of the plurality of twentieth-century historical practice, jumps and bumps suddenly arise—the temporary suspension of chronology in favor of the theoretical approach on the one hand, and the sudden suspension of the theoretical in favor of the chronological on the other—this is because of the heterogeneity of the subject and the need to be explicit about what makes that heterogeneity cohere. If, then, this recounting produces a somewhat eccentric and necessarily truncated image of twentieth-century historiography, it is only because the plurality of our century's historical product is just such an enterprise and the lone historian can only do so much.

For in fact, all twentieth-century historiography, as regards the source of its coherence in each and every example, can be classified along a line that stretches from the externalization of this principle in covering laws or models to its underutilization in what amounts to a particularly modern and specifically twentieth-century notion of discourse. Moreover, this line provides a context for the discussion of each individual historian's example of historical coherence—a basis for assessing that example's relation to the externalization of the principle of coherence—as well as for the discussion of any ambiguities that crop up along the way. Given the heterogeneity of the subject, it is thought best to objectify the individual historian and the example of his practice after the manner of Hegel, emphasizing the individual historian and the historical dialectic even though the Hegelian precedent cannot otherwise be followed. The logical problem of cross-referencing the collective nature of man in order to get at the individual part of him is resolved here by the common stress on social history and the reaction of the unity of historical time.

The example of the externalization of the principle of coherence as applied to the study of history comes to us from mid-century and it comes to us from philosophy. The universal role of reason, but not reason itself, was subordinated but not canceled by Romantics of the nineteenth century. This example comes after the great shocks of the two world wars, and after the experience of the turbulent interwar period, with its disruptive social, political, economic, and cultural dynamism that would not assimilate to tradition. It has been in the realm of philosophy, where the Anglo-American-Austrian stress on historically indifferent logic and analysis replaced the Franco-Italo-German concern for a historically interested existentialism, that intrahistorical (auto-rational) reason has given way to canons of ahistorical rationality.

Logical positivists and analytical philosophers are representative of the twentieth-century attitude that attends rather to epistemology than to process—to the writing rather than the living of history—and if their classification is not very surprising it does confirm the persistence of the rationalistic and historistic tradition into the contemporary phase of the approach to history. In accordance with the shift from substance to knowledge, the kind of reason which this group seeks in history has shifted from pattern to explanation, from continuity of process to the connection denoting the meaning of an event. As these philosophers have extended their insights to a recalcitrant history, among other fields, they have sought to account for the most varied kinds of reality. What we have called the rationalistic and historistic types of approaches to the problem of reason in history, signifying a rationality that is not as well peculiar to history, find expression in the opposing claims of those who espouse "covering laws" for history and those who insist on principles of explanation closer to the procedure of independent historians. The covering-law model, which holds that historians resort to uniformities expressed by general laws for their explanations, whether they avow such a procedure or not, equates historical with extrahistorical rationality in the words of no less an authority than Carl

Hempel, one of the creators of the model. He has written categorically that "the nature of understanding, in the sense in which explanation is meant to give us an understanding of empirical phenomena is basically the same in all areas of scientific inquiry. . . . Our schemata exhibit . . . one important aspect of the methodological unity of all empirical sciences."[1] It should be noted too that Karl Popper, the noted critic of nineteenth-century rationalistic history, rejected for natural sciences as well as historical logic—and thus from the perspective of his own rational history—the kind of inductive generalization on which he found the putatively invalid rational history of the nineteenth century to be based, and in the midst of his apparent concession to a historically congenial proposal of "piecemeal social engineering" he insisted on the essential unity of rational procedures in all fields. "All theoretical or generalizing sciences make use of the same method, whether they are natural sciences or social sciences. . . . The methods always consist in offering deductive causal explanations, and in testing them. . . . The thesis of the unity of scientific method . . . can be extended, with certain limitations, even to the field of the historical sciences. . . . A singular event is the cause of another singular event—which is its effect—only relative to some universal laws."[2]

The reservations which have been expressed about the applicability of the covering-law model to history have often posed countervailing rational canons of explanation which are appropriate to history alone and are therefore classifiable as a historistic rationality. Such, for example, is Dray's advocacy of what he—and others after him—call "rational explanation," referring thereby to the historian's merger of his historical agent's reconstructed professed reasons for an action with the historian's own calculation of the "real" reasons such an agent had for his action.[3] An alternative reservation is to limit such rational explanations to the professed reasons of the agent and to attribute all further explanation to the realm of causes, which may or may not be historistic in location.[4] In any case, however, whether in this form of rational explanation or in the more intricate exposition of a special logic of historical narration,[5] the point is that the contemporary schools of philosophy which have equated pattern and explanation in history and which are famous for their rationalistic philosophy of history have also spawned discussions of historistic equivalents in favor of a more distinctive reason. If the covering-law model is the conceivable limit to the externalization of the principle of coherence as it is applied to the field of historiography, as is here proposed, then surely the spawned discussions of historistic equivalents to this law must count toward the confirmation of this proposition.

At any rate, these examples seen here in outline nonetheless stand for our century's most decisive effort at reestablishing for the issue of historical coherence a basis in certainty which is external to history itself, resting as they do in a supposed universal comprehension of the nature of our understanding of empirical phenomena. Unfortunately, or fortunately, depending on your view of the necessarily pluralistic nature of the historical enterprise, this derivation of historical coherence from an external source is precisely that effort which the phenomena of historicism has shown to be forever problematic. Before we move more deeply into this subject, however, two examples of historians who insisted upon principles of explanation and coherence much closer to the procedures of the independent historian himself are instructive. For, in fact, our century's historiography betrays a greater proliferation of historically interested existentialisms than it does an adherence to any historically indifferent logic.

Friedrich Meinecke, whose long life and career spanned the era before the First World War, the interwar age, and the post–World War II period, was a professional historian whose theorizing about history belongs essentially to the second of these epochs.[6] He was a convinced historicist who looked to history itself, both as a process and as a mode of knowledge, to generate the coherence connecting the individual events and forms that were the essence of history. "The core of historicism," he wrote, "consists in the replacement of a generalizing treatment of historical-human forces by an individualizing treatment."[7] Two of his distinctive, obvious qualities underline this intra-historical emphasis of his. First, his ambivalence about philosophy led him to oppose the intrusion of philosophy into history in the form of political principles and to insist upon philosophical principles induced from history, capping its factuality with generality and constructing a unity for historical events, as well as upon a philosophical sense in the historian.[8] Second, he was the first to welcome historicism as a good thing. Whereas others, like Troeltsch and Mannheim, had noted the cultural importance of historicism but still viewed it primarily as a "problem," as a kind of relativism to be overcome, Meinecke, while far from denying the essentially individualizing meaning of historicism and the problem of the "anarchy of values" which it inevitably raised, characterized it nonetheless as "the highest stage that has been yet attained in the understanding of human affairs," and wrote one of his chief books on its genesis, seeking to solve the problems it raised in its own terms.[9] He could not accept Troeltsch's literal attempts at solving historicism's problem of "the confusion" wrought by the "infinite pluralism of individual values" precisely because he was more historical and therefore more empirical than the theologian and because, although he did not admit it, he was more accepting of historicism than Troeltsch, with his incessant effort to "overcome" it, ever was. In *Die Idee der Staatsräson* (1924) Meinecke took as his theme the "polarity of physical nature and intellect" and he accepted both sides as the stuff of his history, including their implications of a naturalistic causal nexus vis-à-vis ideal teleology.[10] Toward the end of his life, moreover, he claimed that he looked to "a wholly new synthesis of historicism and natural law" and admitted "the typical" and "the recurrent" into association with the unique event as an integral part of historicism itself.[11]

Meinecke's original tendency to define historicism in terms of its doctrine of individuality and to compound this plurality by his emphasis upon the motifs of conflict, duality, and empirical heterogeneity in historical matters made it difficult for him to find factors of stable coherence in history. He attempted to overcome this weakness, while still saving the dominant place of historicism, by introducing the idea of "development" alongside that of "individuality" as parts of historicism's essence, and by defining development as a "continuous coherence of life [*Lebenszusammenhang*] directed at purposes."[12] Through the interaction of the notions of development and individuality, the individual distinctiveness of historical life became powered by the "ideas" that invested the individuality of history in socialized, suprapersonal forms and thereby endowed it "macroscopically" with the continuity of the "unity of human-spiritual life" lending intelligibility and coherence to historical particulars.[13]

By virtue of the flexible qualities which he assigned to individuality, optimally but not ultimately through its marriage with the notion of development, Meinecke sought to develop the universal cultural connections out of the historians' approach to the historical process itself in the historistic mold. Thus intellectual history, in the form of the history of ideas, received his primary emphasis as the seat of the continuity in history. But the historicistic basis of this coherence was never felt to be adequate by Meinecke, and he actually grounded his notions of individuality and development in the secure ground of his *Weltanschauung*— i.e., his philosophy of life— whence he applied it to history, despite his ostensible analysis of the relationship in the opposite direction which posited the primacy of history.[14] Hence he could hold on to his faith in historical coherence when, after the Second World War, he associated his newly won preference for Burckhardt over Ranke as historical thinker with his preference for the idea of individuality (which he associated with Burckhardt) over the idea of development (which he associated with Ranke). To be sure, Burckhardt's cultural pessimism was more to his postwar taste than Ranke's historical optimism, but the fact remains that he was secure about the coherent implications of the new idea of individuality even without the accompanying notion of historical development, thereby confirming the extrahistorical derivation of his faith in the individuality of life's forms.[15]

Like Meinecke, Arnold J. Toynbee, one of the most prominent albeit unrepresentative historians of our age, had a long career that climaxed in work written and published during the years following the Second World War, work that really belongs, for its historical thought, in the interwar era.[16] But unlike Meinecke, Toynbee seems to belong in the antihistoricist camp, since he explicitly attributed to "historicism"—to *Historismus* as he insisted on calling it—the belief in the uniqueness of historical events and in their consequent incommensurability that he rejected in principle.[17] And yet he was himself a product of the historicist emphasis, as here defined, for he admitted always that generalization in every form was ever the problem in history, that induction from history is as adequate and as inadequate as induction in general.[18] In this gear, Toynbee's stress upon the subjection of historians to the conditions of their own time, the consequent relativity of their results, and the use of the comparative method as the road to generalization in history amounted to an admission of his own complicity in the historicism whose individualism he overtly opposed.[19]

It follows that Toynbee opposed those who castigated his generalizations about the present situation of mankind for not being empirical but rather for being imposed on the historical evidence.[20] To understand the conflict, which was largely a matter of different perspectives upon Toynbee's achievement with both sides overvaluing the synthetic function of the historian per se and claiming it for themselves, resort need not be had to Toynbee's increasing religious faith, as evidenced in his late attribution of lawfulness in history to the law of God, which is, by his definition, not "man-made" but rather a translation from the human to the divine sphere through an anthropomorphic metaphysics and its corresponding deterministic "law of nature" which is thence imposed upon the historical destinies of men.[21] Toynbee's belief in a common nature, i.e., in "stable ingredients" which fall short of being immutable but which run through human time and are the real basis of "philosophical contemporaneity" (the ground of Toynbee's confidence in the comparability of civilizations), points to the dual relationship between history on the one hand, and science and art on the other, whereby the latter are deemed to be sometimes within the other times outside of history.[22] The former represents the early and undeveloped, the latter the mature thought of Toynbee. In his early posture, Toynbee denied that "the continuity of history" was genuinely historical in its application to the presumed connection between the lives of different societies, and he insisted that although the law-making capacity was in the province of general science the "rhythmic alternation between two antithetic yet complementary activities, which is native to thought in general and to historical thought in particular, is also native to History itself."[23]

But later Toynbee slipped into the admission that the different kinds of activities were added to rather than comprehended within history. "One must be free to resort to the different methods of the poet, the historian, and the scientist in turn, according to the nature of each piece of the task," he now wrote, and he elaborated on this dictum to concede that historical thinking was as subject to the priority of hypothesis and to the misproportion between theory and induction as any kind of scientific thought.[24] What must be admitted, then, over and above the strictures upon Toynbee's imposed generalizations vented upon him by historians of an individualizing historicist tendency, is that as he went on, and as, admittedly, the conviction of a Christian dispensation in human affairs grew strong in him, his admission of the intrusive quality of his generalizations and of their generic vitalistic derivation increased apace. His emphasis went from the inside to the outside of the historical process for the validity of his historical generalizations.

Like the American "new historians" from the other side, Toynbee helped to bridge the gap between the internal scientific emphasis of the French and the external philosophical explications of the Germans in overcoming the crisis brought on by the caustic impact of historicism. The American "new historians" along with the innovative and influential French "Annalistes" must now be discussed.

The "new history" that featured the innovative approach of historians around the turn of our century was, appearances to the contrary notwithstanding, grounded in historicism and the dissolution of universal values. The specialized, factual, narrowly political history which they overtly deplored had, as we have seen, stable if unexamined extrapolitical principles as their assumptions. The hallmark of the new history was to accept the mobilization and therefore the historization of all knowable human reality and to construct stable syntheses within it, usually with the aid of science and its methods. This "new history" was widespread, affecting James Harvey Robinson, Charles Beard, Carl Becker, and other devotees of historical pragmatism in America, Karl Lamprecht in Germany, and the French school as a school, wherein it took firmest root. Thus the American version of the "new history" upheld the generic scientific method as the fittest means toward establishing valid historical knowledge. It looked to the larger meaning of a "fact or occurrence" as part of "the search for natural laws and their multiform applications" which synthesized the historical accounts of fact and occurrences, and frankly invoked the most recent discoveries of the social sciences as relevant to the coherent "selection of historical facts and their interpretation."[25] When the younger protagonists of "the new history" (Becker and Beard were students of James Harvey Robinson) grew away from the original stress on the orientation of the past toward the present, they gravitated, each in his own inimitable way, even further into the toils of historicism. Becker refused outside assistance and, insisting that "left to themselves, the facts do not speak," that consequently the historian must "give them a certain place in a certain pattern of ideas," he underlined the relativity and variability of purely historical patterns.[26] The later Beard, on the other hand, reacted vigorously against the natural-scientific determinism that grew out of such patterns and turned increasingly to the continental European schema of a philosophical supervention of historicism, pace Croce, Meinecke, and Mannheim, for ways out of his intellectual impasse.[27]

Like the early version of the new history, the approach of Karl Lamprecht, who engaged in an open *Methodenstreit* with his orthodox colleagues around the turn of this century, joined in his campaign an insistence upon collective and unitary history with the candid reliance upon the social sciences of psychology. He prescribed that "the general type of development of peoples must be found," and he postulated both psychic community at the roots of the historical development of a generic national culture and a strict causal relationship among its expressions as its motor.[28]

But the new historians of American and German vintage had little influence outside the continent of North America. Undoubtedly, of the professional historians who reflected the impact of historicism around the turn of our century, the two representative ones were Henri Berr of France and Friedrich Meinecke of Germany, and if, as in the case of idealist philosophy in the twentieth century, there seems to be a continuum in significant historiography between the era before the First World War and the interwar period (including even the years immediately following the Second World War), then we should add the contemporary American "new historians" and Marc Bloch and Lucien Febvre of the later *Annales* school as extensions of Henri Berr and the independent contemporaries, and Johan Huizinga and Arnold Toynbee to Freidrich Meinecke, as explicit historical commentators on historicism.

With this done, Henri Berr's main channel of influence was organizational. In 1900 he founded and edited an impressive journal under the title *Revue de Synthèse historique* (in 1931 the title was changed to *Revue de Synthèse,* and the periodical continued to appear under this title until it was discontinued in 1951), and from 1920 he served as editor of the collection *The Evolution of Humanity (L'Evolution de l'Humanité),* which was designed to include one hundred synthetic volumes on the history of human civilization and which actually sponsored the publication of some sixty-five works down to Berr's death in 1954. But Berr also left an extended written formulation of his ideas in his book *Synthesis in History (La Synthèse en Histoire),* which he published originally in 1911 and then republished, unchanged except for a new preface and appendix, in 1953. In this work he expanded and grounded the prefatory program that he outlined for the first volume of his review, in which he promised treatment of both sociology and psychology as indispensable components of a historical science, with emphasis on the former, and he insisted on the indissolubility of combined thesis and analysis, while emphasizing again the actual preeminence of the former.[29] In this book Berr worked out these principles in such a way as to show both the strength of the French new departure upon which he insisted and the vulnerability of the traditional component of the historical approach which he, willy-nilly, adopted. His strength was his emphasis—far more categorical in the book than in the program—upon what was general and coherent in the new scientific history, based upon his quotation, from the start, of the well-known axiom that "there is science only of the general" and that the consequent "elaboration of the *general*" was the essence of "scientific synthesis" both of nature and of history.[30] His weakness was his emphasis on the circumstance that science was pervasive and that what was general and coherent in history was the result of no characteristic historical operation but was rather the product of a generic scientific approach that had an historical application alongside others.

On the first count—Berr's insistence that generalized connections constituted the definitive aspect of history—he distinguished explicitly between "erudite synthesis," which "consists essentially only in organizing analytical work and collecting its results"—that is, which is oriented primarily toward the particular facts which it collects, classifies, and establishes critically—and authentic scientific synthesis, which unifies the facts and aligns them with their explanatory principles, to the advantage of the latter kind of synthesis in history. By opting for scientific synthesis over "philosophy of history," which he rejected for its apriority, its subjectivity, and its Germanic character, he thought that he was avoiding the alien derivation of patterns in history.[31] In this gear Berr insisted upon the convergence of nature and history from the perspective of historicizing nature as well as naturalizing history. Thus he maintained the applicability of the scientific concepts which made general sense of the otherwise chaotic multiplicity of events to the flow of history as much as to the organization of nature. Thus he insisted that in any kind of science "the spirit works to order the facts," that the relationship of nature to history was one of "unity" to the process of "unification," that such concepts that were thought in conjunction with the sciences of nature as "law," "necessity," and "logic" were also flexible—i.e., temporal and individual— enough in their essence to be compatible with a science of history. Thus, in its essence, a law of nature was always temporally conditioned, and in its historical application it therefore always came to a law of development. Scientific causality is essentially plural and lawful. It seeks uniformities, and in its historical dress it seeks to discover "the relationship of contingent facts to other kinds of causes." For "the human spirit so rejects disorder" that it conceives contingency only in its relation to "order." In general, then, contingency is always mixed with order; the particular case of history as a science studies "the interaction and rearrangement of causes." The study of necessity in human affairs is the study of sociology, but the study of society which is the affair of sociology is by definition partial, and historical synthesis studies social necessity in its ubiquitous relationship with individuality, one of the forms of contingency, as part of its general obligation. Social evolution is necessitous because it is logical, but it is the kind of logic that is "invented" by individuals and is studied by synthetic history.[32]

But if Berr attempted to interiorize order within history, he also by the same token—and on the second count—enthroned a science that was as much outside of history as within it. Time and time again, in his *Synthèse en Histoire*, Berr explicitly rejected the view that history was "a science sui generis." He emphasized the community of all the sciences over and above the distinctiveness of the historical subscience, and he insisted especially on history's postulation of logical assumptions which "impose themselves perhaps on every scholar."[33] Berr's tendency to expand the historical approach to scientific synthesis into the treatment of scientific synthesis as such was confirmed by the new subtitle of his reedited *Synthèse en Histoire*—to wit, *Son Rapport avec la Synthèse générale*—and by the change in title of his review in 1931 from the *Revue de Synthèse historique* to *Revue de Synthèse*. In his explanation of the change, Berr admitted the ambiguity between the conception of the synthesis of knowledge in general and the role of history in that synthesis, and he claimed that the central place of history in scientific synthesis had been so consolidated in practice as well as in theory through the years that the approach to synthesis through history had been "integrated into an organic whole, the positive philosophy," and thus makes possible the direct consideration of the broader program.[34] And so, at the very start of the scientific history for which the French would be so prominent in the twentieth century, they showed the duality of internal and external scientific inspiration with which they would characterize their historical patterning for the remainder of the century.

Berr's younger collaborators, Lucien Febvre and Marc Bloch, wrote the history that Berr had talked of. Just as Berr represented French historical thinking about the social sciences in the period before the First World War, the *Annales* represented it in the interwar period. Though the *Annales* still appears, there is little doubt that the period from 1929 to 1939 was a distinctive one.[35] Febvre and Bloch, founders and editors of the *Annales,* shared with Berr a reverence for Durkheim, the preference for historical synthesis over historical facts, the conviction of the overriding unity of scientific method and concepts, and the consequent ambiguity about the role of historical and generic science in the construction of the synthetic patterns that integrated the facts of history. Hence they perpetuated into the earlier period of the *Annales* the social scientific ambivalence between the internal ordering of historical coherences and the external imposition of generic scientific laws, and they have perpetuated too the predilection for the former which has been characteristic of French social history during this century. Indeed, they emphasized, more than Berr, the privileged position of history as the preferred focus of research in the social sciences.[36] Thus, not only did Febvre himself entitle a collection of his essays "Polemics in Favor of History" (*Combats pour l'histoire*), not only did he confess himself always to have been a historian "by pleasure or by desire" and to have as his goal the reputation of one who "in history . . . saw only history; nothing more," but he saw that "history," par excellence, "experiences the living unity of Science because history is the science of man."[37] But their misgivings about the developing rationality of Western civilization and their general suspicion of historical theories of change, when combined with their contrapuntal insistence upon the construction of totalities, has led to a growing emphasis upon static structures as the only historically demonstrable patterns possible.[38] In the heyday of the

Annales, the socially minded French stressed the totality of life which could be grasped in historical reality, a totality which required a special methodological rigor since it stressed the economic and social facts of ordinary people.

In contrast to the later *Annalistes,* to the generation coming to prominence after the Second World War, the belief in the early period was in the unity conferred by historical continuity. Thus Bloch justified his great book on the medieval *Feudal Society* by arguing that it belonged to a "system of classification, based on the observation of social phenomena" and by defining his purpose as the attempt to "analyze and explain a social structure and its unifying principles."[39] But behind this historical continuity there lay a faith in the unity of all knowledge. Both Bloch and Febvre subscribed to the tenet that "history . . . cannot escape certain principles that govern all knowledge," that there exists "a natural order governed by immutable laws." Moreover, as the dedication of the *Annales* demonstrates, the condition against which they were reacting was not yet that of a false unity but was one of historiographical specialization and fragmentation.[40] Febvre insisted that the famed critical method is not distinctively historical but rather "a universal method applied indiscriminately to the analysis of all forms of human activity" and hence that history was not separate from the other disciplines but was rather their ally in the great endeavor, transcending history and unifying all the disciplines, of man's knowing how to think and how to live.[41]

Like their mentor, Henri Berr, then, the early *Annalistes* were expressing the ambiguity between the subscription to extrahistorical social sciences that furnished the coherence to historical understanding from the outside, and the subscription to a vital order of history that furnished a model for an internal elaboration of historical coherence by the historian. Operationally, the first generation of the *Annales* worked a middle range of historical synthesis that was intermediate between the individual transitory event and the permanent or long-range framework and logic of all human activity and that constituted a literal method and realm of literal historical reason vis-à-vis both the discrete facts and the constant extrahistorical laws of human behavior. Febvre himself insisted that "law . . . is not necessarily universal and eternal; it manifests itself in history; it can be created in history" and that in practice "it is not fair to impose any prophetic guiding lines from outside on a discipline that is in the process of organizing or reorganizing itself." Bloch and he held, correspondingly, that the appropriate object for history was the social milieu, considered on the one hand as the meeting-place of individual freedom and general "necessity," and on the other as having its own coherence since in it "everything is mutually controlled and connected."[42] For Febvre, then, who made no distinction in kind between intellectual and social history, who insisted on the convergence of art and science, and who initiated the salutary *Annalistes'* approach of stressing the general nature of history and its aid by all the "human" rather than the narrowly social sciences, the notice of man's "social" nature was connected with his abridgment of man's infinite individuality and his rejection of the traditionalists' dwelling on the particular "facts" of the past. Febvre associated man's necessary membership in social groups with his measurability by the "problems" and "theories" which constituted the middle level of the human studies in which the historian must reside. "Facts . . . are so many abstractions," called into reality by historians in the service of the questions and responsive hypotheses which the historian asks and answers from his material in order to explain his present society with the aid of the past.[43] History proffers "a rational classification and a progressive intelligibility."[44] Thus Febvre's and Bloch's preference for "historical synthesis" was connected with the necessarily intermediate role of synthesis in ambiguity between the external derivation of patterned history and the internal autonomy of it, an ambiguity which they deliberately implanted in their approach to the continuity of history. They saw synthesis as at once the heart of "a science sui generis," i.e., of a distinctively historical science, and in general of "a scientific synthesis, . . . the endeavor to generalize, to disentangle a complex causality in order to discover general factors, without eliminating any of them apriori."[45] That the synthesis they emphasize could be historical was guaranteed by their insistence on its temporality. When Bloch proposed to "follow the line of time in an inverse direction"—that is, backward through time, from the results of things to their origins—he started not from the temporally distinct present in order to interpret the qualitatively distinct past but rather from "the recent past" in order to "illuminate a very distinct past"—that is through a connection between temporally homogeneous poles.[46]

And yet Febvre was uncertain about the historical core of his scientific syntheses. He was sure that a properly defined history could borrow concepts and techniques from neighboring disciplines, but he was not so sure that these disciplines were much interested in history, and ultimately this negative relationship must of course dry up the external sources for history itself.[47] This ambiguous relationship to the other human disciplines was thus part of the larger ambiguity that afflicted the *Annales* and that prepared the way for jettisoning the external dependence of history altogether.[48] The *Annales* was founded by a genuine collaboration among the disciplines. Along with the historians Bloch and Febvre, a group of geographers, sociologists, psychologists, and the philosopher-sociologist-economist François Simiand, were involved in its initiation.[49] But such collaboration has become increasingly rare, and with its lessening incidence history has been thrown more and more on its own devices. Febvre was a geographer almost as much as he was a historian, and at least two of his early works—one on Franche-Comte (*Les Regions de France: la France-Comte*) and a general study of *La Terre et l'Evolution*—dealt with the principles of geography in their application to history. Moreover, his famed distinction of contingency, necessity, and logic or idea in historical causation can all be considered within history or can be considered as partially derivative from extrahistorical sciences. Thus sociology deals with social necessity and collective psychology furnishes principles for the idea of historical causation.[50] Clearly, an ambiguity in the derivation of historical coherence existed for the early *Annalistes*.

The tendencies of both the American "new history" as well as of the French *Annales* have been in our century fertile enough to have enjoyed rebirth and propagation without ever having suffered death, or, what is more to the point, without ever having successfully resolved the problems faced by historicism and left unresolved by historicism. The more recent installment of the "new history," which took the form of an innovating emphasis upon the social, psychological, and generally scientific aspect of historical knowledge and expression, is a particularly virulent chapter in a long series of eruptions against traditional historiography, and it introduces a new vintage of historians.[51] Like its precursors, the "new" new history insists upon broader levels of facts to be critically determined, but it inveighs against the external and therefore unexamined weaknesses of historical coherence in the Western tradition of historical literature. To be sure, in such contemporary preoccupations as historical demography and "the new urban history" particularly, as well as quantitative history generally, areas of the past that are more popular, more routine and more existential than the elitist discrete facts that used to be defined as historical are now deemed to be historically relevant. But by and large the stress upon this kind of novelty tends to rest with those historians who are traditional in the sense of disregarding the challenge posed by historicism (historians of little interest in the context of the present inquiry) and the socially and politically radical historians, with their doctrine of a more democratic—i.e., egalitarian—history. The essence of this "new history," like "new history" any time, tends to stress the reinforcement of the connective factor in history. In general, the academic radicals who are rationalist in history—that is, those who overtly import their organizing concepts and methods from outside history—tend to tell historians what they should do. Those who are historists in that they covertly import their organizing concepts and methods from outside of history, or who go historism one better by seeking concepts and methods from within history itself— partisans of historicity, in our terminology—tend to tell historians (and others) what they are doing. In either case, as should be clear by now, by virtue of its own unacknowledged borrowing of patterns from other kinds of thinking, traditional historiography has invited the criticism that the academic radicals have visited upon it.

As might have been expected, the correctives which the radicals have invoked tend to espouse the same kind of duality as has been shown in the traditional history that is their target. The radicals, too, in this emphasis upon a more deliberate and more valid kind of coherence in history, have both explicitly imported concepts from outside of history and have insisted upon a novel construction of patterns within the historical process itself. By and large, Americans and Germans have espoused the former alternative, while the French have worked at the latter.

But in other respects the lines of division run differently. In two ways the current historiographical radicalism sees the Europeans taking one line and the Americans another. Thus whereas academic and political radicalism tend to converge in Europe, they tend to diverge in the United States.[52] Again, where the Europeans tend to include the mental life of a culture in their analysis of historical societies and thus to think of all the human arts and sciences in the galaxy of history's neighboring disciplines, the historians of American vintage think more exclusively in terms of the social sciences as their supporting neighbors. In this section we shall underline the American stress on the externality of historical patterns and the French development toward their historical internality. We shall also dwell upon the European version of the generic human sciences and the American limitation of radicalism to its academic form because these distinctions are most appropriate to the stress on the externality and the internality of historical patterns that is here our chief concern.

American behavioral historians, whether of the quantitative or the psychological bent, are at least as concerned with the importation of more reliable methods and concepts of rational proof from the other sciences into history as they are with the exploitation of new kinds of data. Thus one set of spokesmen for quantitatively oriented social history argues that "the social science approach . . . assumes that there are uniformities of human behavior that transcend time and place and can be studied as such; and the historian as social scientist chooses his problems with an eye to discovering, verifying, or illuminating such uniformities."[53] Another set holds that "from the historian's point of view, the value of technical research consists in and is determined by the light it can cast on general problems of historical interpretation."[54] Still a third spokesman directs his complaints about the current vogue of "impressionistic research" and his own proposals for a "genuinely scientific historiography" to the identification and formulation of "potentially verifiable hypotheses" in the service of "valid general theories" which align history with the other social sciences. Although this particular spokesman recommends a plurality of histories and considers history a condition for a viable social science rather than the reverse, it is clear not only that this recommendation for history of organizing concepts and "systematic research methods" stems from the other social sciences but that they represent "the functional equivalent" in the social sciences of the kind of inquiry characteristic of the natural sciences.[55]

The animus against narration in history as an unexamined synthesis of traditional history confirms the primary orientation of social-scientific historians toward the patterning rather than the facts of the old history.[56] This animus goes back to the hostility expressed by a Lucien Febvre toward the primacy of discrete events in traditional history, for according to his perspective the organization of events into a narrative was one of the ways in which the ordering of facts in the old history was made dependent on the priority of the facts, qua individually conceived events, themselves. The preference for analysis over narrative in the current academic radicalism is then a species of explanation rather than a denial of explanation in history.

The leading German representative of academic radicalism in the historical profession frankly looks for "theoretical tendencies, concepts of development, or 'paradigms' " wherewith to organize the "history of society" for which he plumps. If he rejects social scientific disciplines like political science, economics, and sociology as the literal sources of these tendencies, concepts, or paradigms, his resort to a combination of historical materialism and modernization theory involves his going outside the framework of empirical history for his integrating ideas, as his invocation of Marx and Max Weber as the patron saints of his theories attests.[57]

A leading American advocate of psychohistory is equally definite on the necessity of extending the concepts of extrahistorical science into history to serve as the sinews of the connections that we have called historical reason. "Why should history, the one discipline that deals especially with man's past and seeks explanation of that past largely in terms of man's motives, ignore so staunchly the one science . . . which centers itself on research into exactly these areas?" It is, then, "a contribution to the vexing problem of historical interpretation."[58]

European historians have done much less with psychohistory (as Europeans have done little with psychoanalysis in general) than have those of American birth. But in a pioneering article a German historian who tries to initiate a discussion of the field considers the advantages of applying psychoanalysis to history primarily in generalizing terms and its disadvantages primarily in individualizing terms. Thus he includes among its leading benefits its provision of interpretive "categories," especially those that permit historians to proceed from the "fragments" in their sources to the "whole" in which they have been notably interested and that aim at the needed knowledge of psychic "connections" in the past. He defines its primary liability for history as its commitment to "an atomic individualism" which neglects the network of collective conditions in which historical individuals are implicated.[59] A fitting testimonial of the external reference to which radical historiography of recent German vogue addresses its concern for historical coherence is its concluding identification of "social psychology" as the more viable alternative to psychoanalysis for the categories in which "modern historical science" is interested.[60]

It is clear that the *Annales* has been more than its successive editors, Marc Bloch, Lucien Febvre, Fernand Braudel, and E. Le Roy Ladurie have said it was, but we may use them and their friends, meaning especially Pierre Chaunu and François Furet as its representative figures since these are figures that have articulated the theory behind it. Indeed, the latter generations of the *Annales* are different enough from the first to warrant separate treatment. Here we must keep in mind the distinction in our terminology between the historism and the historicism of the early stage of the *Annales,* associated with Bloch and Febvre and flourishing especially during the interwar years, and the later stage—World War II *Annales* and its relations with this terminology. But, also, we must distinguish between the two generations that are easily lumped together in the later *Annales,* that is, between the historists and the authentic advocates of historicity. The first postwar generation (the second *Annaliste* generation overall) is associated with the name and editorship of Fernand Braudel, who repeated the ambiguity inherited

from his mentor and friend, Lucien Febvre, of the first Annaliste generation, but with increasing emphasis on the internal, or historistic, option
within this ambiguity.

This second generation, especially in the later phase of Fernand
Braudel—that is, especially in 1958 and thereafter—converged toward the then contemporary French vogue of structuralism and
together with the prohistorical structuralists constituted the leading
French version of academic historical radicalism, and several points
must be clarified about these developments. From our point of view,
structuralism simply represented the vain attempt at a total internalization of pattern. It represented one of the attempts to construct a
coherence within the world of time and space for the purpose of filling
the vacuum left by the dismantling of absolutes which has characterized historicism in particular and the characteristic thinking of our
century in general. Whether structuralism was deemed to be antihistorical or prohistorical depended on the kind of history that was the
object of consideration—whether, that is, it was the critical history of
tradition or the structural history that was once the rage of France.
This structuralism has been associated primarily with the writings of
Roland Barthes in literature and Claude Lévi-Strauss in anthropology.
Barthes' writings have in general been indifferent to history—he has
tended to reject literary history in favor of the structural analysis of
literary works, and he ranked the writer's "epic time" above "historical time"—and as such both positions are irrelevant to our consideration. But we must note that Barthes' notion of reality was at least
compatible with history properly and structurally done.[61] Barthes affirmed his antipathy to chronology as a tool of historical science by
attributing only structural and linguistic categories to the historian
Michelet and to the profession generally, in his essay on "Historical
Discourse," and he confirmed his positive attitude to "historians who
deal in structures rather than chronologies" by his participation in a
two-year seminar organized by the historically dominated sixth section of the Ecole Practique des Hautes Etudes in Paris.[62]

But Lévi-Strauss's development was more to the specific historical
point, showing the convergence of structuralism and history from the
side of structuralism. Claude Lévi-Strauss himself, whose structural
anthropology has served as the very model of antihistorical structuralism, actually planted himself on both sides of the historical
question, depending on the kind of history he was discussing. Basically,
his position has been one which conformed to the tradition of historism: for its coherences, history is derivative from but compatible with
anthropology. His original attitude toward history, taken before he was

acquainted with the structural history whose structure he insisted was a borrowing from anthropology, insisted on the compatibility of a history devoted to consciousness, and thus the facts, with an anthropology whose forte was in the cultural analysis of connective unconscious phenomena.[63] Lévi-Strauss's later expressions against history are correspondingly directed not against history as such but only against a certain kind of history.

Lévi-Strauss's antihistorical stance, registered for all to see in the final diatribe against Jean-Paul Sartre's *Critique of Dialectical Reason* in the last chapter of *The Savage Mind,* and confirmed by Jean Piaget's castigation of Lévi-Strauss as "ahistorical" on this account, is actually directed against the individualizing historiography and the "derivative" doctrine of an "analytic, abstract continuity" which has been philosophically imposed upon this kind of history to lend coherence to it.[64] From this point of view, "biographical and anecdotal history . . . is low-powered history, which is not intelligible in itself and only becomes so when it is transferred *en bloc* to a form of history of a higher power than itself," and the only way of guaranteeing intelligibility in this kind of history—and therefore coherence—is to leave the historical realm entirely and to use it only "as the point of departure."[65]

But around the same time (in 1960) Lévi-Strauss was giving a lecture in which he justified "the historical dimension" of anthropology. In doing so he admitted that "this declaration in favor of history may come as a surprise, since we have sometimes been reproached for being close to history."[66] But as he went on to elaborate this defense while adopting his positive stance, it became clear that the kind of history he had in mind was "the idea of a structural history."[67] And he could maintain, somewhat later (in 1965, specifically), that "the introduction of structuralist methods into a critical tradition proceeding essentially from historicism is far from presenting a problem. It is the existence of this historical tradition which can alone provide a basis for structural undertakings. . . . Thus, it is history, in conjunction with sociology and semiology, which will enable the analyst to break the circle of timeless confrontation."[68] Since Lévi-Strauss defined a structure as "a system ruled by an internal cohesiveness," the meaning of his preference for a structural history is clear; and as if to make it unmistakable this kind of history was the assumption behind his reduction of the distinction between synchronization and diachronization, between the order of events and the order of structure.[69] It also lay behind his acknowledgment that Braudel reciprocated.[70]

Braudel represents, indeed, a second, transitional generation of the *Annales,* a generation that paralleled Lévi-Strauss and may well have been responsible for his prohistorical turn. Braudel is the figure who causes confusion among the generations of *Annalistes* because he both continued the dependence upon the neighboring human sciences pioneered by his mentor, Lucien Febvre, and he advocated a historical structuralism that linked him to the anthropological and literary structuralists and that prepared the way for the current generation of *Annalistes* and poststructuralists with their historically internal doctrines of serial history and the archeology of historical knowledge.[71] Braudel becomes somewhat less confusing when his two emphases are chronologically spaced out, so that the rationalistic, external emphasis is associated with the early Braudel and the historistic, internal emphasis is associated with the later one.

The document which causes special confusion in this respect is Braudel's *La Méditerranée et le Monde Méditerranéen à l'Epoque de Philippe II*, for it was not published until 1949; but by Braudel's own testimony it was complete in its "main outline" by 1939 and belongs to the early period of the *Annales*.[72] Hence its frank use of geography as an integral part of the most general section of other history, i.e., as the history of "man in his relationship to the environment, . . . a history of constant repetition, ever-recurring cycles" and the equal acceptance of "almost timeless history," slow-changing social history, and traditional *l'histoire événementielle* as three valid levels of the historical past pointed to the rational pattern of the early *Annales*.[73] It goes without saying that Braudel conceived his work as a synthesis, for he accounted "the unity and coherence of the Mediterranean region" to be one of its major truths, and although he did not say so it was clearly the extrahistorical principles that endowed it with these qualities.[74]

The general direction of Braudel's historical thinking has paralleled and reinforced the development hinted at in the successive editions of *The Mediterranean*. But the two phases remain interwoven enough for Braudel to retain something of the original ambiguity of the *Annales* and to remain distinguished thereby from the latest generation of the *Annalistes*, with their unambiguous devotion to the historicity of historical patterns.

The chief emphasis of the later Braudel was the historistic strain that was muted in the early *Annalistes*. Thus he now insisted on the particularity and individuality of the historical enterprise to a much greater extent than did Bloch and Febvre. He squared this with his other emphasis by insisting on the individuality of societies and hence on the open-ended and plural nature of social histories. He also tended to view the relations of history with the other human sciences more as a problem than as an accomplishment: "we need a new music."[75] The older

Braudel is infinitely more interested in establishing the primacy of history—"Is not history, as the dialectics of duration, in its own way an explanation of the total reality of social life?"[76]—and thus of the internality of historical patterning.

The upshot of Braudel's ambiguity has been his growing acceptance of "long-range structures" in history, despite his preference for middle-range or "conjunctural history." Like the first *Annalistes*—especially like his mentor, Lucien Febvre—Braudel still insisted on synthetic or "total history" (*histoire totale*) and he still insisted that history is a science, destined to cooperate with the other social sciences, but he now maintained much more emphatically than he originally did the inimitable historicity of the totality and the centrality of history among the social sciences.[77] Like the early *Annalistes* too, he now turned decisively against the short-term traditional history of events to which so much of *The Mediterranean* was devoted. He obviously prefers the intermediate middle-term history of "conjunctures" or cycles "as the shape of an explanatory scheme in which history may be placed" and which is a natural medium for "a new mode of historical narrative."[78] By "global" Braudel has made it clear that he means "total," "synthetic," or "unitary," and for "the unification of the diverse sciences of man," including the "global science" of history, he still invokes the necessary assistance "of all the human sciences" and especially the homogenizing influence of "the social" aspect of the past and present.[79]

The long-term history of "structures" consists precisely of the comparatively stable organization of material and social factors that is the scene of confrontation between history and the other social sciences and that is the approach to "coherence" optimally leading to the historization of these social sciences and hence to the internalization of historical connections.[80] Hence in the revision of *The Mediterranean* which he undertook late, during the 1960s, Braudel admitted that "by temperament I am a structuralist," and it was in the same period that he praised Lévi-Strauss to the disadvantage of Sartre.[81] At the same time he revised his view of the geographical aspect of the first section to exclude it from history, since it was now seen to refer to "timeless realities." He also excluded the level of discrete events from his notion of history, for he now identified "slow and fast-moving levels" with "structure and conjuncture," and of the two he argued for a "structural history," now identified with very gradually changing economic and social relationships.[82] Like all prohistorical structuralists, who may be said in general to represent what has been most characteristic in penultimate French social thought, Braudel sought to make a historically distinct coherence the paradigm or "model"—to use his term—

for all patterns of the past. The proportions of external and internal influences on Braudel were summed up in his edition of excerpts and articles from Lucien Febvre. The fact that he still looked to Febvre as his mentor showed his loyalty to the externality of the early *Annales*. But the title that he chose, borrowing from Febvre himself—*For an Entirely Separate History (Pour une histoire à part entière)*[83]—corresponded rather to Braudel's own later development than to Febvre's original intentions for this title, although Braudel did this as if Febvre would have loved it. Clearly Febvre would not have.

But a distinction must be drawn between Braudel, who remained faithful to the teachings of Febvre and who correspondingly still thought primarily in terms of the cooperation between history and the other human sciences, and the latest generation of the *Annales*, represented especially by Le Roy Ladurie, Chaunu, and Furet, and standing for a historical internality that goes one step further than even the structuralist emphasis of the older Braudel. This excessive historical internality, to repeat a point made often in these pages, we label "historicity" in contrast to the terms "historism" and "historicism," with which it is too often linked. The chief sign of the innovation instigated by the new generation is the half-understanding wonderment with which Braudel greeted the notion of a "serial history" which was introduced by Pierre Chaunu and which became characteristic of the latest generation of *Annalistes*.[84] Conditioning this upsurge of French historical thinking has been the general move of French thought from a structural to a poststructural phase, represented especially by Jacques Derrida in philosophy and Jacques Lacan in philosophical psychoanalysis, and the movement of the human disciplines in general (arts as well as sciences) away from historicity and thus away from the invitation to collaboration with historians. These movements have had, as their overt signal, the aging of Braudel's contemporaries such as the prohistorical Lévi-Strauss and the equally prohistorical albeit quite different existentialist, Sartre, and have taken the form of philosophy's emphasis on logic and linguistic analysis, the decline and fall of literary and artistic history, and the triumph of nonhistorical behavioralism in the social sciences.[85] As a result, historians have been thrown on their own resources and, for the first time, there has been the development of theories that establish the autonomy of patterns in the past and the derivation of facts from them.

The confusion in the French historiographical scene can be clarified if we make two assumptions: first, the spokesmen for the present *Annales*—Le Roy Ladurie, Furet, Le Goff—furnish the thread of continuity through the maze; and second, these figures are rivalled only by the poststructuralist notions of a Lévy, a Foucault, and a Derrida.[86] Thus Le Goff and Nora spoke of a new history, which they refused to define save to say that it involved an entirely novel definition of the historical enterprise that dismisses the continuity of history as an invalid interpolation of meaning by past historians. Levy, paraphrasing Certeau, insisted that the remnants of continuity in the interpretation of history meant that all history was ficitious, that it "does not exist."[87] In this poststructuralist celebration of historical relativism, two things are clear: first, that the middle-term, conjunctural history, is now out, in favor of a new emphasis on the long term and the event as the necessary components of the new history; and, correspondingly, that both Febvre and Braudel are viewed as representatives of a historiographical past that has little to do with the current tendencies.[88]

Emmanuel Le Roy Ladurie, representative of the third generation of the *Annales,* looks back to Bloch and Febvre as the founding fathers of his school and classifies Braudel with them.[89] Like Bloch and Febvre, he focuses on synthetic problems rather than new facts for his starting points.[90] But unlike Bloch and Febvre, he takes these problems from history itself rather than from man as a whole. Consistent with this preference, he shows a much greater intimacy with "statistical or 'serial' history" and stresses more than Braudel ever did the historical bent of the sciences which Le Roy Ladurie insisted now upon historizing. His interest in attitudes toward death is an exercise in historical psychology which he calls "a strictly historical problem"; he recalls Simiand for his stimulation of historians; and he emphasizes cooperation with non-historians in the more rarified fields of the natural sciences, as if to confirm the historization of the social sciences.[91]

Furet, the current *Annaliste* who has shown himself to be more theoretically minded than the bulk of his colleagues, has taken the concept of "serial history" from the quantitative historian Pierre Chaunu, and turned it into a many-purposed instrument for all historians whose material permits the attribution of primacy to the regular temporal series and of functional derivation to the particular data which compose the series, with the consequent depreciation of the event in favor of the relationship among events by which it is henceforth subordinated. Since the historical series is temporal, it is categorically distinguished from the economic series, which is not: hence it becomes a species of distinctively historical reason.[92]

But the philosopher-historian Michel Foucault was the figure on the French intellectual scene whose denial of membership in the structuralist fraternity seems justified by his stress on historical change, on the cultural mutations he called "epistemes," rather than on the historical constants that were the structuralists' stock-in-trade.[93] Not only did Foucault emphasize the discontinuity of things in his theoretical works, but his empirical historical studies, dealing with the successive treatment of madness in the classical period running from the sixteenth to the eighteenth centuries[94] and the origins of its modern clinical treatment at the turn from the eighteenth to the nineteenth century, with the origins of the clinic and the prison in the eighteenth and nineteenth centuries, and with the history of human sexuality through the ages, all focus on the change from an older, imposed order of things, to a new, human, and internal order at the start of the modern era.[95]

Foucault's theoretical approach is illuminated and his popularity becomes a sign of a representative role when his proposals are viewed from a poststructural perspective.[96] His radical arguments against traditional history and its assumed continuities of the person, of the work, of the genre, and of the theories are so many arguments against the historian's absorption of rational unities from nontemporal reality, and his requirement that unities be reconstructed from the assumption of discontinuity, from the "archaeological" materials composed exclusively of the temporal relationships among bare statements is in fact an argument for a peculiarly historical reason. In his own words, "the essential task was to free the history of thought from its subjection to transcendence." "By freeing [the facts of discourse] of all the groupings that purport to be natural, immediate, universal unities, one is able to describe other unities, . . . the analysis of their coexistence, their succession, their mutual functioning, their reciprocal determination, and their independence or correlative transformations. . . . I have undertaken, then, to describe the relations between statements."[97]

Foucault's empirical studies orient his theoretical position, which is structuralist in its ambiguous attempt to assert transcendencies within the time-space continuum, toward the situation of definitely accounting for historical change. In this context he set himself the problem of explaining the birth of institutions like the asylum, the clinic, the prison at the start of modern times—that is, in the early part of the nineteenth century. Because of his primary interest in coherence, he placed his emphasis in each case upon society's internal ordering impulse vis-à-vis a precedent libertarianism or authoritarianism. Thus, in his view, the clinic originated as "a new coherent unitary model for the formation of medical objects, perceptions and concepts" while accepting as its necessary conditions the revolutionary achievement of the "privileges of the pure gaze prior to all intervention and faithful to the immediate."[98] The implications of this establishment of historical order upon the conditions of historical freedom were spelled out in Foucault's history of insanity, where he stressed that the modern treatment of unreason was at the behest of the dominant reason, that "the stifling anguish of responsibility" was the asylum's libertarian condition for the individual's own affirmation of "the great continuity of social morality" represented by the asylum in its fundamental relationship of discontinuity with its authoritarian past.[99]

To say, as Foucault thus does, that there is only one world of the past, that this world is inhabited only by the traces which are the stuff of history, and that the task of the historian is to construct a unity, a set of discursive regularities appropriate to the discontinuous character of this historical past—surely this is the conceivable limit of history's internalization. At the very least, it concludes the task of this chapter to have set forth along a line a spectrum of various theoretical positions, all held by prominent twentieth-century historians, on the issue of coherence in historiography as well as in history itself.

In conclusion, then, it can be safely said that twentieth-century historians have not been historians of historicism and that no true historicism has yet emerged from this work. The historians more or less contemporary with the crisis manifested by historicism responded in two apparently opposed but actually analogous ways, but they did not respond by becoming historicists and the results of their efforts stretch between the externalization and the total internalization of the principle of coherence. Fragmentation and disjointedness would be the inevitable conditions of the intellectual order they created. To be sure, either explicitly or implicitly, both groups acknowledged the caustic force of the cultural crisis upon the wanted stability of universal processes and values. As we have seen, the more philosophically inclined historians tended to respect the fragmentation of reality and to appreciate the new approaches which perceived it by proceeding after the fashion of the historicist's version of the philosophy of history and after the example of the historicists' response to the dissolution of universals as well, by offering up for consumption new standpoints in rationality; and these standpoints have not been offered up in the spirit of an all-encompassing historicism.

The less philosophically inclined historians, on the other hand, have been either indifferent to or positively reject any speculation about ultimate reality. They believe in the unsteady flow of individual events and their right to make them cohere, generally in narrative, because it is their business to do so, and they ignore other kinds of reality because it is not. As professional historians they are concerned only with the historical process. They see that process as an unceasing flow and they seek to identify connective principles entirely within this flow. Historians do not explicate extrahistorical reality, whether dissolute or stable, as was the habit of the historicists. Neither do they often confess the extrahistorical nature of the sources of coherence in their work. If the sources of coherence for the historical enterprise are somehow dependent upon relations to ultimate reality, then the explanation of those relations can well be left to the philosophers.

In the historians' case, therefore, even after the phenomena of historicism had judged this reliance somewhat illusory, somewhat unstable, and in no sense strictly historical, the external roots of historical coherence have had to remain implicit, largely passed over in silence. Both groups of historians have shown their relation to the crisis of historicism only obliquely, by their willingness to continue to rely upon extrahistorical values when establishing coherence, or, after a fashion more pronounced, by the determination with which they constructed their versions of historical coherence. By and large, albeit with varying degrees of commitment, twentieth-century historians have all been historians of historicity. Twentieth-century historians have been either traditional in the traditional sense of furthering the tenets of historism or they have been traditional in the nineteenth-century, modern sense— hybridized in the aftermath of historicism—of grounding coherence in the concepts and methods of rational proof. If strict reliance upon the concepts and methods of rational proof somehow belies the notion of cultural crisis, that reliance has not hindered historical practice, even if that practice somehow fell short of the possibilities of the Age. Hence historians have differed from the more philosophically minded historicists by taking fragmented reality as a given rather than as a set of circumstances to be explained. That is, the historians have taken a fragmented reality as a point of departure rather than as a condition of the reality they would seek to explicate. Our century's historians have emphasized historical synthesis as the inevitable condition of the intellectual order they would seek to create, or, more frequently but much less significantly, they have ignored the issue of cultural crisis altogether. Nonetheless, either explicitly or implicitly, judged by the relation of coherence in their work to its source, both the philosophers and the historians alike who have been covered here acknowledge that the dissolution of universals is the dominant challenge of the times and that the transcendence of this dissolution through the establishment of a pattern somehow compatible with it is the order of the day. But in either case they have accepted the fragmentation of their reality as a given and are proceeding with the sources of coherence in this work half within history, but with its roots dangling without, all the while accepting the heterogeneity of human reality.

EPILOGUE
A RESPONSIVE MOTIF

Traditional historians, at least the ones most germane to the point of this study, are those historians who still believe in the critical approach to the sources of history, in the individualistic, particularistic, and pluralistic emphasis of the historical enterprise, in the facts as the discrete units delivered by the critical approach and the particularistic emphasis, and in the primacy of politics as both the accessible and the collective facet of past human activity. Defenders of traditional history in this sense have, insofar as they have not simply done business at the same old monographic and textual stand, replied in kind to the challenge of the new historians to the historical patterns which traditional history has for so long taken for granted. Thus, in response to the traditional habit of organizing events in the form of narration, the characteristic response has been to affirm narration and to add analysis to it as a complementary kind of explanation.[1] The reply has had three different forms.

First, some traditionalists have reiterated the individuality, multiplicity, and diversity of historical facts as the characteristic products of history, and they have simply given up on the coherent patterns, whether providential, progressive, or commonsensical, which have born the brunt of the successive attacks by historicism and the new history. This kind of response to these attacks has, in turn, sounded two different specific chords. A few have lamented the nonhistorical derivation of historical patterns and the consequent loss of such patterns with the demise of extrahistorical absolutes to the extent of losing their faith in a history that has to do without such patterns.[2] Others have gloried in the demonstration of exclusive individuality for history, claiming that this is of the essence in history and rejecting patterning that goes beyond the particularistic approach, the plural results, and the planned chaos of history.[3]

Second, some traditional historians have applied to historical patterns the same critical standards that have applied in the historiographical past to the truthful processing of historical facts. Like representatives of the first responsive type, this second type exalts the historian's address to the particularistic and individualistic aspects of the human past; but unlike the first type their reply to the unitary tendencies of the logicians and the social scientists in the ranks of historians is not so much to reject coherence in history itself as to apply the implications of a diversified, plural historical reality to the coherent patterns, both of generalization and of explanation, in history. The result is usually the loosening or the complication or the limitation of historical patterns, in response to the critically ascertained facts of the case.[4] The European aristocracy, for example, gets divided not only in accordance with national cultures, when these are actually influential, but into the several privileged classes, having to do with their specific origin, their progressive or reactionary economic interests, their upper or lower status in the privileged ranks, their geographical locus at the central court or in the variegated countryside. Similarly the bourgeoisie, the correlative group in the processional pattern of unreformed historical tradition, gets broken up by the reformation of historical tradition into the several middle classes that are identified by their specific economic activity, their position at the court or in the towns, and their national allegiance. But, however fragmented, these social groups persist sufficiently to allow for their political representation in the parliaments or in the bureaucracies of their regions; hence, like the aristocracy (and the working classes), they retain sufficient social identity to furnish the roots for the persistence of political coherence, somewhat more sophisticated than but essentially continuous with the historiographical tradition.

The third—and last, for our purposes—kind of response made by traditionally minded historians to the challenge posed to older historical patterns by academic radicalism has lain in their attempt to internalize and thus to historize the roots of the coherence that used to lie in an absolute sphere of reality outside the historical process to which it was applied. Obviously, this activity by traditional historians such as John Pocock and Frank Manuel runs into the similar activity of radicals such as Jacques Le Goff, all of whom try to move the roots of historical coherence from the outside to the inside of history.[5] Whether historians who engage in such activity are classified as traditionalists or radicals depends often enough upon the capricious judgment of the classifier. Thus Carl E. Schorske and Reinhart Koselleck, who are labelled here as traditionalists, have had personal relations with academic radicals in their respective countries, and they have attempted, in the fashion of radicals, to think through their procedures with due regard to the social roots of these methods.[6] They are labeled traditionalists here largely because they have dealt in the aesthetic, philosophical, and administrative coherences that were the stuff of older connections and because they have used generic social concepts that traditional historians originated. But what is important in this context is not their own traditionalism or their radicalism, but rather their interest in internalizing what was external previously. What Schorske has done has been to translate aesthetic categories into historical connections by rooting these categories in the changing, postliberal society of the Viennese bourgeoisie around the turn of this century.[7] What Koselleck has done has been to spell out the "formal temporal structures," which he devised as a novel means of tying early-modern histories to modern history, in terms of a "conceptual history" which is a socialized as well as a temporalized version of the former philosophical idea standing outside of historical societies, all in the service of defining "the unity of history as a science" and "especially of showing its indwelling connections of events."[8]

In any case, these figures are merely exemplary of the constructive responses that have been made to the academic radicals. Whereas it has been primarily French historiography that has represented the internalization of historical patterns among the radicals, an analogous tendency has been represented in other Western historiographies by figures who recognize the centrality of historical coherence as much as the radicals do but who are not themselves tied to the radical camp. They illustrate the crisis of the historical discipline by the anxiety of their response, and they confirm the crisis insofar as their endeavor to establish an authentic historical pattern that is free of external dependence is a spontaneous enterprise independent of the responsive motif. Although it appears that the selection of a common historical pattern or theme has been made impossible by the logical problem faced and left imperfectly resolved by the historicists, this problem has been compounded further by those who have ignored or taken for granted the derivation of coherence in their work. Where the issue has not been skirted, however, the great difficulty modern historians have had in dealing objectively with the issue of unity in general is made a case in point. Historians have either embraced the minority position and come up against the logical problem of casting history in the so-called historicist mode or, most commonly, they have maintained the historian's traditional reliance upon the individual and the particular event: the latter approach stresses the individual as the source of history while the former cannot escape stressing the individual as the symbol of the discipline.

Common ground remains in short supply. What is called for is an admission on the part of historians that they have become, so to speak, hyphenated historians, with some kind of qualifier necessarily attaching to their various roles. Quite clearly, there is no simple past whereof a historian can be pure historian. Despite having to proceed subjectively in this matter, and despite having no more to rely upon as guide than what he finds interesting in the record of the past, the historian must nonetheless persist in the attempt to locate that common theme which resolves this problem in history's favor. Thus, to the problem of the weakness of historical coherence, a weakness which is attested by the centuries of extrahistorical deviation of historical coherence and which has invoked the current cultural malaise of nonhistorians about the value of history as well as the current academic radicalism of the economically, socially, and politically emphatic historians within history, the following personal solution is addressed. This solution is grounded upon two assumptions.

First, the human mind tends ever to coherence; it finds satisfaction only in a kind of unity, which it then identifies with intelligibility. In accordance with this assumption, the problem of historical coherence is a genuine problem; humans are simply not satisfied with the individuality, the diversity, the refractoriness of past human things which has been the implication of the historian's use of the critical method and which has been the strength of modern historiography. Indeed, it can be argued that history is in the trouble that it is in precisely because the historical approach does stress the multifarious in human behavior. A more unified approach, one that validates the connection among events, is required, then, to rehabilitate history in the popular mind.

The second assumption upon which the following proposed solution for the problem of a distinctive historically based coherence is based is the retention of the traditional difference between fact and the connection among facts. This retention flies in the face of recent analyses which have tended to bridge the difference from both ends: facts have been dissolved into tissues of relations, and relations or connections have been accepted as kinds of large or great facts. These arguments are accepted for the perspectives in which historical facts are seen as relations and relations as facts, but not for other perspectives in which facts are seen as facts and relations as relations among facts. For example, the French Revolution can be seen as a tissue of relations with an internal history of subordinate facts or as itself a large fact with relations to other facts, according to the perspective upon it. Even in this solution, what is accepted is that the explanation of a historical fact is its insertion into a larger series of historical facts which thus functions as an explanatory relation and creates its constituent facts to fit the relation. But from the perspective of the problem to be solved here, a difference subsists between the facts of a past case and the relationship or connection which generalizes or explains the facts, both because men have always believed that such a difference does exist and insofar as history has to deal with men's past attitudes it has to take this belief into account, and because for most historians the difference between fact and connection is needed for the crucial difference between truth and subjectivity.

There are two parts to this solution, one referring to the historical process, that is, to history as lived experience, and the other to the historian, that is, to history as it is written. According to the first aspect of the solution, unity in history exists when the agents of history act deliberately in the light of it. We have come to the point, since we no longer believe in an objective reality outside of history, when the only continuity which we recognize in the historical process, in contrast to the input of the historian, is the continuity which is conscious in those who drive or are driven by the historical process itself. This continutiy is obvious in the case of intellectual history because men are always aware of the principles laid down in ancient times and are always thinking in terms of them, whatever their position on the relative merits of ancients and moderns may be. Moreover, in intellectual and cultural history there is always the internal dimension of things wherein thinkers and artists write consciously in response to issues or challenges opened by the prior generation of thinkers and artists. Thus, action in the light of historical continuity is built into the very sinews of the agents involved in intellectual history.

But there is such a deliberate unity in the more concrete spheres of past human activity as well. Not only is there a revolutionary continuity in the mentality of those in 1848 and 1917 who adopted roles made familiar by the great French Revolution of 1789, but there is a spatial historical unity on the part of those who seek to advance or to obstruct a political system which is expanding its sway beyond the local or regional circumstances of its present. In all such cases, where the unity of the past and the historical present is itself a factor to be empirically unearthed, the role of continuity in history is patent, whatever the countervailing role of the discontinuity undoubtedly at hand in each moment of human time may be. In this first aspect of the solution, the scope of history's continuity will vary according to the attitude of the past men toward it. For this aspect of the problem, coherence existed in history because men believed that it existed, and insofar as men believed that it existed, coherence existed.

The second aspect of the solution is to the first like an ontogenetic recapitulation of the phylogenetic development of Western civilization: just as the concern for the validity of historical knowledge replaced the concern for the ontic pattern behind historical reality at the turn of our century, the second aspect of our solution has to do with the historian rather than with the historical process which he records and which is the center of our first aspect. Now, it is clear that at the very least the historian contributes his knowledge of the situation which was in fact unknown or which was in principle unknowable by the historical agent who acted upon it. Such knowledge is by definition a knowledge of relations or of connections, since it has to do either with the motivation of the agent or with the relations between his action and its results for the situation in which he found himself. But, over and above such special knowledge, the historian's selection and organization of his material is as much in the light of his own perspective on human relations as it is in the light of the facts of the past case. In any event the criterion of the historian's contribution must be purely temporal in character. That is, he must operate as if the relations of succession or of simultaneity among the facts of the past establish a connection among them that is stronger than mere juxtaposition and different from, albeit as rational as, logical integration. In short, there is a chronologic which is, for the historian, as telling as syllogistic or propositional logic is for the logician or the social scientist: the touchstone of the historian's selection and organization will lie in that which is revealing for the temporal arrangement of things. From this point of view, it makes little difference whether the historian's method is narrative, descriptive, or analytic; what does make a difference is whether the historian makes his judgment about the coherence of things according to their distribution in time—whether, that is, things subsist before, after, or at the same time as other things.

Now it should be clear that the proposed solution combines elements from what we have called historicity and historism. It exalts historicity—that is, the conformity of historical patterns with the process of history itself—in that, according to it, the pattern which the historian interposes will be patently less extensive in its scope than the general order of things which used to be the temporal expression of an absolute, extratemporal reality. In part because of the growing disbelief in such absolutes, in part because of the obeisance which everybody, including historians, must now give to the discontinuity from the past of the present sovereign moment, and in part because of the tribute that the historian in particular must pay to the individuality of men and things to which the historical enterprise is addressed, the coherence that the historian constructs must be in the realm of the limited connections occupied by motivation, narrative, holistic description, or the analysis of a definite condition. He must not project the general factors in the situation which he has not empirically studied, and he must not draw analogies that go beyond demonstrably identical elements in two or more situations, each of which he has studied. Just as the scope of historical coherence is now more restricted than it was in the past, so the temporal character of the criteria for historical coherence must be more exclusively temporal than it was in the past.

In addition, this solution frankly acknowledges its historism—that is, its derivation of historical connections from principles that lie outside of the process of history itself. It is well known that history, as a discipline, has no subject matter of its own. The question that arises here is one of the relationship between such principled ignorance and the distinctive role of historical knowledge which we have just asserted. It may be fairly asked: knowledge about what? Now it is clear that from this point of view that the historian cannot be a pure historian: he must have expert knowledge of the discipline that occupies the ground whose past he investigates. It should be clear too that the difference between fact and coherence enters here: a historian can know the facts of his field as a hybrid who has the expert knowledge of human behavior he has gleaned from the neighboring discipline that concerns itself with this facet of human behavior; but insofar as he checks on the past of this facet and in general studies its temporal connections he operates as a pure historian. In other words, the historian's extrahistorical knowledge should be invoked for the facts of the past, but his distinctively historical knowledge should be invoked for the coherence of the past.

It has been generally agreed—and much has been made of this consensus of late—that history is a social discipline. The philosophical historians who make the most of the individualistic destiny of history insist that history begins where the individual meets the society in which he is ensconced. The social-scientific historians insist, as we have seen, on the individuality of whole societies and frown upon individual persons. The proposal advanced here would deny that history is necessarily a social discipline, holding instead that it is necessarily a temporal discipline which may or may not be concerned with social facts. According to this proposal, even the negative attitude toward society, which registers the indifference of men to all social circumstances, including their own, is a one-sided view of history that testifies illegitimately to its social character. Some men are socially oriented, while others are not; they could be active in any geographical and social space, so long as the traditions of their primary sphere of activity and the chronological dispositions of their secondary sphere of activity, which help to constitute their historical coherence, are in place. Only so can history avoid the social reductionism that has plagued so many of its most congenial neighboring disciplines.

Paradoxically, the less that history is presently esteemed, the more necessary it becomes. For the less history is worth in the present, the more indispensable is its view of the past because we continue to believe that knowledge of the past is required for living in the present and because history was once highly regarded in the past. But, for both reasons—that is, the kind of past knowledge that is now useful and the ground for history's earlier popularity—it is the specific embodiment of life's coherence that matters rather than the usefulness of past facts. It is to the rehabilitation of historical coherence that the proposals for the revitalization of history must be addressed.

History must be true and it must make sense. These are the requirements which a society demands of its history, and these requirements are what this solution—and this book—is about.

NOTES

Introduction

1. For recent social history which for the most part transcends quantitative methods, see Georg C. Iggers, *New Directions in European Historiography* (Middletown, 1975), passim; for the primarily individual focus of recent psychohistory, see Bruce Mazlish, ed., *Psychoanalysis and History* (New York, 1971), pp. 3, 13; for an analytical view of history from the standpoint of concepts rather than the quantitative techniques of the social sciences, see Robert F. Berkhofer, Jr., *A Behavioral Approach to Historical Analysis* (New York, 1969), passim.

2. See Carl E. Schorske, *Fin-de-Siècle Vienna: Politics and Culture* (New York, 1980), pp. xx-xxi, xxxvii; William J. McGrath, *Dionysian Art and Populist Politics in Austria* (New Haven, 1974); and Roger Shattuck, *The Banquet Years: The Origins of the Avant-Garde in France* (New York, 1968).

3. For the convergence of social and quantitative history, see the argument for "social mathematics" by Fernand Braudel, "History and the Social Sciences," in *Economy and Society in Early Modern Europe*, Peter Burke, ed. (New York, 1972), pp. 25–35; and the casual subsumption of quantification under social history in David S. Landes and Charles Tilly, eds., *History as Social Science* (Englewood Cliffs, N.J., 1971), p. 73.

Chapter One

1. Herodotus, *The Histories*, trans. Aubrey de Selincourt (Baltimore, 1954), pp. 15, 53; Arnaldo Momigliano, *Studies in Historiography* (New York, 1966), pp. 127–30.

2. Thucydides, *The History of the Peloponnesian War*, ed. and trans. R. W. Livingstone (New York, 1943), pp. 43–44, 118, 257. The historian's reliance upon Thucydides has never stressed the irrational elements in his work. To the contrary, historians have tried generally to further their own claim to rationality by relying upon Thucydides as a predecessor.

3. Herodotus, *The Histories*, pp. 15, 19.

4. John H. Finlay, Jr., *Thucydides* (Ann Arbor, 1963), p. 72.

5. Ibid., pp. 70–73, 292–94.

6. Thucydides, *The History of the Peloponnesian War*, p. 45.

7. Ibid., p. 189.

8. For this approach to Israelite history and the historiography, see Millar Burrows's essay on "Ancient Israel" in *The Idea of History in the Ancient Near East*, ed. Robert C. Denton (New Haven, 1955), pp. 101–31.

9. Millar Burrows, "Ancient Israel"; Erich Dinkler, "Earliest Christianity"; Roland H. Bainton, "Patristic Christianity," in Denton, *The Idea of History in the Ancient Near East*, pp. 101–31, 169–236.

NOTES TO PAGES 17-24

10 Eusebius, *The History of the Church from Christ to Constantine,* trans. G. A. Williamson (Baltimore, 1965), pp. 31–32, 76, 112.

11. Karl Löwith, *Meaning in History* (Chicago, 1949), p. 156.

12. St. Augustine, *The City of God,* ed. Vernon J. Bourke, trans. Gerald G. Walsh, Demetrius B. Zama, Grace Monahan, Daniel J. Honan (Garden City, N.Y., 1958), pp. 99, 111, 217, 328, 391–92, 408.

13. Otto, Bishop of Freising, *The Two Cities: A Chronicle of Universal History to the Year 1146 A.D.,* ed. Austin P. Evans and Charles Knapp, trans. Charles Christopher Mierow (New York, 1966), pp. 95–96, 323–24. For the complementary nature of the philosophy in Otto's later *Deeds of Frederick Barbarossa* and in general for the intellectual relationship between the *Two Cities* and the *Deeds,* see Karl F. Morrison, "Otto of Freising's Quest for the Hermeneutic Circle," *Speculum* 55 (1980): 207–36.

14. Otto of Freising, *The Two Cities,* pp. 89, 94, 454.

15. Ibid., pp. 280–82, 322–24, 354.

16. Ibid., p. 31.

17. Ibid., pp. 359, 404–405.

18. Beryl Smalley, *Historians in the Middle Ages,* (New York, 1974), pp. 184–185.

19. Bede, *A History of the English Church and People,* trans. Leo Sherley-Price, (Baltimore, 1955), pp. 33–35.

20. Smalley, *Historians in the Middle Ages,* p. 10.

21. Eusebius, *The History of the Church,* pp. 47, 49.

22. Otto of Freising, *The Two Cities,* pp. 90–91.

23. Were that the case, I would have to cover in some detail the contributions to modern historiography made by the medieval chronicles and Renaissance humanism. See Louis Green, *Chronicle into History: An Essay on the Interpretation of History in Florentine Fourteenth-Century Chronicles* (Cambridge, 1972), chap. 1; Eric Cochrane, *Historians and Historiography in the Italian Renaissance* (Chicago, 1981), chap. 1.

Chapter Two

1. For this historical revolution of the sixteenth and seventeenth centuries, see Julian H. Franklin, *Jean Bodin and the Sixteenth-Century Revolution in the Methodology of Law and History* (New York, 1963); Donald R. Kelley, *Foundations of Modern Historical Scholarship: Language, Law, and History in the French Renaissance* (New York, 1970); George Huppert, *The Idea of Perfect History: Historical Erudition and Historical Philosophy In Renaissance France* (Urbana, 1970); and F. Smith Fussner, *The Historical Revolution: English Historical Writing and Thought, 1580–1640* (London, 1962). There has been academic dispute about the aptness of the idea of "revolution" in its application to the widespread and prolonged advances in critical historiography from the fifteenth through the seventeenth centuries. For the pros and cons of the dispute, see Joseph H. Preston, "Was There an Historical Revolution?" *Journal of the History of Ideas* 38 (1977): 353–64. The issue is obviously of marginal importance here.

2. Kelley, *Foundations of Modern Historical Scholarship*, pp. 22, 24, 45.

3. John Bodin, *Method for the Easy Comprehension of History*, trans. Beatrice Reynolds (New York, 1944), pp. 8, 15. For Pufendorf see my *The Politics of Discretion: Pufendorf and the Acceptance of Natural Law* (Chicago, 1965). See also Hugo Grotius, *Annales et historiae de rebus Belgicis* (Amsterdam, 1658); Jacques Cujas, *Novellarum constitutionum* (Gymnicum, 1569); Guillaume Budé, *De l'institution du prince* (Gregg Press, 1966), a reprint of the 1547 edition.

4. Paolo Sarpi, *History of Benefices and Selections from the History of the Council of Trent*, ed. and trans. Peter Burke (New York, 1967), pp. xxv, 117; Heinrich Ritter von Srbik, *Geist und Geschichte vom Deutschen Humanismus bis zur Gegenwart* (Munich, 1950), 1:95.

5. Jean Mabillon, quoted in R. P. Dom, J. M. Besse, *Les études ecclésiastiques d'après la méthode de Mabillon* (Paris, 1902), p. 91.

6. Franklin, *Jean Bodin and the Sixteenth-Century Revolution in the Methodology of Law and History*, pp. 83–88, 152–53; Emil Clemens Scherer, *Geschichte und Kirchengeschichte an den deutschen Universitäten* (Freiburg, 1927), pp. 135–39.

7. Adalbert Klempt, *Die Säkularisierung der universalhistorischen Auffassung* (Göttingen, 1960), passim.

8. Thomas Hobbes, *The Elements of Law, Natural and Politic*, ed. Ferdinand Tönnies, 2d ed. (London, 1969), pp. 22–25; Thomas Hobbes, *Leviathan* (New York, 1914), pp. 18–23, 41–42; J. G. A. Pocock, *Politics, Language, and Time* (New York, 1971), pp. 149–57.

9. Lucien Lévy-Bruhl, "The Cartesian Spirit and History," in *Philosophy and History: Essays Presented to Ernst Cassirer*, ed. Raymond Klibansky and H. J. Paton (New York, 1963), pp. 191–95; Descartes, "Discourse on the Method of Rightly Conducting the Reason and Seeking for Truth in the Sciences," *The Philosophical Works of Descartes*, trans. Elizabeth S. Haldane and G. R. T. Ross (n.p., 1931), 1:84–85.

10. Descartes, "Rules for the Direction of the Mind," ibid., 1:3–5.

11. Norman Kemp Smith, *New Studies in the Philosophy of Descartes: Descartes as Pioneer* (London, 1952), pp. 63–65.

12. Hobbes, *Leviathan*, pp. 30–32, 41.

13. J. G. A. Pocock, *The Machiavellian Moment* (Princeton, 1975), p. 370.

14. J. G. A. Pocock, *The Ancient Constitution and the Feudal Law: English Historical Thought in the Seventeenth Century* (New York, 1967), pp. 235–39.

15. John Locke, *An Essay Concerning Human Understanding*, ed. A. D. Woozley (New York, 1964), pp. 393–95, 411–12.

16. For Bacon's emphasis, see Francis Bacon, *The New Organon and Other Writings*, ed. Fulton H. Anderson (New York, 1960), pp. 43–45; for Descartes's, see his "Rules for the Direction of the Mind," 1:45, 84–85.

17. Fussner, *The Historical Revolution: English Historical Writing and Thought*, pp. 255, 262–69; James C. Morrison, "Philosophy and History in Bacon," *Journal of the History of Ideas* 38 (1977): 595–606.

18. Pocock, *Politics, Language, and Time*, pp. 159–201. Commentators on

Hobbes's other historical writings—his early translation of *Thucydides* and his later essay in contemporary history—*Behemoth; or, The Long Parliament*—insist, to the contrary, on their subordination to his political theory. See *Hobbes' Thucydides,* ed. Richard Schlatter (New Brunswick, N.J., 1975), pp. xi, xxvii-xxviii (Schlatter's comments essentially repeat his older analysis, "Thomas Hobbes and Thucydides," *Journal of the History of Ideas* 6 [1945]: 362); M. M. Goldsmith, *Hobbes' Science of Politics* (New York, 1966), pp. 234–38.

19. Krieger, *The Politics of Discretion,* pp. 170–200.

20. Friedrich Meinecke, *Die Entstehung des Historismus* (Munich, 1936), 1:63.

21. Felix Gilbert, *Machiavelli and Guicciardini: Politics and History in Sixteenth-Century Florence* (Princeton, 1965), pp. 285, 288–91, 300.

22. Ibid., p. 230.

23. Thus Guicciardini introduced his account of Piero di Medici's reign with the promise: "In these events I will endeavor to show not only the general causes and effects but also in as much detail as possible the origins and sources of all these ills." Guicciardini, *History of Italy and History of Florence,* ed. John R. Hale, trans. Cecil Grayson (New York, 1964), p. 11.

24. Gilbert, *Machiavelli and Guicciardini,* pp. 285, 288–91, 300.

25. Guicciardini, *History of Italy and History of Florence,* pp. 27–28, 69, 85, 111, 145.

26. Gilbert, *Machiavelli and Guicciardini,* pp. 290–91, 295, 301; Guicciardini, *History of Italy* and *History of Florence,* p. ix.

27. Felix Gilbert, *Machiavelli and Guicciardini,* pp. 279, 284–85, 291; Guicciardini, *History of Italy and History of Florence,* p. xix; Krieger, *Ranke: The Meaning of History* (Chicago 1977), p. 115. This criticism is not an indictment of the accuracy of Guicciardini's facts.

28. Bodin, *Method,* pp. 2–3, 8, 157; Julian H. Franklin, *Jean Bodin and the Rise of Absolutist Theory* (Cambridge, 1973), pp. 25–26.

29. Bodin, *Method,* pp. 291–303.

30. George Huppert, *L'Idée de l'histoire parfaite,* trans. Françoise and Paulette Braudel (Paris, 1973), pp. 107–9.

31. Ibid., pp. 29, 93.

32. Pocock, *The Ancient Constitution and the Feudal Law,* pp. 15–17, 29, 122–23, 178–81.

33. Sarpi, *History of Benefices and Selections from History of Council of Trent,* pp. xxiv–xxv, 142.

34. A. Robert Caponigri, *Time and Idea: The Theory of History in Giambattista Vico* (Notre Dame, Ind. 1968), pp. ix–x, 109–13; Isaiah Berlin, *Vico and Herder* (New York, 1976), pp. xvi–xix, 26–28, 73.

35. Berlin, *Vico and Herder,* p. 13.

36. *The New Science of Giambattista Vico,* trans. Thomas Goddard Bergin and Max Harold Fisch (Garden City N.Y., 1961), pp. 351–73.

37. Vico, *Autobiography,* trans. Thomas Goddard Bergin and Max Harold

Fisch (Ithaca, N.Y. 1944, 1963), pp. 117, 121, 123, 139, 146, 155–56; Vico, *The New Science*, pp. 17, 62.

38. Vico, *The New Science*, pp. 18, 22, 52; Vico, *Autobiography*, pp. 166–68.

39. Vico, *The New Science*, p. 21.

40. Ibid., pp. 22, 52–53, 58–59, 62; Vico, *Autobiography*, p. 127.

41. Vico, *The New Science*, p. 60.

42. Ibid., pp. 376–84. Emphasis supplied.

43. Frank Manuel, Introduction, in Johann Gottfried von Herder, *Reflections on the Philosophy of the History of Mankind*, ed. Frank E. Manuel (Chicago, 1968), pp. xiv, xvi–xvii, xx–xxi.

44. Herder, *Reflections*, pp. 4–5.

45. Ibid., p. 5. Herder's emphasis.

46. Ibid., pp. 82–118, 269–70, 398.

47. Ibid., pp. 87–117.

48. Ibid., pp. 20–24. For the influence of contemporary science on Herder, see Berlin, *Vico and Herder*, pp. 146, 150. It should be noted that Berlin rejects the notion of any Herderian overall design linking the plurality of individualities to one another. See ibid., esp. pp. 206–11.

49. For this association, see Charles Coulston Gillispie, *The Edge of Objectivity: An Essay in the History of Scientific Ideas* (Princeton, 1960), p. 200, and Maurice Mandelbaum, *History, Man, and Reason: A Study in Nineteenth-Century Thought* (Baltimore, 1971), p. 58.

50. David Hume, *Dialogues Concerning Natural Religion*, ed. Norman Kemp Smith (Indianapolis, 1947), pp. 19–20; J. B. Black, *The Art of History: A Study of Four Great Historians of the Eighteenth Century* (New York, 1965), pp. 79–80; *David Hume: Philosophical Historian*, ed. David Fate Norton and Richard H. Popkin (New York, 1965), pp. 52–54.

51. *David Hume: Philosophical Historian*, pp. 37–38; J. B. Black, *The Art of History* (New York, 1965), p. 85.

52. David Hume, "Of the Study of History," in *David Hume: Philosophical Historian*, p. 38.

53. Hume, *An Enquiry Concerning Human Understanding*, in *David Hume: Philosophical Historian*, p. 52.

54. David Hume, *A Treatise of Human Nature* (Garden City, N.Y., 1961), pp. 363, 366, 389. Hume's emphasis.

55. Hume, *Enquiry Concerning Human Understanding*, in *David Hume, Philosophical Historian*, p. 52.

56. Hume, *Treatise of Human Nature*, pp. 131–35.

57. Fussner, *The Historical Revolution*, pp. 193–97; Jacques-Bénigne Bossuet, *Discourse on Universal History*, ed. Orest Ranum, trans. Elborg Forster (Chicago, 1976): xix–xxxiii.

58. The rationalist kind if not the historist kind of philosophical historiography serves to refute the recently popular conception of the period as one in which empirical events were considered to be a series of signs representing the

essential reality that was signified and manifesting a connection among one another because a distinction must be drawn between rationalist and historist forms of coherence: the principles of coherence were both different and specific in each case. The refuted conception applies rather to the historist than the rationalist historians whose principles were more constant and more obviously extrahistorical than those principles upon which this judgment was based. See Michel Foucault, *The Order of Things: An Archaeology of the Human Sciences* (New York, 1970), pp. xxii–xxiii, 50–67. The break or episteme that Foucault marks between the Renaissance and the classical period at the start of the seventeenth century is not endorsed by this reading of the sources.

59. Spinoza, *Theologico-Political Treatise*, in *The works of Spinoza*, trans. R. H. M. Elwes. (New York, 1951), 1:4–9, 132–55; Leonard Krieger, "Germany," in *National Consciousness, History, and Political Culture in Early Modern Europe*, ed. Orest Ranum (Baltimore, 1975), pp. 90–91; Lewis W. Spitz, "The Significance of Leibniz for Historiography," *JHI* (1952): 13.

60. Elisabeth Labrousse, *Pierre Bayle: le philosophe de Rotterdam* (Paris, 1959), 2:36, 65–68, 124–25, 280–83, 289, 295–97, 446.

61. Peter Gay, *The Enlightenment: An Interpretation* (New York, 1969), 2:373–76; *Autobiography of Edward Gibbon* (London, 1907), pp. 135–42, 172.

62. Herbert Butterfield, *Man on His Past: The Study of the History of Historical Scholarship* (Boston, 1960), pp. 42–55; Leonard Krieger, "Germany," *National Consciousness*, pp. 93–95.

63. Gay, *The Enlightenment*, 2: 376–77; *Autobiography of Edward Gibbon*, p. 180. The specification of history and philosophy was made for as well as by the general historians in the eighteenth century. Thus the German historian J. G. Meusel praised Gibbon for writing "as befits an historian and philosopher" (*ut Historicum et Philosophum decet*). Quoted in ibid., p. 213.

64. Peter Hanns Reill, "History and Hermeneutics in the *Aufklärung:* The Thought of Johann Cristoph Gatterer," *Journal of Modern History* 45 (1973): 30–31; Srbik, *Geist und Geschichte*, 1:123.

65. Krieger, "Germany," in *National Consciousness*, p. 93.

66. Ibid., pp. 95–97.

67. Voltaire, *Philosophical Dictionary* trans. Peter Gay (New York, 1962), 2:419–20.

68. J. B. Black, *The Art of History*, pp. 37–44; Voltaire, *The Age of Louis XIV*, trans. Martyn P. Pollack (London, 1926), pp. 4–5.

69. Descartes, "Discourse on the Method of Rightly Conducting the Reason," in *The Philosophical Works of Descartes*, 1:92; Voltaire, *The Philosophy of History* (New York, 1965), pp. 21, 32, 45–46, 60, 80; Black *The Art of History*, pp. 1, 23, 52.

70. Lord Bolingbroke, *Historical Writings*, ed. Isaac Krannick (Chicago, 1974), pp. xx, 25, 28–29.

71. Keith Michael Baker, *Condorcet: From Natural Philosophy to Social Mathematics* (Chicago, 1975), pp. 344, 346, 355–60; Condorcet, *Selected*

NOTES TO PAGES 50-57

Writings, ed. Keith Michael Baker (Indianapolis, 1976), pp. 210–11, 215, 226, 254–58.

72. Kant, "Idee zu einer allgemeinen Geschichte in weltbürgerlicher Absicht," in *Immanuel Kant's Sämtliche Werke* (Grossherzog Wilhelm Ernst Ausgabe, n.p., n.d.), 1:223, 227, 229, 237–40.

Chapter Three

1. For the association of science and philosophy, see Charles Coulston Gillispie, *The Edge of Objectivity: An Essay in the History of Scientific Ideas* (Princeton, 1960), p. 200; and Maurice Mandelbaum, *History, Man, and Reason: A Study in Nineteenth-Century Thought* (Baltimore, 1971).

2. Georg Wilhelm Friedrich Hegel, *Lectures on the Philosophy of World History. Introduction: Reason in History,* trans. H. B. Nisbet from the German edition of Johannes Hoffmeister (Cambridge, 1975), p. 27.

3. Ibid., pp. 27–44.

4. Ibid., pp. 27–29.

5. Hegel, *Philosophy of Right.* trans. T. M. Knox (Oxford, 1967): 167; Jerrold Seigel, *Marx's Fate: The Shape of Life* (Princeton, 1978), pp. 31, 398.

6. Hegel, *Lectures on the Philosophy of World History,* p. 27.

7. G. W. F. Hegel, *The Phenomenology of Mind,* trans. J. B. Baillie (New York, 1931), pp. 86, 90–91, 104.

8. For the logical interpretation of the dialectic, see especially Richard Kroner, *Von Kant bis Hegel* (Tübingen, 1921, 1924); for the historical interpretation, see especially Herbert Marcuse, *Hegel's Ontologie und die Grundzüge einer Theorie der Geschichtlichkeit* (Frankfurt am Main, 1932).

9. Hegel, *The Phenomenology of Mind,* pp. 70–71. For the variant translation of "the time process does raise philosophy to the level of scientific system" as "the time has come for the elevation of philosophy to a science," see *Hegel: Texts and Commentary,* ed. and trans. Walter Kaufman (Garden City, N.Y., 1966), pp. 12–13.

10. Hegel, *Phenomenology of Mind,* pp. 89–95, 100; Kaufman, *Hegel: Texts and Commentary,* p. 62.

11. Hegel, *Phenomenology of Mind,* pp. 799–800.

12. For Mandeville, see his *Fable of the Bees; or Private Vices, Public Benefits* (new ed., Oxford, 1924) (Mandeville insisted privately that he did not really mean the subtitle, but the idea was associated with him nonetheless and would have a significant career); for Kant, see his "Idea for a Universal History with a Cosmopolitan Intent," in *The Philosophy of Kant: Immanuel Kant's Moral and Political Writings,* ed. and trans. Carl J. Friedrich (New York, 1949), pp. 116–17, 130.

13. Hegel, *Lectures on the Philosophy of World History,* p. 89. Hegel referred to the cunning of reason, its characteristic mediatory function, in the philosophically respectable context of his synoptic *Encyclopedia of the Philosophical Sciences* as well as in the more informal lectures on world history. "Reason is as cunning as it is powerful," he wrote in the *Encyclopedia.* "The

cunning consists in the mediating activity by which it allows objects to react upon one another in accordance with their own nature without intruding directly into this process and yet accomplishes its own purposes thereby." Georg Wilhelm Friedrich Hegel, *Werke* (Berlin, 1843), 6:382.

14. Hegel, *Werke,* 6:807.

15. Hegel, *Lectures on the Philosophy of World History,* p. 29. Emphasis in the original.

16. Hegel, *Phenomenology of Mind,* pp. 807–8.

17. *Hegel's Philosophy of Right,* pp. 216–19.

18. Note Karl Hegel's testimony to the greater philosophical emphasis in his father's earlier lectures on the philosophy of history. Georg Wilhelm Friedrich Hegel, *The Philosophy of History,* ed. and trans. Charles Hegel and J. Sibree (rev. ed., New York, 1944), p. xi.

19. Hegel, *Lectures on the Philosophy of World History,* p. 29.

20. Ibid., pp. 74–75.

21. Ibid., pp. 31–43.

22. Ibid., pp. 42–43.

23. Hegel, *Philosophy of Right,* p. 10; Hegel, *Lectures on the Philosophy of World History,* p. 66.

24. Hegel, *Philosophy of Right,* pp. 10–11.

25. Hegel, *Phenomenology of Mind,* p. 114; Hegel, *Lectures on the Philosophy of World History,* pp. 58–59, 64, 92–94.

26. Hegel, *Lectures on the Philosophy of World History,* p. 134.

27. Ibid., pp. 116–24, 130.

28. Ibid., pp. 66–67.

29. Hegel, *The Philosophy of History,* pp. 456–57.

30. Ernst Cassirer, *The Problem of Knowledge: Philosophy, Science, and History,* trans. William H. Woglom and Charles W. Hendel (New Haven, 1950), pp. 227–28; Krieger, *Ranke,* pp. 50, 98.

31. Srbik, *Geist und Geschichte,* p. 179.

32. Frederick von Schlegel, *The Philosophy of History,* trans. James Burton Robinson (New York, 1893): 65–66, 469, 474.

33. Ibid., pp. ix–x, 65–73, 476; Harry Elmer Barnes, *A History of Historical Writing* (New York, 1962), p. 195.

34. Quoted in Srbik, *Geist und Geschichte,* p. 179, and in John Herman Randall, Jr., *The Career of Philosophy* (New York, 1965), 2:259.

35. Schelling, *Die Weltalter, Erstes Buch,* in Friedrich Wilhelm Joseph Schelling, *Sämtliche Werke: 1811–1815* (Stuttgart, 1861), 8:200–201, 203–6, 261, 269.

36. Ibid., 8:254–60; Arthur O. Lovejoy, *The Reason, The Understanding, and Time* (Baltimore, 1961), pp. 81–84.

37. Schelling, *Die Weltalter,* in *Sämtliche Werke,* 8:202, 207.

38. *The Positive Philosophy of Auguste Comte,* trans. and ed. Harriet Martineau (London, 1893), 2:130–31; Mandelbaum, *History, Man, and Reason,* pp. 67–68.

39. *The Positive Philosophy of Auguste Comte,* 2:69–71, 150, 154–55;

Auguste Comte, *A General View of Positivism*, trans. J. H. Bridges (Stanford, n.d.), p. 371.

40. Comte, *A General View of Positivism*, pp. 48–49.

41. August Comte, *Système de politique positive, ou Traité de sociologie, Instituant la Religion de l'Humanité* (Paris, 1853), 3:vii, 3–4.

42. Auguste Comte, *Cours de philosophie positive*, 4th ed. (Paris, 1877), 6:409–11.

43. For Marx's view of history as a part of natural history, see Karl Marx, *Economic and Philosophical Manuscripts*, in Karl Marx, *Early Writings*, ed. and trans. T. B. Bottomore (New York, 1963), p. 164.

44. On the successive distinctions in the views of Marx and Engels on history, from history as humanization, through history as practice, to history as the phenomena of natural law, see Helmut Fleischer, *Marxism and History*, trans. Eric Mosbacher (New York, 1973), pp. 12–37. For a point of view that attributes the rational inevitability of a determined process to the passage from capitalism to communism in Marx, the mere empiricism of unexplained and therefore undetermined process to earlier societies, and therefore the proportions of coherence and fact to opposite phases of history from the one advanced here, see William H. Shaw, *Marx's Theory of History* (Stanford, 1978), pp. 82–148.

45. Karl Marx and Friedrich Engels, *The German Ideology: Parts I and III*, ed. R. Pascal (New York, 1947), pp. 15, 40–41.

46. Ibid., p. 27.

47. Ibid., pp. 115–16.

48. Thus· "The fact is . . . that definite individuals who are productively active in a definite way enter into . . . definite social and political relations. Empirical observation must in each separate instance bring out empirically, the connection of the social and political structure with production. . . . This method of approach is not devoid of premises. . . . Its premises are men, . . . in their actual, empirically perceptible process of development under separate conditions. . . . When reality is depicted, philosophy as an independent branch of activity loses its medium of existence. At the best its place can only be taken by a summing-up of the most general results, abstractions which arise from the observation of the historical development of men." Marx and Engels, *The Germany Ideology*, pp. 13, 15.

49. Marx, *Economic and Philosophical Manuscripts*, in Karl Marx, *Early Writings*, pp. 155, 162–64. Emphasis in the original.

50. Marx and Engels, *The German Ideology*, pp. 18, 30–31, 37, 68.

51. Ibid., pp. 7, 16, 38, 40–49, 65.

52. Ibid., pp. 24–25, 38, 57. Emphasis in the original.

53. Ibid., pp. 70, 75.

54. Karl Marx, *The Class Struggles in France, 1848–1850*, in Karl Marx, *Selected Works*, ed. V. Adoratsky (London, 1942), 2:192, 276; Leonard Krieger, "Marx and Engels as Historians," *Journal of the History of Ideas* 14 (1953): 384–487.

55. Karl Marx, *Capital*, Frederick Engels, ed. (New York, 1967), 1:20.

56. Frederick Engels, *Dialectics of Nature,* ed. and trans. Clemens Dutt (New York, 1940), pp. viii, 26.

57. Ibid., p. 27.

58. Quoted in editor's introduction to Friedrich Engels, *The German Revolutions,* ed. Leonard Krieger (Chicago, 1967), pp. xxiv–xxvii.

59. Frederick Engels, *Herr Eugen Dühring's Revolution in Science: (Anti-Dühring),* ed. C. P. Dutt, trans. Emile Burns (New York, 1939), pp. 27–29.

60. Ibid., pp. 15–16.

61. Frederick Engels, *Dialectics of Nature,* ed. and tràns. Clemens Dutt (New York, 1940), p. 244.

62. Ibid., p. 154.

63. Engels, *Anti-Dühring,* p. 31.

64. Ibid.; Engels, *Dialectics of Nature,* p. 26.

65. Engels, "Notes to 'Anti-Dühring,' " in *Dialectics of Nature,* p. 314. Emphasis in the original.

66. Engels, *Dialectics of Nature,* p. 27. Emphasis mine. For the force of the natural model in Engels's conception of history, see Leonard Krieger, Introduction, in Friedrich Engels, *The German Revolutions,* xx.

67. See above, pp. 76–78.

68. Karl Marx, *Grundrisse: Foundations of the Critique of Political Economy,* trans. Martin Nicolaus (New York, 1973), pp. 85, 94, 99. Emphasis in the original.

69. Ibid., p. 97.

70. Ibid., pp. 89, 107.

71. Karl Marx, *Capital: A Critique of Political Economy,* ed. Frederick Engels (New York, 1967), 1:8, 565, 633.

72. Ibid., 1:10, 358, 620–21.

73. Leonard Krieger, "Marx and Engels as Historians," *Journal of the History of Ideas* 14 (1953):399.

74. Marx, *Capital,* 1:542.

75. Ibid., 1:169; 3:399, 883. Thus Marx could state reprovingly that the power of capital over labor "appears as a power with which capital is endowed by Nature," although actually it is "a historical form peculiar to, and specifically distinguishing, the capitalist process of production." Ibid., 1:333–34.

76. Ibid., 1:19–20.

77. Ibid., 1:359; 3:883–84.

78. Ibid., 1:486–88, 566; 2:16.

79. Marx and Engels, *The German Ideology,* pp. 27–28, 66–67, 70.

80. Shaw, *Marx's Theory of History,* pp. 83–113. Shaw does not make a point of the hardening, but his argument for Marx's notion of the inevitable transition from capitalism to socialism is actually based largely on the later works of Marx.

81. John Stuart Mill, *A System of Logic, Ratiocinative and Inductive,* 8th ed. (New York, 1941), pp. 597, 607.

82. Ibid., pp. 597–98, 607–9.

83. Ibid., pp. 604–5.

84. John Stuart Mill, *On Liberty*, ed. David Spitz (New York, 1975), pp. 16–52; Mill, *System of Logic*, p. 605.

85. For the institutions, equipment, and attitudes of independent practicing historians in this "great age of history," see Felix Gilbert, "European and American Historiography," in John Higham, with Leonard Krieger and Felix Gilbert, *History* (Englewood Cliffs, N.J., 1965), pp. 320–39.

86. Henry Thomas Buckle, *On Scotland and the Scotch Intellect*, ed. H. J. Hanham (Chicago, 1970), pp. xiii–xv, 157. I use "positivistic" loosely, in the general sense of a doctrine asserting the priority of general laws over the facts from which they are derived, on the model of the natural sciences. It is generally agreed that Buckle was not a positivist in the narrow sense of discipleship under Comte and the Comteans. See W. M. Simon, *European Positivism in the Nineteenth Century* (Ithaca, 1963), pp. 219–20.

87. Quoted in Gargan's introduction, Hippolyte Adolphe Taine, *The Origins of Contemporary France*, ed. Edward T. Gargan (Chicago, 1974), pp. xv, xvii, xxvi–vii, and in G. P. Gooch, *History and Historians in the Nineteenth Century* (Boston, 1959), p. 226.

88. Taine, *Origins of Contemporary France*, pp. 4–6, 163.

89. Ibid., pp. 136, 163, 243–45, 294.

90. On this neglect, see Gargan's introduction in ibid., pp. xiii–iv.

91. Quoted in Felix Gilbert, *History: Choice and Commitment* (Cambridge, Mass., 1977), p. 17.

92. Johann Gustav Droysen, *Historik,* ed. Rudolf Hübner (Munich, 1937), pp. 12–16, 258ff. 287, 365; Srbik, *Geist und Geschichte*, 1:371–74.

93. Gooch, *History and Historians,* pp. 131–44; Heinrich von Treitschke, *History of Germany in the Nineteenth Century*, ed. Gordon A. Craig (Chicago, 1975), pp. xiv–xxi.

94. François Guizot, *Historical Essays and Lectures,* ed. Stanley Mellon (Chicago, 1972), pp. xxvi–xxvii, xxiv–xxv, xxiv.

95. Ibid., pp. 141–43, 160–65.

96. Quoted in Douglas Johnson, *Guizot: Aspects of French History, 1787–1874* (London, 1963), pp. 330–32.

97. Guizot, *Historical Essays and Lectures,* pp. 267–68, 278–79.

98. Ibid., pp. 28, 196–99.

99. Quoted in Johnson, *Guizot,* pp. 332, 375–76.

100. Ibid., pp. 321–22. The point here is not intended to bear on either side of the well-worn issue which pits the subordination of Guizot's (and his contemporaries') history to his politics against his subordination of his politics to his history. Since he indubitably historized his political categories, the question of the priority of either is not nearly so important, for the perspective here, as the fact of the political provenance of the categories which he employed for the coherence of his history.

101. Guizot, *Historical Essays and Lectures,* pp. 90–91, 129–36.

102. Johnson, *Guizot,* p. 374.

103. Roland Barthes, *Michelet par lui-même* (Paris, n.d.), pp. 21, 29–30, 33–35, 179–82.

104. Jules Michelet, *History of the French Revolution*, ed. Gordon Wright, trans. Charles Cocks (Chicago, 1967), pp. xiii, 3, 17, 22–23, 27, 30.

105. Ibid., pp. 6–7.

106. Lord Acton, *Essays in the Liberal Interpretation of History*, ed. William H. McNeill (Chicago, 1967), pp. 7–8 (the article in question—"Mr. Buckle's Thesis and Method"—was actually written by Acton's co-editor of the *Rambler*, Richard Sampson, but its ideas, particularly the advocacy of an individuality which Buckle was criticized for neglecting, were approved by Acton); John Emerich Edward Dalberg-Acton, First Baron Acton, *Lectures on Modern History*, ed. John Neville Figgis and Reginald Vere Laurence (London, 1930), pp. 7, 15–18.

107. Acton, *Lectures on Modern History*, pp. 8–12.

108. Ibid., p. 13.

109. Ibid., p. 12.

110. Acton, quoted in Gertrude Himmelfarb, *Lord Acton: A Study in Conscience and Politics* (Chicago, 1962), p. 132; see also pp. 144–69; Acton, *Essays in the Liberal Interpretation of History*, pp. xiv–xvi; Acton, *Lectures on Modern History*, p. 12.

111. Himmelfarb, *Acton*, pp. 168–74.

112. John Lothrop Motley, *The Rise of the Dutch Republic* (London, 1896), 1:7–13, liv.

113. John Lothrop Motley, *Democracy, The Climax of Political Progress and the Destiny of Advanced Races: An Historical Essay* (London, 1869), p. 6.

114. Ibid., p. 5.

115. Motley, *Rise of the Dutch Republic*, 1:lv.

116. On Prescott, see William H. Prescott, *The History of the Conquest of Mexico*, ed. C. Harvey Gardiner (Chicago, 1966), pp. xvi–xxiv, and George Bancroft, *The History of the United States of America from the Discovery of the Continent*, ed. Russel B. Nye (Chicago, 1966), p. x.

117. Bancroft, *History of the United States*, p. xiv. Bancroft's emphasis.

118. Ibid., pp. 3, 6.

119. Ibid., p. 5.

120. Ibid., p. xv.

121. Ranke, *Geschichten der romanischen und germanischen Völker von 1494–1514*, in *Fürsten und Völker*, ed. Willy Andreas (Wiesbaden, 1957): 4; Ranke, *Preussische Geschichte*, ed. Willy Andreas (Wiesbaden, 1957), 1:51; Fustel de Coulanges, quoted in Fritz Stern, ed. and trans., *The Varieties of History* (New York, 1973), pp. 179, 188, 190.

122. Niebuhr quoted in Stern, *Varieties of History*, pp. 48–49.

123. Leopold Ranke to Heinrich Ranke, March 1820, in *Das Briefwerk*, ed. Walther Peter Fuchs (Hamburg, 1949), p. 18; Ranke, *Aus Werk und Nachlass*, vol. 4, *Vorlesungseinleitungen* (Munich, 1975), pp. 124, 127; Krieger, *Ranke*, p. 20.

124. G. P. Gooch, *History and Historians in the Nineteenth Century,* new ed. (Boston, 1959), p. 202; Trygve R. Tholfsen, *Historical Thinking: An Introduction* (New York, 1967), pp. 187, 193–94, 197–210; Stern, *Varieties of History,* p. 185; Numa Denis Fustel de Coulanges, *The Ancient City: A Study of the Religion, Laws, and Institutions of Greece and Rome* (Garden City, N.Y., n.d.), p. 94.

125. Krieger, *Ranke,* p. 137.

126. Ibid., p. 361.

127. Jacob Burckhardt, *Force and Freedom: Reflections on History,* ed. James Hastings Nichols (Boston, 1964), pp. 53, 82, emphasis in original; Karl J. Weintraub, *Visions of Culture: Voltaire, Guizot, Burckhardt, Lamprecht, Huizinga, Ortega y Gasset* (Chicago, 1966), p. 166.

128. Burckhardt, *Force and Freedom,* pp. 83–85, 94, 97; Wientraub, *Visions of Culture,* pp. 123–24.

129. Fustel de Coulanges, *The Ancient City,* pp. 13–14; Fustel de Coulanges, *Histoire des Institutions Politiques de L'ancienne France* (Paris, 1889–91), 1:xii–xiii; 2:xi–xii; 3:2; 4:iv–v; Tholfsen, *Historical Thinking,* pp. 197–210.

130. It should be pointed out that at least in the cases of Ranke and Burckhardt, appreciation has been much greater in a synthetically minded posterity than in their empirically minded contemporaneity, and even in the instance of Fustel contemporary respect was for his scientific treatment of the facts rather than for his insistence upon unspecialized coherence.

131. Krieger, *Ranke,* pp. 233–43.

132. Ibid., pp. 25, 69–75.

133. Ibid., p. 132.

134. Ibid., pp. 291–92.

135. Ibid., pp. 291, 335.

136. Ibid., pp. 13, 20, 273–342.

137. Burckhardt, *Force and Freedom,* pp. 168–69; Weintraub, *Visions of Culture,* p. 151.

138. Weintraub, *Visions of Culture,* p. 153; Burckhardt, *Force and Freedom,* pp. 85, 87, 153, 163–64. Emphasis in the original.

139. L. de Gérin-Ricard, *L'Histoire des Institutions Politiques de Fustel de Coulanges* (Paris, 1936), p. 8; Tholfsen, *Historical Thinking,* pp. 207, 209; Stern, *Varieties of History,* p. 186.

140. For this identification and association, see especially Fustel's protestations linking his notion of history as an impartial and textual "science" with his theses of the constructive Roman impact and the negligible Germanic impact on Gallic society and government, in Fustel de Coulanges, *Histoire des Institutions Politiques,* 1:xii–iii, 324–29; 2:560, 3:ii, 651; 4:462–63. For the inaugural lecture in which Fustel de Coulanges confessed his notion that man was a distinctive being whose "laws, institutions, art, and science . . . are in flux" and who himself "cannot remain immutable," see the published translation of the lecture in Stern, *Varieties of History,* pp. 179–80. For the article against the

German historians, see Gooch, *History and Historians in the Nineteenth Century*, p. 203.

Chapter Four

1. Popper's definition of historicism differed from the nominalist one used here precisely in its countervailing attribution of a generalizing method and an essential identity behind the historical changes it registered (Popper himself distinguished his "historicism" from the historism which was close to its opposite), but the common elements in the two meanings should not be overlooked either: both in Popper's usage and in its putative relativized opposite, extrahistorical reality was itself historicized, thus lending history its coherence out of the pattern behind its own principles of change. For Popper's view, see Karl R. Popper, *The Poverty of Historicism* (New York, 1961), pp. 7–34. For the many meanings of historicism, see Dwight E. Lee and Robert N. Beck, "The Meaning of 'Historicism'," *American Historical Review* 59 (1953–54): 568–77; for the term itself, see George G. Iggers, "Historicism," in *Dictionary of the History of Ideas* (New York, 1973), 2:456–68. It should be noted, however, that the anachronistic application of the term "historicism" to the relativistic thinking of pre–World War I, as embodied in the writing of Dilthey, Croce, and Max Weber, is followed in this chapter on the model of Maurice Mandelbaum, *The Problem of Historical Knowledge,* new ed. (New York, 1967), pp. 88–93, and of Carlo Antoni's Italian title, *Dallo Storismo alla Sociologia* (Florence, 1940), rather than Igger's essay, which distinguishes between relativism and historicism in the prewar period and rejects the latter appellation for it. See Iggers, "Historicism," p. 461.

2. Benedetto Croce, *Teoria e storia della storiografia* (Bari, 1963), pp. 4, 16; *History as the Story of Liberty,* trans. Sylvia Sprigge (New York, 1941), p. 34.

3. Croce, *Teoria,* pp. 6–7, 14–15; *History,* pp. 23, 35, 163.

4. Croce, *My Philosophy and Other Essays on the Moral and Political Problems of Our Time,* trans. E. F. Carritt (London, 1949), pp. 228, 230.

5. Croce, *Teoria,* pp. 52–53; *History,* pp. 32–35, *My Philosophy,* pp. 222, 231. It should be noted that although Croce defined history, as contrasted with chronicle, by its vitality and present-mindedness rather than by "connectedness" as such, he did say that those who defined it by the latter quality had "a right idea" (*un giusto sentimento*). *Teoria,* p. 10.

6. Croce, *My Philosophy,* p. 176.

7. Croce, *History,* pp. 17, 21.

8. Croce, *Teoria,* pp. 43–72.

9. Ibid., pp. 51–52.

10. Croce, *History,* p. 90.

11. Ibid., p. 78.

12. Ibid., p. 90.

13. Croce, *My Philosophy,* p. 225.

14. R. G. Collingwood, *The Idea of History,* ed. T. M. Knox (New York, 1956), p. xix.

15. Ibid., pp. 176–77.

16. Ibid., p. 231.

17. Ibid., pp. 248–49.

18. Ibid., pp. 287, 303.

19. Ibid., p. 231.

20. Wilhelm Dilthey, *Gesammelte Schriften*, 4th ed. (Stuttgart, 1964), 5:9–10. For Dilthey's starting point in his deep conviction about the current separation of thought from life and theory from practice, see Michael Ermarth, *Wilhelm Dilthey: The Critique of Historical Reason* (Chicago, 1978), pp. 16–17.

21. Hajo Holborn, "Wilhelm Dilthey and the Critique of Historical Reason," in *History and the Humanities* (Garden City, 1972), pp. 132–33; Wilhelm Dilthey, *Pattern and Meaning in History*, ed. H. P. Rickman (New York, 1962), pp. 23–33.

22. The expression, beamed at Dilthey, was Rudolf Haym's. See Ermarth, *Dilthey*, pp. 66–67.

23. Ibid., p. 345.

24. Dilthey, *Schriften*, 5:139, 241, 317, 303–31, 414.

25. Ibid., 5:330, 343–45, 415–16; Holborn, *History and the Humanities*, pp. 147, 152.

26. Ermarth, *Dilthey*, pp. 348–49.

27. Ibid., pp. 15, 22.

28. Heinrich Rickert, *Kulturwissenschaft und Naturwissenschaft*, 4th and 5th ed. (Tübingen, 1921), pp. 13–30.

29. Rickert, *Die Grenzen der naturwissenschaftlichen Begriffsbildung* (Tübingen and Leipzig, 1902), pp. 315–16, 570–99.

30. Rickert, *Die Probleme der Geschichtsphilosophie: Eine Einführung*, 3d ed. (Heidelberg, 1924), pp. 146–56.

31. Carlo Antoni, *From History to Sociology: The Transition in German Historical Thinking*, trans. Hayden V. White (Detroit, 1969), pp. 17–23.

32. Ernst Troeltsch, *Der Historismus und seine Überwindung: Fünf Vorträge*, with an introduction by Friedrich von Hugel (Darmstadt, 1966), pp. 1–2.

33. Troeltsch, *Gesammelte Schriften*, vol. 3, *Der Historismus und seine Probleme* (Tübingen, 1961), p. 772.

34. Troeltsch, *Der Historismus und seine Probleme*, pp. 1, 7.

35. Ibid., viii.

36. Ibid., 8–9.

37. Walther Hofer, *Geschichtsschreibung und Weltanschauung: Betrachtungen zum Werk Friedrich Meineckes* (Munich, 1950), pp. 333–34.

38. Troeltsch, *Der Historismus und seine Probleme*, pp. 111–12, 198–99.

39. Troeltsch, *Historismus und seine Überwindung*, pp. 3–4.

40. Troeltsch, *Schriften*, 3:109–13.

41. Ibid., 3:116–18.

42. Karl Heussi, *Die Krisis des Historismus* (Tübingen, 1932).

43. Heussi wrote a doctoral dissertation at Leipzig and crowned his career with a professorial chair at Jena in the faculty of theology with a specialty in church history. In addition to the usual manuals and atlases for the teaching of church history, Heussi specialized in the origins of monasticism and in the great names in church history such as Augustine, Meister Eckhart, and Johann Mosheim. See also ibid., pp. 6–38.

44. Ibid., pp. 56–91.

45. Ortega y Gasset's *Meditaciones del Quijote.*

46. Ortega y Gasset, "History as a System," in *Toward a Philosophy of History* (New York, 1941), pp. 212–13, 216, 217. Emphasis in the original.

47. Ibid., pp. 224–26, 231.

48. Ortega y Gasset, *An Interpretation of Universal History,* trans. Mildred Adams (New York, 1973), pp. 298–301.

49. Oswald Spengler, *The Decline of the West* (New York, 1939), 1:5–6, 8–15.

50. Ibid., 1:7–8; H. Stuart Hughes, *Oswald Spengler: A Critical Estimate* (New York, 1962), p. 7. Emphasis in the original.

51. Spengler, *Decline of the West,* 1:5. Emphasis in the original.

52. On the dubiety of the early Simmel's definition of historicism, see Karl Heussi, *Die Krisis des Historismus,* pp. 4–5; on the tendency of historicism to develop into a more stable sociology, see the study by Carlo Antoni, *From History to Sociology,* which contains essays on Max Weber, Wilhelm Dilthey, and Ernst Troeltsch. His main point—the unremitting search by historicists for stable relationships within the historical world—is applicable to the whole school.

53. Rudolph H. Weingartner, "Georg Simmel," *The Encyclopedia of Philosophy* (New York, 1967), 7:442–43; Michael Landmann's introduction to Georg Simmel, *Brücke und Tür: Essays des Philosophen zur Geschichte, Religion, Kunst und Gesellschaft,* ed. Margaret Susman and Michael Landmann (Stuttgart, 1957), pp. ix–xi.

54. Georg Simmel, *The Problems of the Philosophy of History: An Epistemological Essay,* ed. and trans. Guy Oakes (New York, 1977), pp. viii, 176. "It is necessary to emancipate the self from historicism in the same way that Kant freed it from naturalism" (pp. viii–ix, from the preface to the second edition [1905]).

55. Quoted by Landmann, in Simmel, *Brücke und Tür,* p. ix.

56. Simmel, *Problems of the Philosophy of History,* p. 42.

57. Simmel, "Das Problem der historischen Zeit" (1922) and "Vom Wesen des historischen Verstehens" (1918), in *Brücke und Tür,* pp. 52–60.

58. Mandelbaum, *The Problem of Historical Knowledge,* pp. 101–19.

59. Simmel, "Vom Wesen des historischen Verstehens," pp. 76–85.

60. Simmel, *Problems of the Philosophy of History,* pp. 200–202.

61. Simmel, *The Philosophy of Money,* trans. Tom Bottomore and David Frisby (Boston, 1978), pp. 7, 55, 168–72.

62. Ibid., pp. 168–75, 204–17, 446–70.

63. Ibid., p. 172.

64. *The Sociology of Georg Simmel,* ed. and trans. Kurt H. Wolff (Glencoe, Ill., 1950), pp. 3–13.

65. Ibid., pp. 16–84.

66. Ibid., p. 8. Emphasis in the original.

67. Simmel, "Der Begriff und die Tragödie der Kultur," in Georg Simmel *Philosophische Kultur: Gesammelte Essays,* 3d ed. (Potsdam, 1923), pp. 236–40.

68. Simmel, "Vom Wesen der Kultur," in *Brücke und Tür,* pp. 91–94, "Die Zukunft unserer Kultur," in ibid., pp. 95–97; "Der Begriff und die Tragödie der Kultur," in *Philosophische Kultur,* pp. 242–56, 263–67.

69. Wolfgang J. Mommsen, *The Age of Bureaucracy: Perspectives on the Political Sociology of Max Weber* (Oxford, 1974), pp. 1–5.

70. Ibid., pp. 10–19.

71. Ibid., p. 12; Max Weber, *Gesammelte Aufsätze zur Wissenschaftslehre* (Tübingen, 1922), p. 267; Max Weber, *Wirtschaft und Gesellschaft* (Tübingen, 1922), p. 9.

72. Weber, *Wissenschaftslehre,* pp. 215–18, 268.

73. Ibid., pp. 276–78.

74. Ibid., pp. 275–77.

75. Max Weber, *Gesammelte Aufsätze zur Religionssoziologie* (Tübingen, 1920), 1:11–13, 536–37.

76. Ibid., 1:1–12.

77. Max Weber, "Ueber einige Kategorien der verstehenden Soziologie," in *Wissenschaftslehre,* p. 405.

78. Ibid., pp. 230, 404–5; *Wirtschaft und Gesellschaft,* p. 5.

79. Ibid., pp. 9–10. On Weber's development from the emphasis upon comparative history to one upon comparative sociology, note his later subsumption of the *Protestant Ethic,* written at an earlier time as part of a comparative history, under the rubic, "the sociology of religion" (*Religionssoziologie,* passim).

80. Weber, *Wirtschaft und Gesellschaft,* p. 10.

81. Weber, *Gesammelte Aufsätze zur Wissenschaftslehre,* p. 415; *From Max Weber: Essays in Sociology,* ed. and trans. H. H. Gerth and C. Wright Mills (New York, 1946), pp. 55, 147.

82. Ibid., pp. 51, 247–48; *Gesammelte Aufsätze zur Religionssoziologie,* 1:11.

83. Weber, "Politics as a Vocation" in *From Max Weber,* pp. 120–21, 125–28.

84. Wolfgang J. Mommsen, *The Age of Bureaucracy: Perspectives on the Political Sociology of Max Weber* (Oxford, 1974), pp. xiii–xiv, 82–83, 96.

85. Weber, *Wirtschaft und Gesellschaft,* pp. 9–11; *Basic Concepts in Sociology,* trans., H. P. Secher (New York, 1963), p. 54.

86. Weber, *Wirtschaft und Gesellschaft,* p. 12.

87. Emile Durkheim, *The Rules of Sociological Method,* ed. George E. G.

Catlin, trans. Sara A. Solovay and John H. Mueller (New York, 1964), pp. 15–17.

88. Ibid., pp. 101–12, 129–40.

89. Robert N. Bellah, "Durkheim and History," in Robert A. Nisbet, ed., *Emile Durkheim* (Englewood Cliffs, N.J., 1965), pp. 154–62; Steven Lukes, *Emile Durkheim: His Life and Work* (New York, 1972), pp. 58–65.

90. Lukes, *Durkheim*, pp. 61–62.

91. Quoted in Bellah, "Durkheim and History," p. 158.

92. Claude Lévi-Strauss, *Structural Anthropology,* trans. Monique Layton (New York, 1976), 2:5–9, 24–25, 44–48.

93. Durkheim, *The Elementary Forms of Religious Life,* trans. Joseph Ward Swain (New York, 1965), p. 465.

94. Quoted in Bellah, "Durkheim and History," p. 176.

95. Mandelbaum, *The Problem of Historical Knowledge,* p. 67; Karl Mannheim, *Ideology and Utopia: An Introduction to the Sociology of Knowledge,* trans. Louis Wirth and Edward Shils (New York, n.d.), pp. 70–71.

96. Mannheim, "Historicism," *Archiv für Sozialwissenschaft und Sozialpolitik,* 52 (1924): 1–6, 58–60.

97. Mannheim, *Man and Society in an Age of Reconstruction; Studies in Modern Social Structure,* trans. Edward Shils (New York, 1940), p. 177; *Ideology and Utopia,* pp. 247–50.

98. Mannheim, *Man and Society,* p. 178.

99. Mannheim, *Ideology and Utopia,* pp. 82–83, 95–96, 22–36; *Man and Society,* pp. 178–90.

100. Thus for Lukács: Georg Lukács, *History and Class Consciousness: Studies in Marxist Dialectics,* trans. Rodney Livingstone (Cambridge, Mass., 1971), pp. 70–73. For Horkheimer: Max Horkheimer, *Critical Theory: Selected Essays,* trans. Matthew J. O'Connell and others (New York, 1972), pp. v–ix. For Marcuse: Herbert Marcuse, *Soviet-Marxism: A Critical Analysis* (New York, 1951), pp. 4, 19–20.

101. Marcuse, *One-Dimensional Man,* (Boston, 1964), pp. 11, 15, 18, 123, 158–60, 226–27.

102. Ibid., p. 142.

103. Walter Benjamin, *Illuminations,* ed. Hannah Arendt, trans. Harry Zohn (New York, 1969), pp. 255–63.

104. Theodor W. Adorno, *Negative Dialectics,* trans. E. B. Ashton (New York, 1973), pp. 317–20, 358–59.

105. Susan Buck-Morse, *The Origin of Negative Dialectics: Theodor W. Adorno, Walter Benjamin, and the Frankfurt Institute* (Hassocks, England, 1977), pp. xii–xiii, 46, 50–51.

106. Oscar Handlin makes this point in his *Truth in History* (Cambridge, Mass., 1979), p. 407.

Chapter Five

1. Carl G. Hempel, "Explanation in Science and History," in *Philosophical Analysis and History,* ed. William H. Dray (New York, 1966), pp. 123–24.

2. Karl R. Popper, *The Poverty of Historicism* (New York, 1961), pp. 62–64, 98, 130–31, 143–45.

3. William Dray, *Laws and Explanations in History* (Oxford, 1957), pp. 123–26.

4. For this alternative, see Patrick Gardiner, *The Nature of Historical Explanation* (Oxford, 1952), pp. 123–37; Morton G. White, *Foundations of Historical Knowledge* (New York, 1965), pp. 182–218; Robert F. Berkhofer, Jr., *A Behavioral Approach to Historical Analysis* (New York, 1969), pp. 51–59.

5. Arthur D. Danto, *Analytical Philosophy of History* (Cambridge, 1968), pp. 233–66.

6. Meinecke himself referred to his article of 1925 on "Causality and Values" as his theory of history. Until then, he had devoted himself to the writing of concrete history. Hans Herzfeld, "Friedrich Meinecke: Der Geschichts-Denker," in *Historische Theorie und Geschichtsforschung der Gegenwart* (Berlin, 1964), pp. 99–101.

7. Meinecke, *Die Entstehung des Historismus* (Munich, 1936), 1:2. The famed Dutch historian, Johan Huizinga, was also a part of that illustrious generation whose historical thinking is essentially of interwar vintage, and his example might very well have served to introduce that of Meinecke's. Although he insisted upon the mediating position of the Netherlandish culture in Europe and his own historical work tended to be pan-European in scope, his historical thought classified him as a historicist on the German model, and although he was less explicit on this score than Friedrich Meinecke, he represented the same kind of antinaturalistic immersion in the individual and the same kind of dissatisfaction with this immersion as did the bulk of the German or Germanic historicists. For Huizinga emphasized the variability and the plurality of all cultural history in particular and of history in general. "Its [cultural history's] task is to determine a morphology of the particular, before it can make bold to consider the general," he wrote categorically. "Let us, for the time being, be pluralists above all." Johan Huizinga, *Men and Ideas: History, the Middle Ages, the Renaissance,* trans. James S. Holmes and Hans van Marle (New York, 1959), pp. 58, 64. See also Carlo Antoni, *From History to Sociology,* pp. 204–6. But since he assigned an active role to the historian, bestowing on him the function of eliciting the forms and the structure of phenomena, he was never entirely happy with the individualizing results of the historian's endeavor, and even in his masterpiece, *The Waning of the Middle Ages,* he took on the task of seeking out "the common feature of the various manifestations of civilization of that epoch." Huizinga, *The Waning of the Middle Ages: A Study of the Forms of Life, Thought, and Art in France and the Netherlands in the XIVth and XVth Centuries* (London, 1924), p. 6. Since by definition he could hardly find the stability he sought within history, he tended as he grew older to find it outside history. The *Homo Ludens* which he wrote as a speech in 1933 and as a book in 1938 was a disquisition on the idea of play behind all of human culture and fully confirms the verdict of his commentator that "Huizinga betrays his metahistorical interests by the choice of his subject matter and the increasing

emphasis on social interrelations." Huizinga, *Homo Ludens: A Study of the Play-Element in Culture* (Boston, 1955), esp. pp. 1–27; Bert F. Hoselitz, Introduction, in Huizinga, *Men and Ideas*, p. 11. If we note in addition that he turned to constant relationships beyond history then we have the telling story of Johan Huizinga.

8. Hofer, *Geschichtsschreibung und Weltanschauung*, pp. 7–13. In Meinecke's own terms, his position "indeed makes no metaphysical assumptions, but is pressed to meta-physical consequences." Meinecke, *Staat und Persönlichkeit: Studien* (Berlin, 1933), p. 62.

9. Meinecke, *Die Entstehung des Historismus*, esp. 1:5; "Allgemeines über Historismus und Aufklärungshistorie," in Friedrich Meinecke, *"Aphorismen und Skizzen zur Geschichte* (Leipzig, 1942), pp. 11–18.

10. Meinecke, *Machiavellism: The Doctrine of Raison d'Etat and Its Place in Modern History*, trans. Douglas Scott (New York, 1965), pp. 6–12.

11. Meinecke to H. Ritter von Srbik, January 18, 1951, and Meinecke to Kähler, July 11, 1941, in Friedrich Meinecke, *Ausgewählter Briefwechsel*, eds. Ludwig Dehio and Peter Classen (Stuttgart, 1962), pp. 307, 377.

12. "Ein Wort über geschichtliche Entwicklung," in Meinecke, *Aphorismen und Skizzen zur Geschichte*, p. 96.

13. Ibid., pp. 102–9.

14. This is the argument of Meinecke's most sophisticated commentator to date, Hofer, *Geschichtsschreibung und Weltanschauung*, pp. 471–74, 519–39.

15. Meinecke, "Ranke and Burckhardt," in Hans Kohn, ed., *German History: Some New German Views*, trans. Herbert H. Rowen (Boston, 1954), pp. 145, 154; Meinecke to L. Dehio, July 21, 1947, and Meinecke to Kähler, April 16, 1947, in *Ausgewählter Briefwechsel*, p. 282, 514.

16. His afterthoughts are post–World War II. But *A Study of History*, the real basis of his fame, goes back for its inspiration to the period immediately following the First World War. The first six volumes were published by 1939, the next four, which ended the main body of the work, in the years following hard on the end of World War II, from 1946 to 1954, and the final two volumes of reconsiderations by 1961.

17. Arnold J. Toynbee, *A Study of History* (New York, 1961), 12:16, 562.

18. Ibid., 9 (1954): 173–216; 12:22–68.

19. Ibid., 1:1–16, 147–62.

20. Ibid., 12:259–68, 563–68; Pieter Geyl, *Debates with Historians* (New York, 1958), pp. 114–15, 129, 165–80; Gerhard Masur, *Geschehen und Geschichte: Aufsätze und Vorträge zur europäischen Geistesgeschichte* (Berlin, 1971), pp. 182–85.

21. Toynbee, *A Study of History*, 9:168–73.

22. Ibid., 1:172–74; *Civilization on Trial* (New York, 1948), p. 8; *Change and Habit: The Challenge of Our Time* (New York, 1966), p. 10.

23. Toynbee, *A Study of History*, 1:43–44, 50.

24. Ibid., 12:40–47.

25. James Harvey Robinson, *The New History: Essays Illustrating the Modern Historical Outlook,* new ed. (New York, 1965), pp. 15, 24, 48–100.

26. Carl L. Becker, *Everyman His Own Historian: Essays on History and Politics* (New York, 1935), p. 251.

27. Morton G. White, *Social Thought in America: The Revolt against Formalism* (New York, 1949), pp. 22–35; Cushing Strout, *The Pragmatic Revolt in American History: Carl Becker and Charles Beard* (New Haven, 1958), pp. 50–61.

28. Karl Weintraub, *Visions of Culture* (Chicago, 1966), pp. 162–77.

29. Henri Berr, "About Our Program," in *The Varieties of History,* ed. Fritz Stern, trans. Deborah H. Roberts, new ed. (New York, 1973), pp. 250–55; H. Stuart Hughes, *The Obstructed Path: French Social Thought in the Years of Desperation. 1930–1960* (New York, 1968), pp. 26–27.

30. Berr, *La Synthèse en Histoire: son Rapport avec la Synthèse générale,* new ed. (Paris, 1953), pp. 5–23. Emphasis in the original.

31. Ibid., pp. 15–42, 138–401.

32. Ibid., pp. 30–32, 48–53, 63–68, 109–11, 113–14, 151–52, 168–75.

33. Ibid., pp. 138–44, 226–27, 250–51.

34. Berr, "Au Bout de Trente Ans," *Revue de Synthèse* 1 (1931): 3–5.

35. Fernand Braudel, "Personal Testimony," *Journal of Modern History* 44 (1972): 461.

36. Ibid., p. 463.

37. Lucien Febvre, *Combats pour l'histoire* (Paris, 1953), pp. v, 12–13, 17–18, 31.

38. Georg G. Iggers, *New Directions in European Historiography* (Middletown, 1971), pp. 73–77.

39. Marc Bloch, *Feudal Society,* trans. L. A. Manyom (Chicago, 1961), pp. xvii, xx.

40. Henri Berr and Lucien Febvre, "History," in *Encyclopedia of the Social Sciences* (New York, 1932), 7:361; Bloch, *The Historian's Craft* (New York, 1953), p. 135; *Annales d'histoire économique et sociale* 1 (1929): 1–2.

41. Febvre, *Combats pour l'histoire,* pp. 24, 30–33, 55–60.

42. Lucien Febvre, *A New Kind of History,* ed. Peter Burke (New York, 1973), p. 42; *Encyclopedia of Social Sciences,* 7:361–62, 365; Bloch, *The Historian's Craft,* p. 188.

43. Febvre, *Combats pour l'histoire,* pp. 12–15, 20–25, 30, 117, 224.

44. Bloch, *The Historian's Craft,* p. 10.

45. Febvre, *Encyclopedia of Social Sciences,* p. 361. Emphasis in the original.

46. Bloch, *Les caractères originaux d l'histoire rurale française,* new ed. (Paris, 1960), pp. ix–x, xiv.

47. Febvre, *Combats pour l'histoire,* pp. 14, 32–33, 282, 291–94, 300–301, 313.

48. See below, pp. 158–60.

49. Fernand Braudel, *Ecrits sur l'histoire* (Paris, 1969), p. 103. "With them . . . history was seized with all the sciences of the human."

50. Palmer A. Throop, "Lucien Febvre: 1878–1956," in S. William Halperin, ed., *Some Twentieth-Century Historians: Essays on Eminent Europeans* (Chicago, 1961), pp. 280–97.

51. For the current use of the term "new history" by academic radicals, see the analyses in Jean Glenisson, "France," in George G. Iggers and Harold T. Parker, eds., *International Handbook of Historical Studies: Contemporary Research and Theory* (Westport, Conn., 1979), pp. 178–79, and Jacques Le Goff and Pierre Nora, eds., *Faire de l'histoire*, 3 vols. (Paris, 1974), 1:x–xiii. See also the primer *Historians and the Living Past: The Theory and Practice of Historical Study,* by Allan J. Lichtman and Valerie French (Arlington Heights, Ill., 1978), pp. 122–24.

52. For an example of the European convergence, see E. J. Hobsbawm, "From Social History to the History of Society," *Daedalus* 100 (1971): 20–43, where the dating of social history only from the decade of the 1950s obviously has to do with Hobsbawm's convergence of academic and social radicalism.

53. *History as Social Science,* ed. David S. Landes and Charles Tilly (Englewood Cliffs, N.J., 1971), p. 9.

54. *The Dimensions of Quantitative Research in History,* ed. William O. Aydelotte, Allan G. Bogue, and Robert William Fogel (Princeton, 1972), p. 7.

55. Lee Benson, *Toward the Scientific Study of History: Selected Essays* (New York, 1972), pp. 2–8, 196–201, 255–58, 312–26.

56. E.g, Robert F. Berkhofer, Jr., *A Behavioral Approach to Historical Analysis* (New York, 1971), pp. 271–73.

57. Hans-Ulrich Wehler, "Vorüberlegungen zu einer modernen Gesellschaftsgeschichte," in *Industrielle Gesellschaft und politisches System* (Bonn, 1978), pp. 304, 10–20.

58. Bruce Mazlish, in *Psychoanalysis and History,* ed. Bruce Mazlish, rev. ed. (New York, 1971), pp. 2–3.

59. Hans-Ulrich Wehler, "Geschichtswissenschaft und Psychohistorie," *Innsbrucker Historische Studien* 1 (1978): 203–5, 212.

60. Ibid., 1:212–13.

61. Roland Barthes, *Essais critiques* (Paris, n.d.), pp. 10–11; Hans Robert Jauss, "Geschichte der Kunst und Historie," in Koselleck and Stempel, eds., *Geschichte: Ereignis und Erzählung* (Munich, 1973), pp. 199–203.

62. Roland Barthes, ed., *Michelet par lui-même* (Paris, n.d.); "Historical Discourse," in Michael Lane, ed. *Introduction to Structuralism* (New York, 1970), pp. 145–55.

63. Claude Lévi-Strauss, *Structural Anthropology,* trans. Claire Jacobsen and Brooke Grundfest Schoepf (New York, 1963), pp. 1–25.

64. Claude Lévi-Strauss, *The Savage Mind* (Chicago, 1966), pp. 245–69, esp. 263. This is an English translation of *La Pensée sauvage,* originally published in 1962. See also Jean Piaget, *Structuralism,* ed. and trans. Chaninah

Maschler (New York, 1970), pp. 108, 122, and Marc Gaboriau, "Structural Anthropology and History," in Lane, ed., *Introduction to Structuralism*, pp. 156–69.

65. Gaboriau, "Structural Anthropology and History," pp. 261–62.

66. Claude Lévi-Strauss, *Structural Anthropology*, trans. Monique Layton (New York, 1976), 2:12–15.

67. Ibid., p. 16.

68. Ibid., p. 276.

69. Ibid., pp. 17–18. The second condition which Lévi-Strauss specified as definitive of structures—the "transformations through which similar properties are recognized in apparently different systems"—is not relevant to this discussion.

70. Ibid., p. 16; Fernand Braudel, "History and the Social Sciences," in Peter Burke, ed., *Economy and Society in Early Modern Europe* (New York, 1972), pp. 27, 31, 33–34, 38. This article is a translation of Fernand Braudel, "Histoire et sciences sociales: 'La longue durée'," *Annales: Economies, Société, Civilisations* 13 (1958): 725–53.

71. Although he does not account for himself, Braudel himself has formally confirmed the existence of distinctive periods in the history of the *Annales*. Fernand Braudel, *The Mediterranean and the Mediterranean World in the Age of Philip II*, trans. Sian Reynolds (New York, 1972), 1:15.

72. Ibid., 1:15.

73. Ibid., 1:20–21.

74. Ibid., 1:14.

75. Braudel, *Ecrits sur l'histoire*, pp. 86–94, 115–21.

76. Braudel, "History and the Social Sciences," in Peter Burke, ed., *Economy and Society in Early Modern Europe: Essays from Annales* (New York, 1972), p. 25. The article was originally published in 1958. See, too, in this regard Braudel's *Civilization and Capitalism* series, in three volumes, and make no mistake: I consider Braudel a twentieth-century historian of the first rank.

77. For a discussion of *histoire totale* in Braudel, see J. H. Hexter, "Fernand Braudel and the *Monde Braudellien*," *Journal of Modern History* 44 (1972): 511.

78. Ibid., 44:498–510; Braudel, "History and the Social Sciences," pp. 16–18.

79. Braudel, *Ecrits sur l'histoire*, pp. 103–14.

80. Braudel, "History and the Social Sciences," p. 17.

81. Braudel, *The Mediterranean*, 2:1244.

82. Ibid., 2:1239–42, quoted in Hexter, "Braudel," p. 504.

83. Lucien Febvre, *Pour une histoire à part entière* (Paris, 1962).

84. Braudel, "Pour une histoire sérielle: Seville et l'Atlantique (1504–1650)," in Braudel, *Ecrits sur l'histoire*, pp. 135–61.

85. Lawrence Stone, "History and the Social Sciences in the Twentieth Century," in Charles F. Delzell, ed., *The Future of History* (Nashville, 1977),

pp. 7–10, 12, 29, 38; René Wellek, "The Fall of Literary History," in Reinhart Koselleck and Wolf-Dieter Stempel, eds., *Geschichte—Ereignis und Erzählung* (Munich, 1973), pp. 428, 439–40.

86. Jacques Le Goff and Pierre Nora, *Faire de l'histoire*, 1:xiii; Michel de Certeau, *L'écriture de l'histoire* (Paris, 1975), pp. 9–23; Bernard-Henri Lévy, *La barbarie à visage humain* (Paris, 1977), pp. 61–73, English translation, *Barbarism with a Human Face,* trans. George Holoch (New York, 1979), pp. 44–54; Glenisson, "France," in Iggers and Parker, eds., *International Handbook,* pp. 178–90.

87. Levy, *Barbarism,* p. 54.

88. E.g., on the distance from Febvre, see Certeau, *L'écriture de l'histoire,* pp. 18–19.

89. Emmanuel Le Roy Ladurie, *The Territory of the Historian,* trans. Ben and Sian Reynolds (Chicago, 1979), p. 18.

90. Ibid.. In this regard, see as well François Furet's fine essay, "Beyond the *Annales,*" *Journal of Modern History* 55, no. 3 (September 1983): 389–410, esp. 409–10.

91. Ibid., pp. viii, 7, 282.

92. Pierre Chaunu, *Histoire quantitative ou histoire sérielle* (Geneva, 1968); François Furet, "Quantitative History," in *Historical Studies Today,* eds. Felix Gilbert and Stephen R. Graubard (New York, 1972), pp. 47–48.

93. On Foucault, see especially Allan Megill, "Foucault, Structuralism and the Ends of History," *Journal of Modern History* 51 (1979): 452–503; Mark Poster, "Foucault's True Discourse," *Humanities in Society* 2 (1979): 155–56, with particular reference to Foucault's recent *The History of Sexuality,* trans. Robert Burty, vol. 1 (New York, 1978), and Hayden V. White, "Foucault Decoded: Notes from Underground," *History and Theory* 12 (1973); 24, 27–28, 45, 49, or Foucault's own theoretical writings, in *The Order of Things: An Archaeology of Human Science,* pp. xiv, xxii–xxiii, and *The Archaeology of Knowledge,* trans. A. M. Sheridan Smith (New York, 1972), pp. 15–17.

94. For my position on Foucault's interpretation here, see my *An Essay on the Theory of Enlightened Despotism* (Chicago, 1975), p. 55.

95. Foucault, *The Order of Things,* p. 7; *Madness and Civilization: A History of Insanity in the Age of Reason,* trans. Richard Howard (New York, 1965); *The Birth of the Clinic: An Archaeology of Medical Perception,* trans. A. M. Sheridan Smith (New York, 1975); *Discipline and Punish: Birth of the Prison,* trans., A. M. Sheridan Smith (New York, 1975); *The History of Sexuality.*

96. See Allan Megill's *Prophets of Extremity: Nietzsche, Heidegger, Foucault, Derrida* (Berkeley, 1985) for an illuminating discussion of Foucault, although I must add that his thesis seems to hold truest for Derrida. These four thinkers are not all of world-historical significance.

97. Foucault, *The Archaeology of Knowledge,* pp. 29–31, 203.

98. Foucault, *Birth of the Clinic,* pp. 25–26, 29–30, 51, 88–122.

99. Foucault, *Madness and Civilization,* pp. 243–69.

Epilogue

1. H. Stuart Hughes, *History as Art and as Science: Vistas on the Past* (New York, 1964), pp. 68–71; Jacques Barzun, *Clio and the Doctors: History, Psycho-history, Quanto-History* (Chicago, 1974), pp. 151–58.

2. Hayden White, *Metahistory: The Historical Imagination in Nineteenth-Century Europe* (Baltimore, 1973), pp. 1–2, 7–21, 426–29; Martin Duberman, *The Uncompleted Past* (New York, 1971), pp. 42–59, 335–56.

3. E.g., Barzun, *Clio and the Doctors*, pp. 92–95; Oscar Handlin, *Truth in History* (Cambridge, Mass., 1971), pp. 408–10.

4. E.g., J. H. Hexter, *Reappraisals of History: New Views in History and Society in Early Modern Europe* (New York, 1961); J. H. Plumb, *Death of the Past* (Boston, 1970); Geoffrey Elton, *The Practice of History* (New York, 1967); Alfred Cobban, *The Social Interpretation of the French Revolution* (Cambridge, 1965).

5. Thus the rehabilitation of political history by the *Annaliste* Jacques Le Goff in his "Is Politics Still the Backbone of History?" *Daedalus* 100 (1971): 1–13. Obviously political, economic, and social histories are not the only kind of histories to have had their patterns internalized of late, for the arts as well as the social sciences have grown tendencies that are inimical or indifferent to history. Thus, whereas there used to be spokesmen for the application of structural linguistics to history, the historical indifference of the sociolinguists themselves has led to historians' stressing historical languages as the coherent context for the interpretation of past individuals. Hence historians have had themselves to historize their principles, and the radicals, whatever their faults, should not be criticized for forcing the traditionalist's hand in this regard. As this work shows, these considerations were overdue. For the hopeful application of structural linguistics to history, see Nancy S. Struever, "The Study of Language and the Study of History," *Journal of Interdisciplinary History* (1974); see J. G. A. Pocock, *Politics, Language, and Time* (New York, 1971), pp. 9–18.

6. Stone, "History and Social Science in the Twentieth-Century," p. 38; Iggers, *New Directions in European Historiography*, pp. 116–17.

7. Carl F. Schorske, "Dialogues," *Daedalus* 98 (1969): 930–32.

8. Reinhart Koselleck, "Geschichte, Geschichten, und formale Zietstrukturen," in Koselleck and Stempel, eds., *Geschichte*, p. 212; "Über die Theoriebedürftigkeit der Geschichtswissenschaft," in Werner Conze, ed., *Theorie der Geschichtswissenschaft und Praxis des Geschichtsunterrichts* (Stuttgart, 1972), pp. 13–17.

INDEX

Acton, Lord, 92–93
Adorno, Theodor W., 132, 133–34
Analytical philosophy, 139, 159
Annales: and Durkheim, 148; historical
continuity, 149; interdisciplinary
cooperation, 151; later generation of
Annalistes, 154–55, 159–60. *See also*
Bloch, Marc; Braudel, Fernand;
Chaunu, Pierre; Febvre, Lucien; Furet,
François; Le Roy Ladurie, Emmanuel
Antiquarianism, 18th century, 46–47
Augustine, Saint, 16, 17–18
Auto-rationality. *See* Rationality

Bacon, Francis, 29–30
Bancroft, George, 95–96
Bayle, Pierre, 46
Beard, Charles, 145
Becker, Carl, 145
Bede, The Venerable, 21–22, 23
Benjamin, Walter, 133
Benson, Lee, 194 n.55
Beri, Henri: nature and history, 147;
scientific history, 146; synthesis of
knowledge, 147–48
Bloch, Marc, 148, 149; "historical
synthesis," 150
Bodin, Jean, 25, 34–35
Bolingbroke, Henry St. John, 49
Braudel, Fernand, 154; and Febvre, 158,
159; and historism of early *Annalistes,*
157–58; geography, 157, 158; global
science of history, 158; historical
structuralism, 157
Buckle, H. Thomas, 85–86
Burckhardt, Jacob, 100; aesthetics and
historical coherency, 103–4

Chaunu, Pierre: historicity and "serial
history," 159
Christianity and historiography:
Catholic-Protestant rivalries, 35–36; in
the Middle Ages, 21. *See also*
Augustine, Saint; Eusebius; Joachim of
Floris; Mabillon, Jean; Otto of
Freising; Paulus Orosius; Schelling,
Friedrich von; Schlegel, Friedrich;
Toynbee, Arnold; Universal history,
Christian; Vico, Giambattista

City of God and the City of Man. *See*
Augustine, Saint; Otto of Freising
Coherency, historical: 19th century
historicism, 135–36; 19th century
views of rationalism and historism,
52–53, 177 n.58; beginnings of
historicism, 28; early modern
rationalists, 28–32; extra-historical
coherence, 33–35; Hegel and
Romanticism, 62; in medieval
historiography, 22–23; lack of in 20th
century historiography, 138, 162–63,
167; "paradigms" and German radical
historians, 153; secularization, 27–28;
the "philosophical historians," 46–47.
See also Bodin, Jean; Burckhardt,
Jacob; Comte, Auguste; Condorcet,
Marie-Jean-Antoine-Nicolas; Facts,
historical; Foucault, Michel;
Guicciardini, Francesco; Hegel, Georg
W. F.; Herder, Johann Gottfried von;
Historicism; Hume, David;
Machiavelli, Niccolò; Ranke, Leopold
von; Vico, Giambattista
Collingwood, Robin George: historian's
consciousness, 113–14; philosophy
and history, 112–13
Comte, Auguste: changes in his historical
method, 67; law of progress, 65; law
of the three periods, 65; philosophy
and history, 66; sociology, 66, 67
Condorcet, Marie-Jean-Antoine-Nicolas,
marquis de, 49–50
Critical history: and ancient history, 13;
and traditional historians, 164;
compared to radical history, 6–8; four
phases of development, 8–10. *See also*
Fustel de Coulanges, Numa Denis;
Niebuhr, Barthold; Ranke, Leopold;
Sources, historical
Croce, Benedetto: and Ranke, 111;
historicism and universal principles,
110; influence of, 112; philosophy and
history, 110–11
Cultural presentism, 2

Descartes, René, 29
Dilthey, Wilhelm: and hermeneutics,
115; historical reason, 114;

199